CW01402427

Electronic products

LONGMAN

Contents

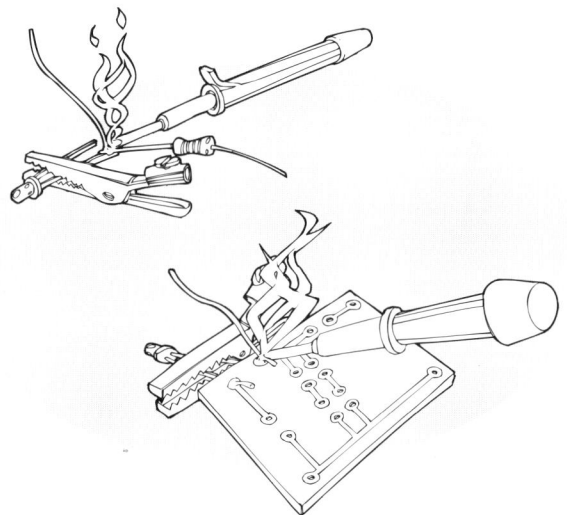

Part 1 Learning D&T at 14–16

What will I design and make?

Earlier you used a range of very different materials for designing and making – textiles, food, resistant materials such as wood, metal and plastic, graphic media and technical components. At 14–16 you are allowed to specialise. You have chosen to specialise in designing and making using electronic components. This means that you will be using electronic components, some mechanical components and a range of resistant materials. At 14–16 you are expected to work to a higher standard in both designing and making and the quality of your products should be better than at an earlier stage. The 14–16 course lasts only two years and you simply do not have enough time to gain the extra skills, knowledge and understanding needed to improve your work in more than one area. The sort of things that you will design and make are shown below.

This area of designing and making is usually called **electronic product design.**

RISE &
SHINE
SENSOR
SYSTEM

◘ *Designing and making at 14–16 is a real challenge. Your products should be good enough for the shops or public display*

Of course, there is more to design and technology than designing and making and in your 14–16 course you will also learn about the way design and technology work in the world outside school. In particular, you will study how industry produces electronic products and the effects that manufacturing these products have on people and places.

How will I learn?

If you do design and technology the Nuffield way then your teacher will use three different teaching methods. These are described below.

Resource Tasks

These are short, practical activities. They make you think and help you to learn the knowledge and skills you need to design and make really well.

Case Studies

These describe real examples of design and technology in the world outside school. By reading them you will find out more than you can through designing and making alone. Case Studies help you to learn about the way firms and businesses design and manufacture goods and how those goods are marketed and sold. You will also learn about the impact that products have on the people who use them and the places where they are made.

Capability Tasks

These involve designing and making a product that works. When you tackle a Capability Task, you use what you have learned through doing Resource Tasks and Case Studies. Capability Tasks take a lot longer than either Resource Tasks or Case Studies. Your teacher will organise your lessons so that you do the Resource Tasks and Case Studies you need for a Capability Task as part of the Capability Task. In this way your teacher makes sure that you can be successful in your designing and making.

The way these methods work together is shown here.

I did these Resource Tasks:

SRT1	Identifying needs and likes
SRT5	Attribute analysis
CRT1	Communicating to the client
CRT4	Communicating to the user
MfRT1	Manufacturing enclosures
CRT1	Making and testing a radio

I read these Case Studies:
The clockwork radio
A radio revolution

So I was able to design and make this two-way radio for my gran. She uses it to find out who is at her front door.

Resource Tasks for gaining knowledge, skills and understanding

You will be given a Resource Task as an instruction sheet like the one below. All Resource Tasks are laid out in the same way. You will see that they are different to the ones you used earlier.

code number title

clear instructions

crt 4 Communicating to the user

communicating resource task 4

1 Choose an electronics-based product from the list below:
- personal stereo
- multi test meter
- portable radio/CD/tape player.

2 Use drawings and brief notes to show the following for the product you have selected.

Personal stereo

How the batteries are replaced

How the headphones can be adjusted

How tapes are fitted

Multi test meter

How the batteries are replaced

How to set the adjusting control(s) to read different units

How to read the scale

How to use the test probes

Portable radio/CD/tape player

How the batteries are replaced

How the mains lead is connected

How CDs are fitted into the player

How the function selection switch is set

3 Make some rough sketches first to develop ideas for text, illustrations and layout.

4 Make a neat copy. Use IT facilities if you have them, especially for text.

Further/homework
Give your guide to a friend and ask them to do a user trip on it.

Work out your own user trip evaluation sheet.

© The Nuffield Foundation 1997

page 1/1 crt 4

Learning
How to use graphical skills to produce a user guide.

Student's book
Communicating your design proposal, page 112

Timing
180 minutes

Equipment and materials
- pencil crayons
- felt tip markers
- drawing equipment
- stencils or dry transfer lettering
- computer and printer
- desk top publishing and graphics software
- access to one of the following: personal stereo, multi test meter, portable radio/CD/tape player

Type of task
Extension

Other subjects
IT

statement of what you will learn through doing the task

reference to the parts of the *Student's Book* you will need

time you should spend on each task

Equipment and materials section tells you what you will need

Type of Resource Task – recap, extension or new ideas

Other subjects section tells you which other subjects you need to use for this task

More about Resource Tasks

There are three types of Resource Task.

Recapitulation Resource Tasks

These are tasks that go over things that you probably did previously. They are very useful for reminding you of things you may have forgotten about or for catching up on things you have missed.

Extension Resource Tasks

These are tasks which take an idea that you were probably taught earlier and develop it further. They are useful both for revising ideas you developed earlier and for helping you to use them in a more advanced way.

New ideas Resource Tasks

These are tasks which deal with knowledge and understanding that are new to 14–16 year olds. It is unlikely that you will have done this work previously. They are important in helping you to progress.

Your teacher may:

- organise the lesson so that everyone is doing the same Resource Task;
- set different students different tasks;
- allow you to choose from a range of Resource Tasks.

Sometimes you will work on your own and sometimes as part of a team.

Your teacher may introduce a sequence of Resource Tasks by talking to the whole class

4

Case Studies for awareness and insight

There are two types of Case Studies for 14–16 year olds.

The first types deals with 'large' technologies. These are the technologies which significantly affect the way people live. Often they are associated with a particular time in history. It is important that you read these Case Studies because they will help you to understand the way that technology influences our lives.

The second type deals with products that are similar to those that you will be designing and making. They describe:

- how the designs were developed, manufactured, marketed and sold;
- how the products work;
- how the products affect people who make them, those who use them, and others.

A particular Case Study may deal with just one of these or with all of them. It is important that you read these Case Studies because they will help you to design like a professional designer.

It is easy to lose concentration when you are reading a Case Study so they all contain questions which you should try to answer while you are reading them. It is often useful to discuss your answers with a friend. This will help both of you to think about and make sense of the study.

The Case Studies also contain Research Activities. You will often be set these as homework as they involve finding out information that is not in the Case Study. This will help you to learn how to seek new information as well as giving you further understanding of design and technology.

A student presents her electronic Case Study to the class

Capability Tasks for designing and making

Each of the products you design and make as a 14–16 year old will be from a group of product types. These groups of product types are called **lines of interest**. For example, you might design and make a product that was from the line of interest 'security devices'. Your product could range from a tamper alarm for push bikes to a system to protect a collection of precious jewels on display in a public museum. Certain sorts of knowledge, skills and understanding are useful for designing security products. These might include an understanding of sensors, operational amplifiers, logic gates and noise – making circuits, plus knowledge of materials and manufacturing processes – all of these are needed to design and make products in this area.

We have identified seven lines of interest for Capability Tasks in the area of electronics. Some possible products from each line of interest are shown opposite. Note that one of the lines of interest is different in that it uses the technology of the other lines of interest. This is called a multiple line of interest.

During your 14–16 course you will have the opportunity to work in at least three different lines of interest. If you worked in only one line of interest, although you would end up knowing a lot about that particular part of design and technology, there would be other parts you would know nothing about at all. If you were to work in many more than three lines of interest, you wouldn't have the time to study anything in depth and you would end up knowing very little about any part of design and technology. So working in three lines of interest will enable you to gain a reasonable level and range of understanding and skill in design and technology knowledge.

sensing devices

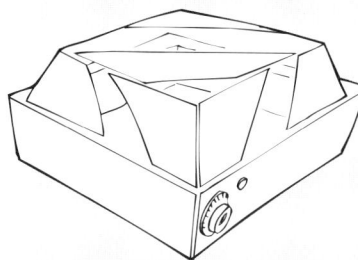

measuring devices

electronic novelties

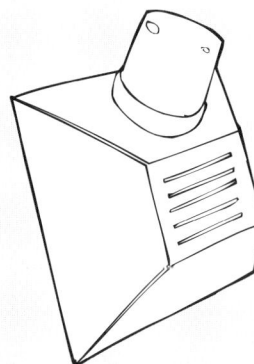

security devices

control systems

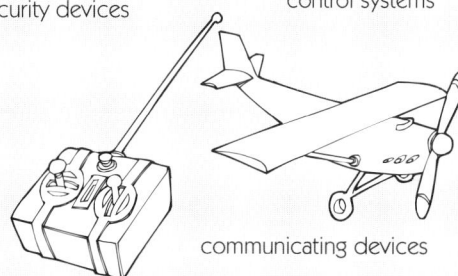

communicating devices

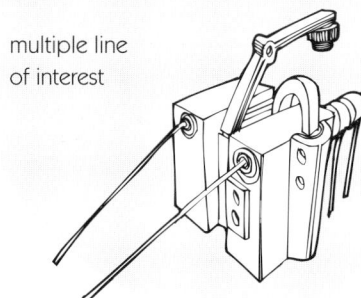

multiple line of interest

Managing three Capability Tasks

If you are following a full GCSE course, it is likely that you will tackle three Capability Tasks during year 10, each one from a different line of interest. Your teacher will work out with you which ones the class will tackle. In year 11 you can revisit a line of interest or tackle a new one. The one in year 11 will probably be used for your GCSE coursework. This makes sense because you should be better at designing and making in year 11 than you are in year 10.

It will be quite a struggle to fit three complete Capability Tasks into year 10, so your teacher may organise the lessons so that you only do part of some of these tasks. You will certainly need to do one complete Capability Task, where you design, make and test a well-finished product.

In another Capability Task you might only produce a working model of the product. This means you don't have to spend a lot of time making the finished article. In another Capability Task you might produce only a series of design proposals as detailed, annotated sketches. This cuts down the time you spend on the Capability Task even further.

Your teacher may give the class a design brief plus a specification and ask you to design and make a product that meets these requirements. Your teacher might even give you the brief, the specification and circuit layout and ask you to make the product so that you will learn about the manufacturing process. Of course, it is important that you carry out the Resource Tasks and Case Studies needed for each of these Capability Tasks. In this way you will acquire a lot of design and technology knowledge, understanding and skill and still keep in touch with designing and making. This will put you in a strong position to tackle a full Capability Task in year 11.

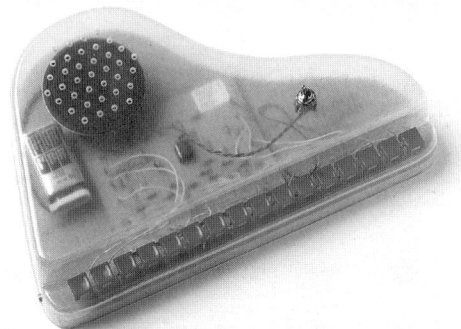

Up to design proposals

Up to a working model

Up to the finished product

🔲 *A Capability Task can be work completed at different stages*

Ensuring your designing makes sense

You will be working to a brief which summarises the following information about your product:

- what it will be used for;
- who will use it;
- where it might be used;
- where it might be sold.

This will help you to think about the design of your product. It will also help you to write the specification. You will need to use the brief and the specification as references for your designing. By checking your design ideas against the brief and specification, you will be able to see whether they are developing in sensible directions.

This checking is often called reviewing and it is very important. If you fail to review your work at the correct times you will almost certainly waste a lot of time and your design ideas are likely to be inappropriate and, in some cases, may not work at all.

First review

Once you have some ideas for your product, in the form of quickly drawn, annotated sketches, you should carry out your first review by comparing your ideas with the requirements of the brief and the specification. Ask yourself the following questions for each design idea.

- Will the design do what it is supposed to?
- Will the design by suitable for the users?
- Will the design fit in with where it might be used or sold?
- Is the design likely to work?
- Does the design look right for the users and sellers?
- Have I noted any special requirements the design will need to meet later on?

Any design ideas that do not get a 'yes' for all these questions will need to be rejected or adjusted. In this way you can use the first review to screen out any design ideas that will not meet your requirements. You can do this screening in two ways:

- on your own by just sitting, thinking it through in your head and making notes against each design idea;
- working in a group and explaining your ideas to other students who can check them out against the questions. This takes longer and you will have to help the others in the group to check out their design ideas. However, the extra time is usually well spent as others are often more rational in their criticisms of your ideas than you are.

Whichever way you choose, it will be important to discuss your review findings with your teacher.

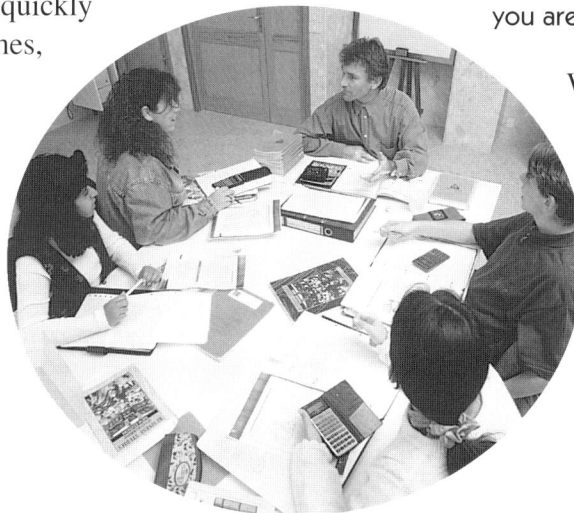

Second review

By screening your early ideas you will be able to focus your efforts on developing a single design idea and on working out the details of that design. You will present these details as a mixture of annotated sketches, rendered presentation drawings and working drawings (sometimes called plans).

To make sure that your designing is still developing in a sensible direction, you need to ask the following questions before you begin making the product.

- Am I sure that the working parts of the design will do what they are supposed to?
- Am I sure about the accuracy with which I need to make each part?
- How long will it take me to make and assemble all the parts of my design?
- Have I got enough time to do this?
- If not, what can I alter so that I have a design that I can make on time and which still meets the specification.
- Will the materials and components I need be available when I need them?
- Will the tools and equipment be available when I need them?
- Am I sure that I can get the final appearance that I need?
- Have I got enough time for finishing?
- Is there anything I can do to be more efficient?

You are probably the only one who can answer these questions, but it will be worth checking your answers with your teachers as they are likely to know about any hidden traps and pitfalls.

Evaluating the final products

Here are examples of the ways in which you can evaluate your design once you have made it. You can find out more about them in the Strategies section (pages 66–93). It will be important to use all these different methods in coming to a judgement about the quality of your design.

User trip

By interviewing the user this student was able to find out what he did and didn't like about the talking toy he had designed and made.

Performance specification

Gupta designed a returnable radio to be used at sporting events. Fans could listen to the commentary and watch the game. The specification for the equipment was as follows.

- It should use earphones.
- It must be easy to use and not require holding.
- It must appeal to a wide range of fans.
- The outer covering should be customisable for different fixtures and/or different sports.

Gupta was surprised to find how easily the earphone connection became broken when fans waved their arms about. It is important to design your product to meet all the specification requirements.

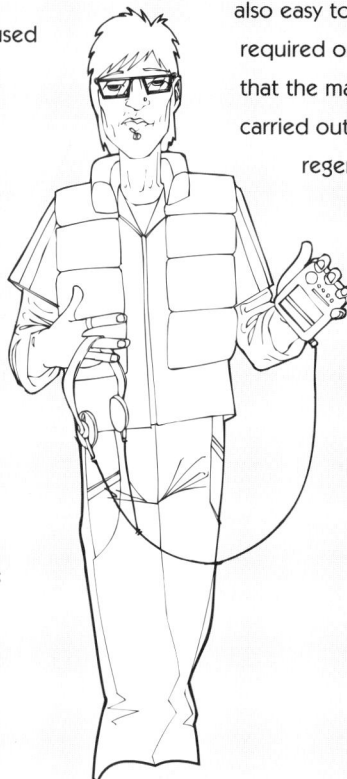

Winners and losers

Jane had developed the design for an automatic watering system for her parents' greenhouse. She could make it as her D&T Nuffield Project and when the family went on holiday the plants would be OK. What she had forgotten was that her father usually asked the elderly couple who lived next door to water the plants. They wouldn't be needed now.

By thinking about winners and losers, Jane quickly realised that they might feel hurt and upset if they felt they weren't needed.

Appropriateness

Fred designed a simple-to-assemble card shell for a 'recyclable, green radio'. The internal circuitry was also easy to produce. Overall, the workers required only two days' training. Fred hoped that the manufacture of the radio could be carried out in a depressed area, as part of a regeneration scheme.

By asking the questions on page 92, he was able to decide whether his design was appropriate.

Thinking about how well your product meets its specification

One way to do this is to discuss your product with some other students. Give your product a blob score for each part of the specification – 5 blobs if it meets that part really well, 3 blobs if it meets it moderately well, 1 blob if it meets it only poorly and no blobs if it fails to meet this part of the specification. The next part is the tricky bit. Explain to the other students in the group why you have given the scores you have. Their job is to question your judgements. Your job is to convince them that the judgements are correct. If you do this, you will be in a good position to move on to looking at your own progress.

Looking at your own progress

At the end of a Capability Task it is important to look back at what you have done and reflect on your progress. The following sets of questions will help you with this.

Feeling good about what you have done

- Am I proud of what I made?
- Can I explain why?
- Am I proud of the design I developed?
- Can I explain why?

Understanding the problems

- What sorts of things slowed me down?
- Can I now see how to overcome these difficulty?
- What sorts of things made me nervous so that I didn't do as well as I know I can?
- Do I know where to get help now?
- What sorts of things did I do better than I expected?
- Was this due to luck or can I say that I'm getting better?
- Were there times when I concentrated on detail before I had the broad picture?
- Were there times when I didn't bother enough with detail?
- Can I now see how to get the level of detail right?

Understanding yourself

- Were there times when I lost interest?
- Can I now see how to get myself motivated?
- Were there times when I couldn't work out what to do next?
- Can I now see how to get better at making decisions?
- Were there times when I lost my sense of direction?
- Can I now see how to avoid this?

Understanding your design decisions

- With hindsight can I see where I made the right decisions?
- With hindsight can I see where I should have made different decisions?
- With hindsight can I see situations where I did the right thing?
- With hindsight can I see where I would do things differently if I did this again?

Part 2
Using other subjects in D&T at KS4

Using science

At 14–16 you will be able to use science when you are tackling Capability Tasks. This is different to using science in a Resource Task. In a Resource Task you will be told to use science in the Other subjects section. In a Capability Task you have to choose when to use science.

Your science lessons will teach you two main things. First, how to carry out scientific investigations. If you need to find something out in a Capability Task – say, the strength of shell structures made from different materials, or the variation in temperature in a nest while eggs are being incubated – then you can use your science to help you to plan the investigation and design the necessary experiments. Second, in science you will acquire scientific knowledge and understanding which could be useful to you in a Capability Task. The information in the table below will help to remind you of the science you are likely to find useful. Note that some of the science is from previous courses well as from 14–16.

Uses of science in designing electronic products

The activity	Science likely to be useful	
Designing shell forms to house circuits	The properties and uses of materials (KS2/7–11); Force and pressure (KS3/11–14); Stiffness of materials (KS4/14–16)	
Understanding electrical components	Simple circuits, switches and dimmers (KS2/7–11); Power, current and voltage in circuits (KS4/14–16)	
Exploring user interface design	The properties and uses of materials (KS2/7–11); Planning experimental procedures (KS3/11–14 and KS4/14–16); Obtaining evidence (KS3/11–14 and KS4/14–16); Analysing evidence and drawing conclusions (KS3/11–14 and KS4/14–16); Considering the strength of the evidence (KS3/11–14 and KS4/14–16)	
Understanding communication systems	Electromagnetic spectrum (KS3/11–14); Frequency, amplitude and wavelength (KS4/14–16)	

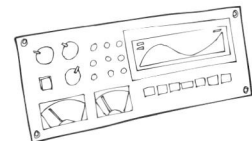

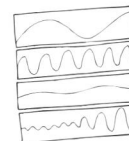

Using mathematics

At 14–16 you will need to use your understanding of mathematics to help your design and technology. You will be able to use mathematics when you are tackling Capability Tasks. This is different from using mathematics in a Resource Task. In a Resource Task you will be told to use mathematics in the Other subjects section. In a Capability Task you have to choose when to use mathematics. Often you will use mathematics without realising it. The panel below shows some examples.

You use mathematics whenever you ...

... measure anything

... calculate anything

... assemble anything

... work out a decoration

... conduct a survey or use a questionnaire

... use or make a working drawing

... plot a graph

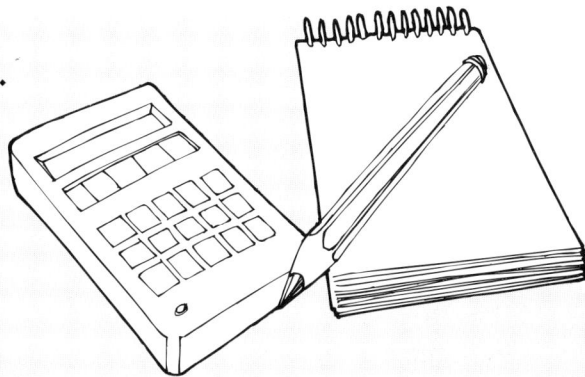
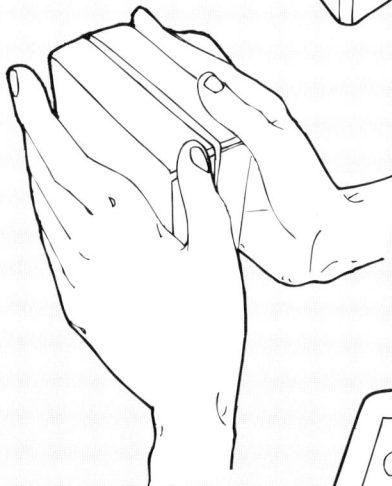
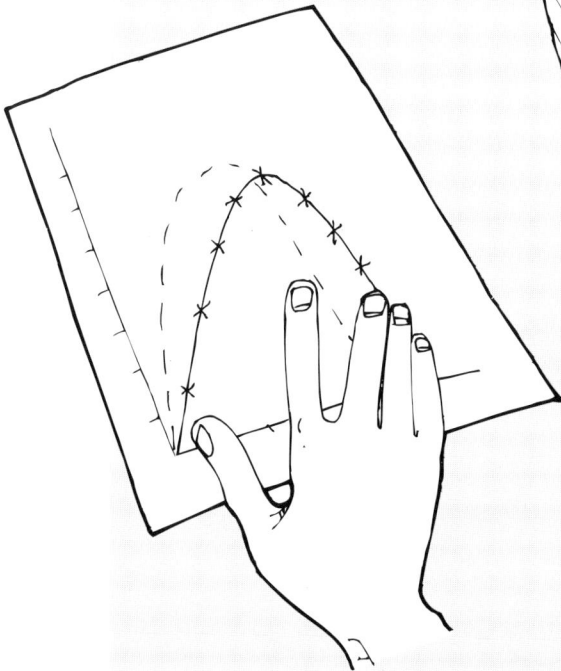

Using art

At 14–16 you will need to use your understanding of art to help your design and technology. You will be able to use art when you are tackling Capability Tasks. This is different from using art in a Resource Task. In a Resource Task you will be told to use art in the Other subjects section. In a Capability Task you have to choose when to use art. The example below shows how some students have used art in developing the design for the appearance of frost alarms for a variety of different pets which might be kept out of doors.

Using information technology

At 14–16 you will need to use your understanding of information technology to help your design and technology. You will be able to use information technology when you are tackling Capability Tasks. This is different from using information technology in a Resource Task. In a Resource Task you will be told to use information technology in the Other subjects section. In a Capability Task you have to choose when to use information technology.

The examples on the right show how one student used information technology, in the form of electronic circuit modelling software, to evaluate his design ideas and then CAD software to design the layout for the required printed circuit board.

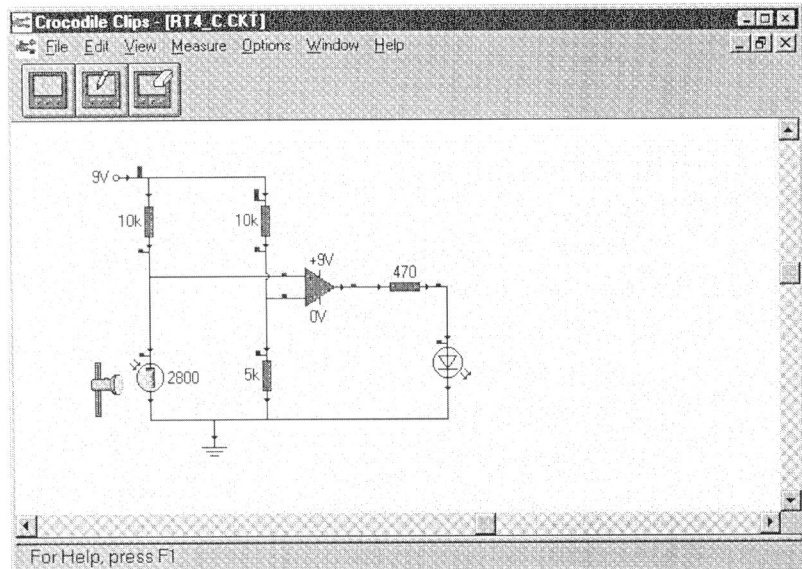

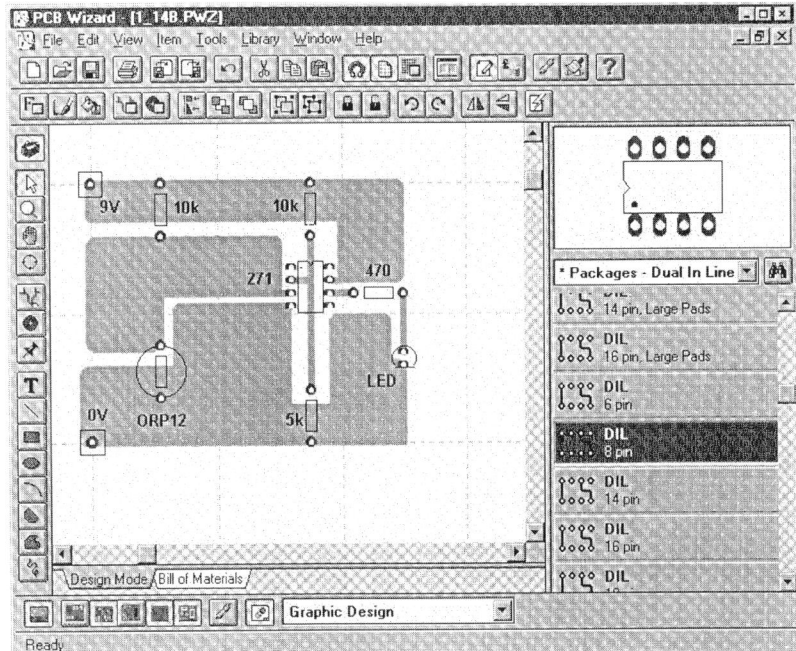

Part 3
How you will be assessed at GCSE

Writing your own Capability Task

It is likely that the Capability Task you tackle in year 11 will be the one that will be used for your GCSE coursework. This makes sense because you should be better at designing and making in year 11 than you are in year 10. Here are some guidelines to help you.

Designing the Capability Task

1 Deciding on the line of interest

Ask yourself the following questions.

- Do you want to revisit a line of interest from year 10, or do you want to try something new?
- Which Resource Tasks did you enjoy most? Are these linked to a line of interest?
- Is there a group of students in your class who want to work on a particular line of interest?

2 Justifying your decision

Ask yourself these questions.

- Who will benefit from the product you are going to design and make?
- Will you be successful at designing and making this sort of product?
- Can you afford to make this sort of product?

3 Sorting out any extra learning that might be necessary

It is not difficult to identify particular areas of design and technology knowledge that are likely to be helpful for your task. Discuss this with your teacher and identify Resource Tasks that could be useful.

4 Identifying any Case Studies that might provide useful background reading

Read and make notes listing those points that are relevant to your task.

5 Drawing up a 'Using other subjects' checklist

- Discuss this with your D&T teacher.
- Check with your other subject teachers if you think they can help.

6 Working with other people

There may be parts of your Capability Task that could benefit from a team approach – carrying out a survey, collecting reference materials, brainstorming ideas, for example. You will need to organize these carefully so that everybody's task is improved.

Tackling the Capability Task

7   Writing a design brief and developing a specification

You must remember that you are expected to design and make a quality product that meets demanding criteria. These should take into account how it could be manufactured, how it might be repaired or maintained and how it might be sold.

8   Generating design ideas

You will need to show where your ideas come from. Make sure you keep a record of your early thoughts.

9   Developing your ideas

You will need to keep a clear record of how your ideas have developed.

10   Making presentation drawings and working drawings

These should show what your design will look like and how it can be made.

11   Planning your making

12   Making your design

13   Evaluating the final product

Make sure you use a range of techniques.

14   Putting on a display

You should mount a display that shows your work to best advantage. It should describe the following:

- your ideas and where they came from;
- how they developed;
- presentation and working drawings;
- your schedule for making;
- your evaluation.

Writing your own Case Study

You may have to write your own Case Study as part of your GCSE assessment. Here are some guidelines.

Which product?

You should choose an everyday item that is manufactured. You should be able to examine it, use it yourself, see others use it and evaluate it. Here are some possibilities:

- walkman;
- digital watch;
- pocket calculator;
- pager;
- mobile phone;

What should it describe?

Your study should describe the following:

- what the product looks like;
- what the product does;
- how it works;
- who uses it and what they think of it;
- how it's manufactured;
- the impact the product has made on the way people live.

You might also describe:

- how the product has changed over time;
- other products that do a similar job.

How many words?

No more than about 2000 words. (One side of A4 paper filled with typing is about 500 words.)

What about pictures?

It is important to use illustrations as well as text. You can use any of the following:

- your own illustrations drawn directly onto the page or pasted in place;
- illustrations photocopied from books or magazines and pasted in place;
- your own illustrations scanned onto disc and printed in place;
- illustrations taken from a library on CD-ROM and printed in place.

What about layout?

If possible use desk-top publishing (DTP) software to produce your Case Study. If this is not available use word processing (WP) software to lay out the text. If this is not available use a typewriter.

What about the overall length?

A reasonable mixture of text and pictures will give you a length of about 12 sides of A4.

What about special features?

You can make your Case Study:

- *attractive* by producing an illustrated cover;
- *easy to look through* by numbering the pages, using headings and producing a title page and contents page;
- *easy to understand* by using illustrations with notes and captions.

Examination questions

You may have to take a final written examination paper at the end of year 11 as part of your GCSE assessment. This paper will be made up of different sorts of questions. Here is a guide to these questions and how to answer them.

Interpreting a short Case Study

In this sort of question you will be given two or three paragraphs to read and one or two pictures to look at. The writing and the pictures will describe an aspect of design and technology from the world outside school. You will then have to answer a series of questions based mainly on what you have read. Some will involve finding a piece of information from the text. If you read the text carefully, you can always get these questions right. Some will involve explaining something that is described in the text. These are more difficult as they will require you to use your design and technology knowledge and understanding. Some will ask you to make a judgement about the effects of the design and technology described. These are the most difficult but if you think carefully you will be able to use your design and technology awareness and insight to make judgements and give good reasons to back them up.

Presenting and interpreting information

In this sort of question you will be given data from some design and technology research and asked to present it in a way that makes it easy to understand. The data may come from very different sources. It could be about consumer preferences, the results of testing a material or component, production figures for different manufacturing methods, or sales figures for different products. Once you have presented the data, you will be asked questions that require you to interpret it.

Why is it like that?

In this sort of question you will be given information about a product in the form of annotated illustrations and text. You will be asked to explain different features of the design, such as:

- why a particular material has been chosen;
- why particular components have been chosen;
- why a part is the shape and form that it is;
- how particular parts work together to turn the input into the output;
- what would happen if certain things were changed;
- how particular parts might be manufactured;
- how the design might be improved.

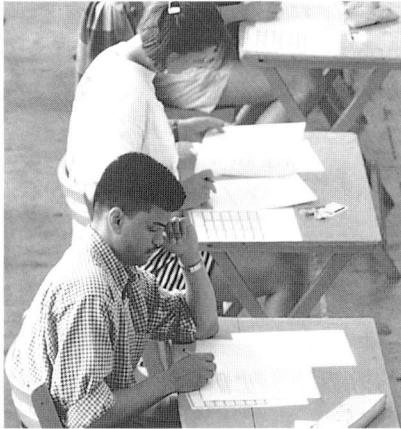

You will have to use the design and technology knowledge and understanding you have gained throughout years 10 and 11 to give correct answers.

What could you use for that?

In this sort of question you will be given a short technical design problem. You will be presented with an incomplete design to which there are several different possible solutions. Your task will be in three parts:

1 to describe some of the possible solutions by means of simple annotated sketches;
2 to compare these solutions;
3 to state clearly which you think is the best, with reasons.

Again, you will have to use the design and technology knowledge and understanding you have gained throughout years 10 and 11 to give correct answers.

Exam questions ②

Question 1 is taken from the Northern Examination Board GCSE Specimen Paper.
It deals with sensors, transistors and relays

1 An egg producer wants to fit an automatic lighting system to a chicken hut.
The two main specifications for the system are:
- the hut lights must come on automatically as dusk falls;
- the system must be run from a renewable energy source.

(a) Add to the track layouts below, the circuit symbols required to build a potential divider for the input to the system. (3)

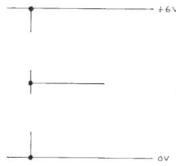

(b) State what the effect would be if you reversed the position of the components you have drawn. (1)

(c) The switching stage of the circuit is accomplished with a transistor. At what voltage does the transistor start to switch on? (1)

(d) A suitable transistor is the npn type BFY 51 shown below
What is the small tag on the casing for? (1)

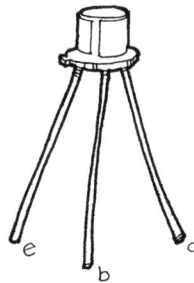

(e) The three legs of the transistor must be connected the correct way round in the circuit. Give the name for each of the legs in the space below and add a short description to explain how each of the legs is connected in a circuit.
The leg labelled e is called the   and is normally connected to (3)
The leg labelled b is called the   and is normally connected to (3)
The leg labelled c is called the   and is normally connected to (3)

(f) Below is the circuit diagram showing the switching stage of the system.
   (i) Add the important detail which is missing from the transistor symbol
      and briefly describe why it is part of the usual symbol. (3)

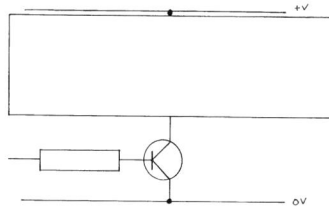

   (ii) Explain the purpose of the 1k resistor (2)

(g) The transistor illustrated has a hfe (gain) of 40. Calculate the base current
   when the collector current is 400mA.

The formula   ....
Insert the values   ....
The answer   ....   (4)

(h) A 12V sport light powered by a lead acid battery is to be used to provide the light in the
   chicken huts. A relay could be used as an interface. The circuit symbol for the relay and its
   contacts is shown below.

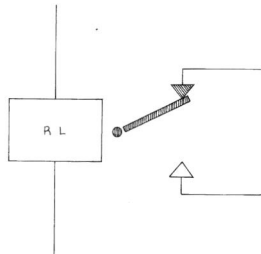

Using the information you have been given throughout the question draw a complete circuit
diagram for the system. The block diagram below may be helpful.

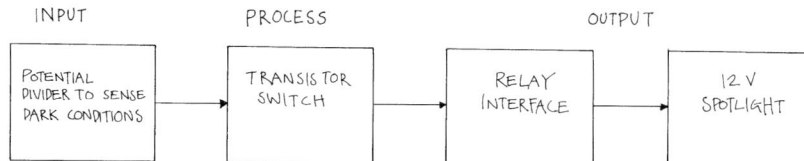

(i) (i) Name a type of transistor which could be used in place of the relay. (1)
   (ii) Give one reason for your choice. (1)
   (j) Use sketches and notes to describe how you would satisfy the requirements run the
      system from a renewable energy source. (10)
(Total 48 marks)

Questions 2 is taken from the Edexcel Examination Board GCSE Specimen Paper. It deals with monostable circuits and component selection.

2   A toy company has designed a circuit to go inside a toy car in order to control the motor which drives the wheels.
The circuit is shown below.

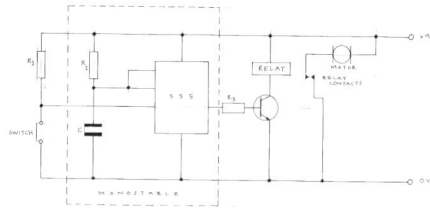

(a) (i)   State how this circuit can help to prolong the life of the battery.   (2)
(ii) A member of the company, who knows very little about electronics, comments, 'it is not very sensible to expect a child to keep his finger on the switch to make the toy work'.
Explain what is wrong with this comment.   (1)
(iii) State TWO things which the designer would need to think about before building this circuit.
                                                                                                            (2)
(b) State why a relay is used in this circuit.   (2)
(c) The company has decided to build the circuit on copper clad board. The diagrams show the circuit for a monostable and a partly completed layout diagram of it.

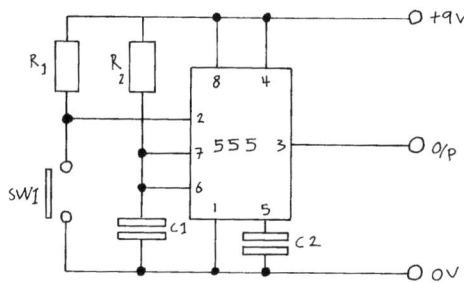

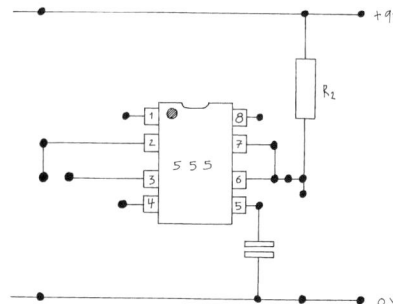

Complete the layout diagram by adding the following:
   (i)   resistor R1;
   (ii)   capacitor C1;
   (iii) switch SW1;
   (iv)   connections to pins 8 and 1.   (5)
(d) The system is now extended so that a buzzer alerts the child when the toy is about to switch off.
Here is a block diagram of the new design.

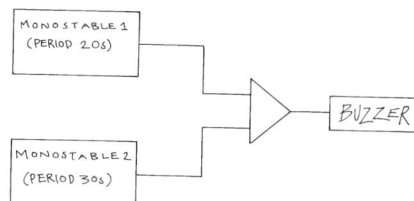

   (i)   Stage how long the buzzer will sound if both monostables are triggered at the same time. (1)
   (ii) Explain how the system operates. You may like to use a timing diagram to help you.   (4)
(Total 17 marks)

General Case Studies

Public transport In London

The early Victorians had rutted and cobbled streets with poor drainage and no road system as such. Today we have crowded buses, trains and tubes as well as an increasing number of vehicles creating more pollution and slowing traffic down. Are today's London residents and commuters any better off than their Victorian predecessors?

Early victorian scene

Horses galore

The horse has played a key role in the development of public transport systems in cities across Europe. In 1829 the first regular horse bus service – carrying just 12 people – provided a fixed route service from the City of London to Paddington. It ran every three hours with a fare of one shilling (5p). This was a considerable sum of money at the time and so the service catered mainly for the wealthy. Its success encouraged other operators to set up services on other routes. This was the beginning of London's public transport system.

P Pause for thought

What is the future for public transport in London or any of Britain's other major cities?

Competition and cobbled streets

More operators in the market-place meant they had to compete for passengers. This made operators invest in ways of carrying more people. This resulted in the introduction of back-to-back seating on the tops of buses in 1850. These seats were accessed by a ladder – it took another 30 years to get a proper stairway to the top of the horse-drawn bus!

The size of the bus and therefore the number of passengers it could carry was limited by the power of the horses. A significant advance was made in 1861 with the introduction of horse-drawn trams. These had wheels which ran on steel tracks laid in the road. This made it easier for the horses to pull their loads which meant that buses could be made larger or more passengers could be carried on the existing buses.

Travelling in 1870

P **Pause for thought**

What else might be used to power buses and trams? Why weren't these used in 1850?

Trams provided a cheaper form of transport with lower fares. This meant that more people could afford to use them to get to and from work. By 1900 many suburban areas of London were served by tram routes.

Powering the way forward

In 1906 there were around 50 000 horses working in London, transporting more than 2 000 000 people per day. But the days of horse-drawn transport were numbered. Towards the end of the nineteenth century operators explored other power sources, such as steam, electricity and diesel fuel. Their aim was to become more competitive by making their vehicles either faster or able to carry more passengers. Experiments with steam-powered trams were short lived and electricity proved to be the ideal power source. From 1901 overhead power lines or road-embedded conduit systems were installed.

The main problem with electric trams was that they were not very manoeuvrable. The power lines and tracks were often laid down the middle of the road. People had to dodge the traffic passing on either side to get on the tram!

Horses could not compete with these clean, quiet, reliable and larger capacity vehicles, and with the simultaneous introduction of the diesel motor bus, the horse's demise was complete.

The trolley bus: more manoeuvrable than the tram because it did not need rails

Trolley buses were introduced in London in the 1930s. They had already been used successfully in other cities for over two decades. They did not run on rails, though they were powered using overhead electric cables in a similar way to the trams. This meant they were more flexible as their manoeuvrability was limited only by the reach of their overhead power links. After World War II, from 1945 onwards the diesel-powered motor bus became the dominant form of public transport above ground and trolley buses ceased operation in London in 1962.

London electric tram in 1908

Going underground

London pioneered the underground railway system. It began with railway carriages pulled by a steam engine in 1863. This system was dirty and noisy and was replaced in 1890 by a deep-level electric system – the first in the world. Most of the central part of London's existing underground system was developed between the two wars, the outer reaches being developed after World War II. The London Underground is still being developed today with links to the Docklands Light Railway and the Jubilee line extension to the south of the River Thames.

Back above ground

The tram has not been totally forgotten. European cities such as Amsterdam have operated tram systems successfully for many decades and cities in England are beginning to follow suit. Manchester and Sheffield

Question

1 As public transport became more comprehensive, reliable and affordable, London changed. People could consider living further away from their workplace, knowing that they could get to work by public transport.

What effect do you think this had on the areas surrounding London and in the Victorian slum sites within the city?

launched new tram systems in the early 1990s. London Transport is exploring the possibility of a Tramlink between Wimbledon and Croydon using existing rail lines. As a virtually emission-free form of transport and one that can maximize the use of rechargeable power sources, tram systems are an attractive proposition for congested and polluted cities.

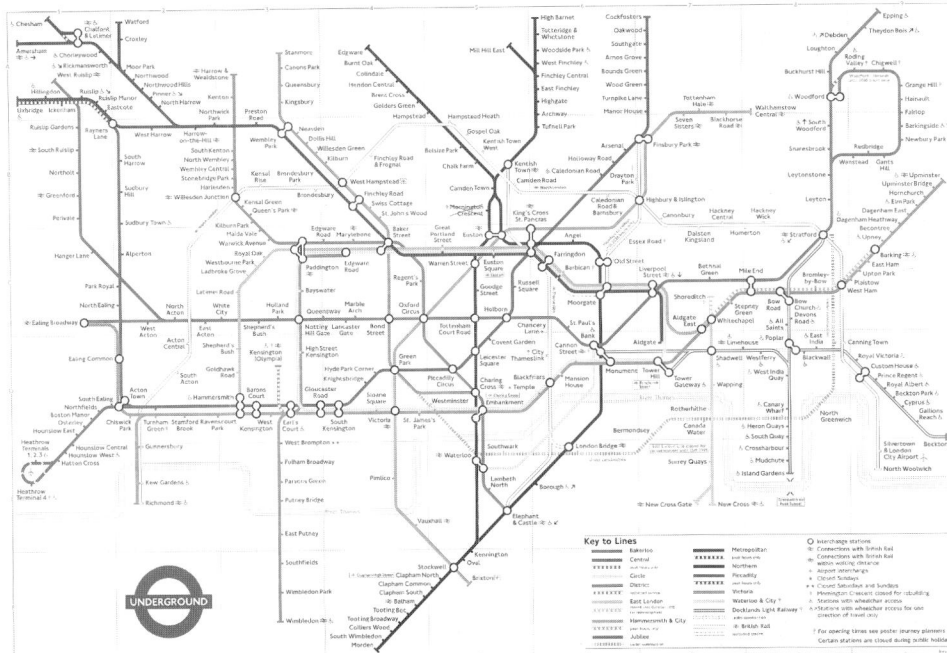

The modern tube map, first designed in 1933, shows only the sequence of stations and the connections

Ownership and intervention

Until the end of the nineteenth century individuals or companies owned various bus and tram routes. In 1891 London City Council started buying tramway companies and by 1899 they owned seven of the largest operations. By doing this the council was able to ensure that transport routes met the needs of the areas they served and the tram became the cornerstone of a public-owned transport system.

In 1933 the London Passenger Transport Board, a public body, was set up with powers to take over all bus, tram, trolley buses and underground services in London and adjacent counties. Today, bus routes are being offered for sale to private companies to manage. London Transport reported in 1994 'substantial savings of 15–20 per cent of previous operational costs … achieved from the tendering process.'

By the year 2001 it is planned that all bus routes will have been put out to tender to private companies. Over a period of 100 years public transport in London will have gone almost full circle, from private to public ownership and then back again.

Installing and managing the system

Public transport in London calls on all aspects of design and technology – civil engineering, mechanical and electrical engineering, large-scale manufacturing, advanced data capture and information handling systems, extensive maintenance and staff development.

London Transport has used the latest electronic and information technology to develop ticket vending machines and ticket reading machines linked to entry/exit points.

R Research activity

Find out about the public transport in your area. Try to answer these questions:

1 What are the bus routes?
2 How frequently do the buses run?
3 What is the cost of a journey from the outskirts to the city centre?
4 What concessions are available?

You might present your information in the form of a display including an annotated map.

Modern designs keep improving transport in London

The 'look' of London Transport has been developed through corporate identity programmes that cover signage, uniforms, livery for vehicles, promotional materials and stationery.

General case studies

DIY medical testing

Some products could not be designed if the designers didn't understand the science behind the way the product works. Obvious examples are motor cars, radios and televisions, microwave ovens and thermal blankets. The science behind these products is mainly physics and chemistry. Now new medical products are being developed which depend on an understanding of biology. For example, in the past a doctor would test for diabetes by sticking a finger into a sample of urine and licking it to see if it tasted sweet. Nowadays the doctor would use a chemical test strip developed specially to test for sugar.

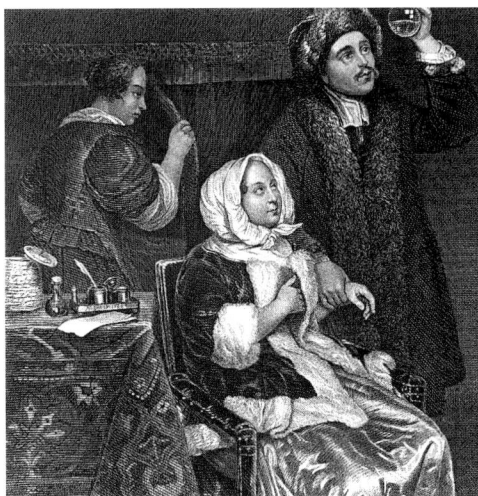

▶ Old-style medical testing

Some medical tests are so simple and reliable that anyone can carry them out. A new type of product has therefore come onto the market – do-it-yourself medical testing kits.

P **Pause for thought**

What medical conditions might people want to test themselves for?

Testing for pregnancy

When a woman becomes pregnant she produces a chemical called human chorionic gonadotrophin (hCG). This chemical is present in a woman's urine when she is pregnant. In order to find out if she is pregnant, therefore, a woman can test for hCG in her urine.

Until fairly recently the only way to test for hCG was to inject the urine sample into a female animal such as a mouse or toad. If hCG was present then the woman's urine would cause the animal to produce eggs. If she was not pregnant there would be no hCG so no eggs would be produced. This test had many disadvantages:

- it had to be carried out by a laboratory technician;
- it took several days;
- sometimes the animals had to be killed to find out if eggs had been produced.

Biologists have discovered that our white blood cells produce antibodies as part of our defence system against attack by viruses, bacteria and certain chemicals, generally called antigens. The antibodies protect us by recognizing and combining with the antigens and rendering them harmless. The white blood cells produce particular antibodies to fight particular antigens.

In 1975 two scientists discovered how to produce large amounts of antibodies outside the body in a fermenter. This enabled scientists to produce a wide range of antibodies in large quantities, including one that could recognize and combine with hCG and nothing else. They knew this could form the basis of a reliable and accurate pregnancy test. Now it was up to product designers to develop an easy-to-use pregnancy testing kit.

Here's what they developed …

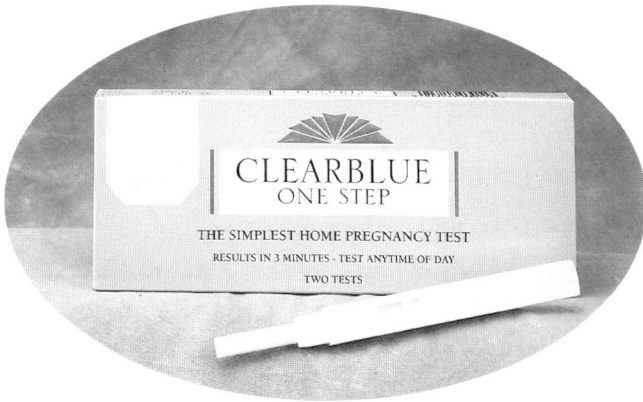

The Clearblue One-step pregnancy testing kit

The pregnancy testing kit

To carry out the test a woman urinates onto the absorbent sampler.

There are two windows in the test kit. A blue line appears in the smaller of the two windows to show that the test is complete and has worked correctly. If the test is positive a line will appear in the large window, showing that the user is pregnant.

How it works

How the test kit works is explained below.

R Research activity

Find out the meanings of the following terms:
monoclonal antibodies
hybridoma cells.

Q Questions

1 Why is the small window important?

2 Why is urine used for the test rather than blood?

3 a What are the advantages for a woman in knowing that she is pregnant as soon as possible after she has conceived?

  b Are there any disadvantages in knowing as soon as possible?

4 Why is it important for the test to be reliable and accurate?

5 Why is it important for the test to be easy to use?

6 What changes would you make to the test kit if it were to be used in a hospital laboratory?

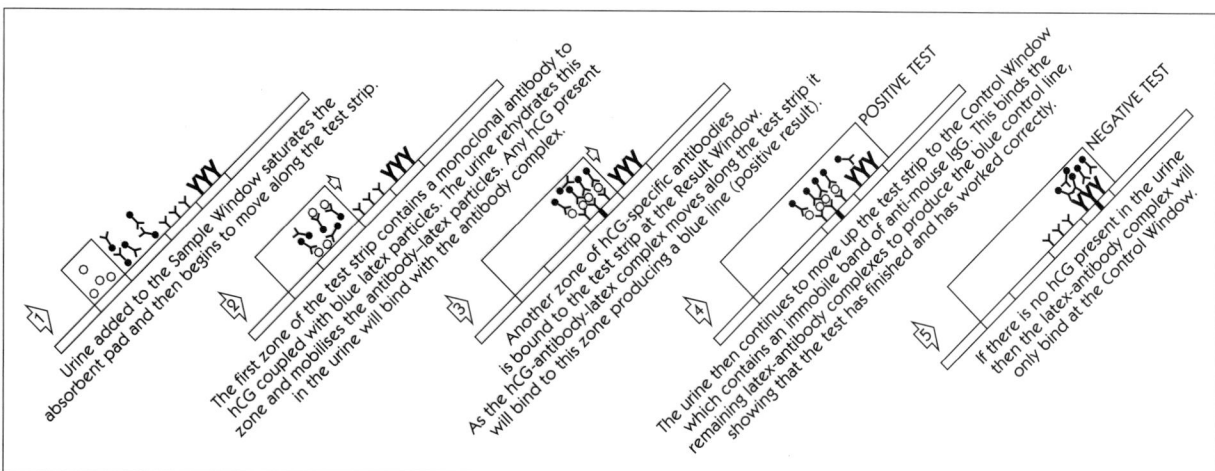

1 Urine added to the Sample Window saturates the absorbent pad and then begins to move along the test strip.

2 The first zone of the test strip contains a monoclonal antibody to hCG coupled with blue latex particles. The urine rehydrates this zone and mobilises the antibody–latex particles. Any hCG present in the urine will bind with the antibody complex.

3 Another zone of hCG-specific antibodies is bound to the test strip at the Result Window. As the hCG-antibody–latex complex moves along the test strip it will bind to this zone producing a blue line (positive result).

4 POSITIVE TEST The urine then continues to move up the test strip to the Control Window which contains an immobile band of anti-mouse IgG. This binds the remaining latex-antibody complexes to produce the blue control line, showing that the test has finished and has worked correctly.

5 NEGATIVE TEST If there is no hCG present in the urine then the latex-antibody complex will only bind at the Control Window.

3

Information – the power to change lives

The way we communicate with other human beings and the speed with which we receive information have influenced dramatically the kind of world we live in today.

The start of books

Five hundred years ago most people were illiterate and relied upon word of mouth to receive information. Books were only available to closed religious orders and were laboriously copied by hand. In 1448 a German goldsmith, Johan Gutenberg, invented a way of printing whole pages using movable type. Gutenberg used this method to produce the first printed bible in 1456.

William Caxton was the first Englishman to develop a printing business. He printed his first book in the English language in 1474, called *The Recuyell of the Historie of Troye*.

P **Pause for thought**

What is the possible connection between books becoming more widely available and schools opening?

As printing became faster, books were published on all sorts of subjects. As more books became available more people learned to read. It was also around this time that the first schools were opened.

How books shaped people's ideas

In France, the illegal and elicit distribution of cheaply printed books called 'Chap' books became commonplace by the late 1700s. One of these Chap books informed the ordinary people about the enormous excesses of the monarchy. Chap books helped to kindle a sense of national identity which ultimately lead to the French Revolution and the overthrow of the monarchy.

P **Pause for thought**

Can you think of examples where the press is criticized for printing stories about royalty ?

Information from books added to the resentment that caused the French Revolution

Information becomes important for business

In 1605, the year of the Gunpowder Plot, the first newspaper was printed, in Antwerp, Holland. The first British newspaper was called the *Daily Courant* and first appeared in 1702. At that time newspapers were read mainly by businessmen and merchants because they contained stories from other parts of the world which were important to trade and politics.

Questions

Working in a group discuss the following.

1 With new industry new jobs develop. What jobs do you think were created to operate the newspaper industry?

2 How do you think newspapers got their news two centuries ago as compared with today?

3 **a** Who decides what news is printed in the newspapers?

   b What might influence their decisions?

Pause for thought

Despite technological advances news is still passed on by word of mouth today. Journalists often interview on-the-spot witnesses or experts before writing up the stories for the newspapers.

New inventions and discoveries for mass communication

By the end of the nineteenth century Sir Alexander Graham Bell, a Scottish scientist, had invented the telephone and Guglielmo Marconi had invented the radio. It was now possible to communicate rapidly with people across the world. Radio had such potential for mass communication that the government set up the British Broadcasting Company in 1922, later to become the British Broadcasting Corporation (BBC).

Radio made it possible for people to hear the voices of politicians and other important people for the first time. The people of Britain would have heard Neville Chamberlain's famous announcement that Britain was 'now at war with Germany' in September 1939 on the radio.

By the mid 1930s nearly every family had a radio – for many a major source of news and entertainment. Radio stars were as popular as pop stars are today

Radio with pictures

During the 1920s John Logie Baird, another British scientist, was working on the idea of talking pictures. The BBC immediately became interested in his idea and started to develop television, transmitting its first programme in 1929. However it was not until the coronation of Queen Elizabeth II was televised in 1953 that large numbers of people hired TV sets and started to watch television regularly.

In the 1970s satellite communications were developed so pictures could be transmitted as they happened from anywhere in the world.

P Pause for thought

How much time do you spend each day listening to the radio and watching television?

Q Questions

Working in a group discuss the following.

4 Do you think that television and radio have changed our lives for the better or the worse?

5 Do you think television influences people's opinions?

6 Do you think it right that the government can censor what we watch?

Mass communication has changed our lives forever

Television is thought to have a very strong influence on people because of its power to shape our thoughts and ideas. The government regulates what we see on television and has the right to veto a programme if it thinks the content is not in the national interest.

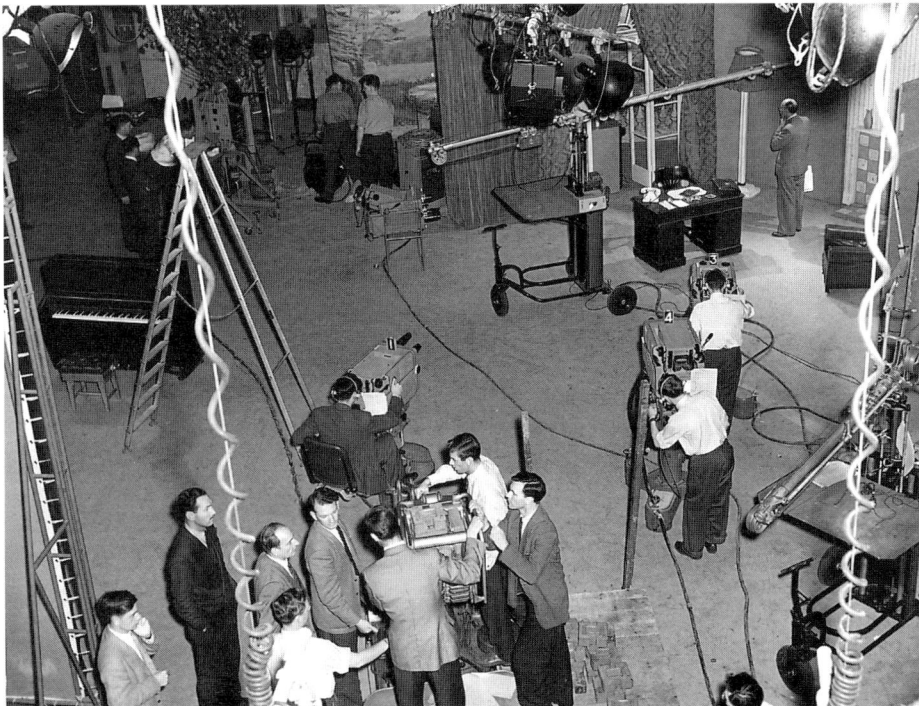

At first there was only one channel and pictures were transmitted in black and white. By the 1960s ITV, the first commercial channel, had been given a licence to broadcast and later, in the mid 1960s, colour was introduced

Reporters covering wars, the World Cup or the Olympic Games all use satellite communications, so we can see events as they happen, wherever they are taking place in the world

R Research activity

Find out about access to the Internet in your area by answering these questions.

1 Can you log onto the Internet at home?

2 Can you log onto the Internet at school?

3 Can you log onto the Internet in the local library?

4 Do your parents log onto the Internet where they work?

5 Is there an Internet users' service for hire in your town?

Use the answers to these questions to comment on how much the Internet is used in your area.

Information is power

Today almost everyone needs information for work, leisure, education and for the day-to-day running of our lives. We can access the information we need very quickly, almost instantly in some cases, through using information technology. A single CD-ROM can hold the information of many encyclopaedias, and high street banks' on-line computers can give instant information about personal finances at cash points throughout the country.

Having relevant information enables people to make decisions and to have more control over their lives. By using computers, phone lines and satellite links, the Internet allows people to exchange ideas and information with anyone in the world. It lets people communicate cheaply and rapidly without the information being edited or censored by a publisher, broadcaster or government. Communication via the Internet is a two-way process, meaning that anyone who transmits information on the Internet can have a dialogue with whoever receives the information anywhere in the world.

Using a CD-ROM to access information

Designing our surroundings

Our surroundings and the buildings we live and work in play an important role in how we feel about ourselves, and the world we live in. People work better if they have an environment which is comfortable and stress free.

Architects design environments to help people work better. When designing a new building the architect will consider factors that affect people such as:

- the air they breath;
- the opening and closing of windows;
- the temperature;
- the lighting, both natural and artificial;
- sources and level of noise;
- the closeness of other people.

P Pause for thought

> Try to remember an occasion when you felt uncomfortable in a room or building. What was it that made you feel that way?

Designed for work

When the architects were designing the Powergen building in Coventry they wanted to make it as energy efficient as possible as well as a good place to work. They decided to use a computer system to monitor the temperature, air flow and lighting. The computer uses the data it receives from sensors around the building to keep a constant check on all these things and to adjust them to save energy. It can open and close windows, turn on lights and so forth when the data it receives indicates that this is necessary. However, individual workers can override the computer, if they want to, at any time. This makes people feel happier because they are in control of their environment and the computer system is still able to save on wasted energy.

The architects were also asked to find ways to improve people's ability to work. Some modern buildings have been found to make people working there feel sick. **Sick Building Syndrome (SBS)** has been associated with factors such as air-conditioning systems, bad lighting and lack of building hygiene. Architects now know more about SBS and the subsequent rise in standards of materials handling during construction has largely eliminated SBS from new buildings today.

Q Questions

1 Make a list of the environmental factors that affect whether you can settle down to do your homework.

2 Make a list of the environmental factors that might affect whether an office worker can work efficiently.

3 Compare your two lists to identify the things they have in common.

▲ *The environment inside the Powergen Building is computer controlled*

Designed to prevent crime and vandalism

When the Docklands Light Railway was being designed the architects knew that the railway went through tough, crime-ridden areas of London and that many of the stations were to be unmanned during large parts of the day. Any solutions they proposed would need to meet three targets:

- prevent crime;
- improve passenger safety;
- require minimum maintenance and repair.

3

Very little glass is used in the station designs as glass is often vandalized and needs replacing regularly. All the materials used in the construction of the stations have been chemically treated to make graffiti easy to clean off.

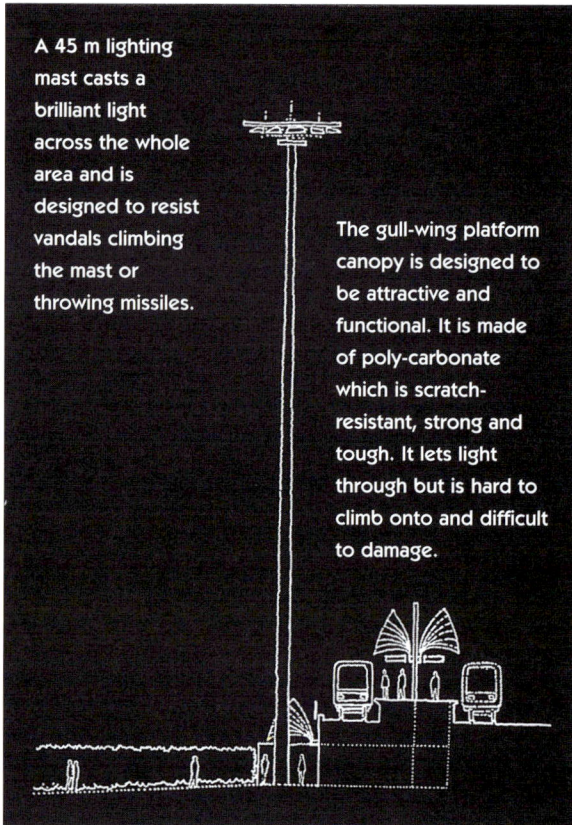

A 45 m lighting mast casts a brilliant light across the whole area and is designed to resist vandals climbing the mast or throwing missiles.

The gull-wing platform canopy is designed to be attractive and functional. It is made of poly-carbonate which is scratch-resistant, strong and tough. It lets light through but is hard to climb onto and difficult to damage.

R ### Research activity

Make a sketch (or take a photograph) of a building, and its surroundings, that is poorly designed or misused. Add notes to show what is wrong. List some of the ways which would improve the environment for everyone living or working there.

◗ *These designs have helped make Docklands safer*

◗ *Looking down from the top of the lighting mast note the thorny hedge next to the path that leads to the ticket booth. This protects passengers from ambush by muggers. The ticket booth is designed to resist ram raiding even by a JCB.*

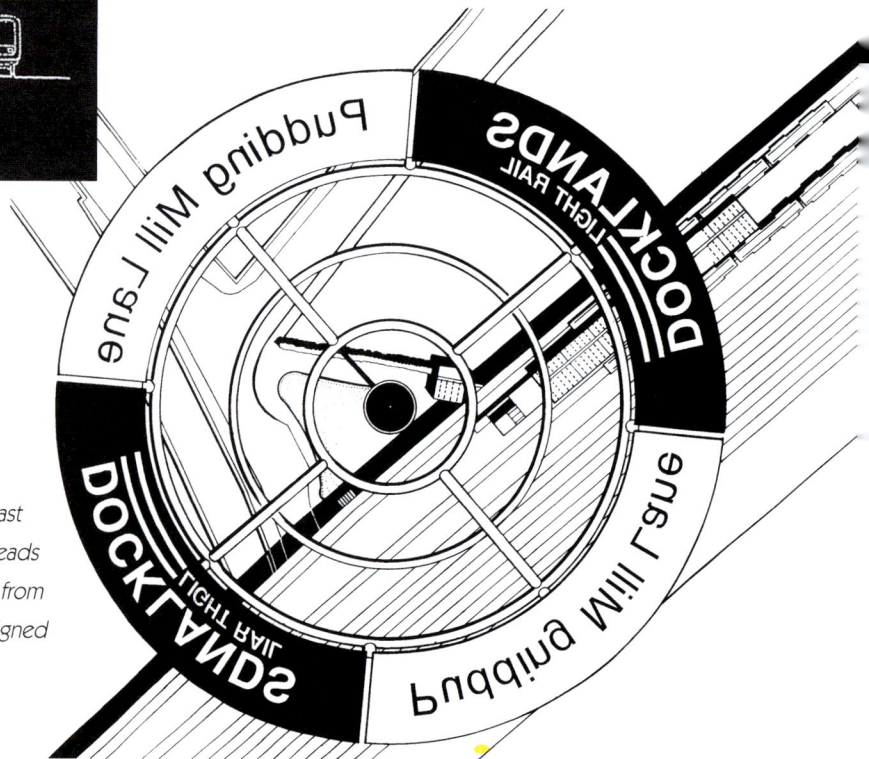

Focused Case Studies

Sensing devices - joist/wiring detector

At one time detecting electrical cables or pipes or wooden studs in partitions or ceiling joists was a hit-and-miss affair. To detect a ceiling joist you simply made lots of tiny holes in a row across the ceiling with a bradawl until you found a joist. Then you repeated this procedure until you found the next one, and so on. It was a reliable method but it took a long time and slightly damaged the ceiling.

These products are sold in DIY shops and builders' merchants and are aimed at a wide range of users – professionals, amateurs, male and female.

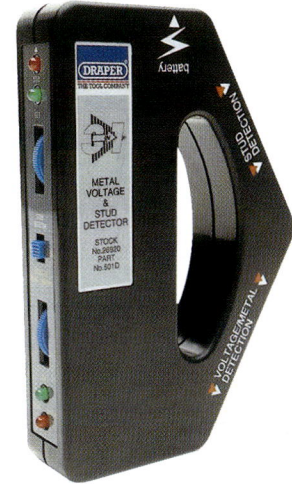

Draper Tools, 3-in-1 combined metal, voltage & stud detector

P Pause for thought

Why can't you use the bradawl method for locating water or gas pipes or electrical cables?

Detecting live cables is particularly important as workers have been seriously injured as a result of getting it wrong. In one case a plumber died when the micro bore metal tubing he was laying under the floor touched an old but still live metal cable. Power-drills are heavily insulated to protect the user against the danger of hitting live cables but the risks of injury are still there.

In order to help to control such risks, special 'tester' screwdrivers and electronic detectors were developed.

The combined metal, voltage and stud detector shown here was designed to locate live or dead electric cables, water pipes, nails and other metal objects. It was also designed to locate wooden studs in partition walling without causing surface damage.

3-in-1 detector features include:

- metal voltage and stud detectors combined in one unit;
- instant visual and audible warning;
- low power consuming LEDs (light emitting diodes) and buzzer indicators;
- powered by one 9V PP3 battery;
- fast, accurate, easy use;
- detailed instruction booklet supplied with instructions on correct use;
- the product conforms with safety directives.

Q Questions

The 3-in-1 detector is not a very stylish product. By means of sketches show how you would improve its appearance.

Using the product

The 3-in-1 detector needs to be set correctly by the user to gain optimum performance. The detailed instruction book is designed to promote correct setting and usage.

For metal/voltage detection the detector is used as shown in the illustration. The setting up procedure for detecting wooden frames is similar but in this mode the detector cannot distinguish between a wooden baton and a pipe or cable, therefore the detector has to be used again, in voltage/metal mode, to check.

P Pause for thought

How might a product designer try to ensure that instructions for usage are not only clear, but are actually read by the user?

Operating instructions

- The user selects the voltage/metal detecting option. A green LED comes on.

- The user adjusts a dial upwards until red, green LEDs come on and the buzzer sounds.

- The unit is held as in the illustrations and moved horizontally (sideways) across the surface.

- When the unit detects a metal object the red LED and a continuous buzzer tone come on.

- If the detected object is a current-carrying conductor then there will be a blinking, red LED and a beeping buzzer sound.

Cautionary notes

- If a conductor is shielded by a metal conduit the detector will only show the presence of the metal.

- Metallised fibres in a wall (say, for fireproofing) may spread the area of voltage pick-up.

- If the wall is rubbed or banged, static electricity may be generated - this will cause a false reading.

- Wearing jewellery on the hands may cause a false reading.

3-in-1 detector used in metal/voltage mode

How it works

The detector uses electromagnetic induction to detect hidden metal. When a magnetic field passes over a metal object, small electric currents are induced in the metal. These currents are called eddy currents and, in their turn, they produce small magnetic fields. In a metal detector there are coils of wire arranged so that in the absence of metal any eddy currents cancel out. However, in the presence of metals an overall eddy current is produced. This current is small but can be amplified to give a signal. If the metal object is 'live', that is a wire carrying an electric current, then there is an additional magnetic field which gives rise to more eddy currents in the coil and these too can be detected.

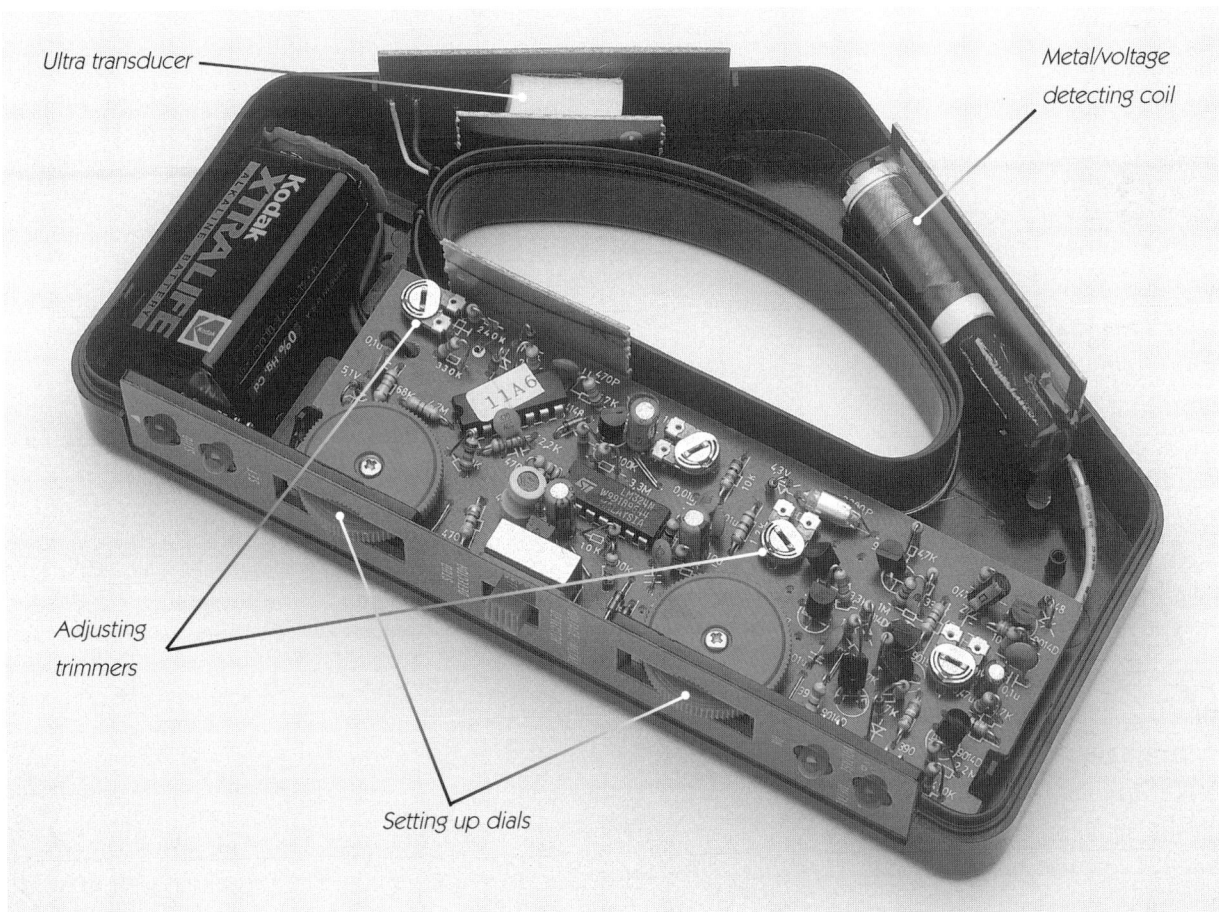

Ultra transducer

Metal/voltage detecting coil

Adjusting trimmers

Setting up dials

Questions

1 Draw a systems diagram to explain how the 3-in-1 detector works. You may find it useful to read pages 86-88.

Research activity

Talk to your science teacher about electromagnetic induction. Identify three applications and describe how they work.

Measuring devices – exercise cycle

Exercise equipment can be used in a gym or at home. It is important to follow a personal exercise programme designed for an individual's use, otherwise it can be unsafe.

The controls and displays on exercise equipment allow users to set up the machine for particular activities and then measure and communicate the user's performance. This is motivating for users as they can set achievable targets and make progress. The user interface needs to be easy to use and read while exercising – even under sweaty conditions! It should not interfere with the exercise in any way and should be in a position that maximises performance. The Tectrix BikeMax shown here is a state of the art exercise cycle.

BikeMax's large, easy-to-read display includes:

- miles per hour [mph] and watts;
- distance and programme/level;
- RPM and average speed;
- calories and calories per hour;
- time remaining and elapsed time;
- easy to follow prompts are displayed, including a 'Help' key;
- BikeMax modes include: a built-in fitness test; group and solo race modes; a custom programme mode and 101 pre-set workouts;
- in exercise mode BikeMax delivers a standard workout based on time and a constant workload, not pedal speed;
- in bicycle mode the workout is based on distance, not time. The faster the user pedals, the faster the workout is completed. There are 18 speeds which simulate a racing bike's gear ratios;
- with SmartLink feature, users can 'daisy chain' up to 8 BikeMax units together for a group race programme;
- SmartLink also lets gym staff connect up to 8 BikeMax units to a personal computer in order to control the workout or simply monitor, record and track users' progress;
- the seat on the BikeMax clicks up for height adjustment. The user pulls the seat up until it has reached the right height. A release knob allows it to be lowered. The oversized seat shape was designed to provide riders with a comfortable, supportive shape without sacrificing durability;
- the bike is driven by a cable drive system, not a chain.

BikeMax specifications

US patents:	5 089 960; and one pending
Min. pedalling speed:	10 rpm
Speed range:	2 – 30 mph
Pre-set programmes:	101 (plus custom programme)
Programme times:	5 – 60 minutes
Fitness test mode:	12-minute test, YMCA protocol
Solo race mode:	race to a caloric or distance goal against an electronic pacer
Group race: mode	2 to 8 BikeMax units (simultaneously) via SmartLink
Communications:	SmartLink uses RS-232 with telephone-type connectors
Power : requirements:	60 watts, 1/2A @ 110 VAC, 1/4A @ 250 VAC
'Daisy chaining':	up to 10 BikeMax units can share one 10-amp outlet
Dimensions:	56" (H), 26" (W), 51" (L)
Weight:	150 lb
Shipping dimensions:	22" (H), 51" (W), 53" (L)
Shipping weight:	200 lbs
Warranties:	institutional – 1 year parts and labour home – 4 years parts /1 year labour

- The control panel on BikeMax is designed to be easy to read. The designers feel that this helps to motivate the user because it constantly challenges their performance.

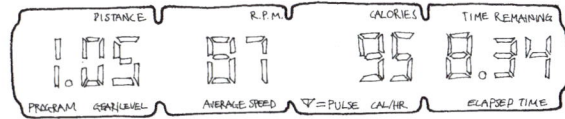

- The control panel can display ten different categories of performance data.

- The control panel includes on/off controls for bicycle simulation modes.

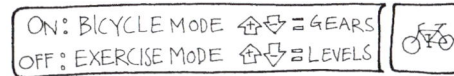

BikeMax has a special HELP key to promote quick and easy programming.

Tectrix exercise equipment includes a wireless heart rate monitor called the CardioTouch monitor. It is pressure sensitive and detects the pulse rate.

Research has indicated that workout benefits can be maximised by raising your heart rate and maintaining it within specific training zones for specific lengths of time. These zones are based on age and weight and reflect activity levels that range from 60 to 90 per cent of maximum heart rate. It is thought that the body burns stored fat with the greatest efficiency within these zones. The designers of the CardioTouch system have presented this information in an easily accessible way as shown in the panel overleaf.

The information needed by people using the Tectrix CardioTouch Heart Rate Monitor

1

- Monitoring your heart rate and keeping within specific training zones is the key to more efficient workouts

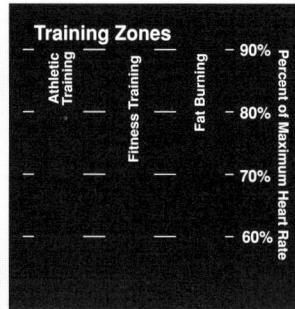

Training Zones

Athletic Training | Fitness Training | Fat Burning

Percent of Maximum Heart Rate
- 90%
- 80%
- 70%
- 60%

2

- The CardioTouch Heart Rate Monitor is designed to help the user optimise their workout according to their age, weight and level of fitness.

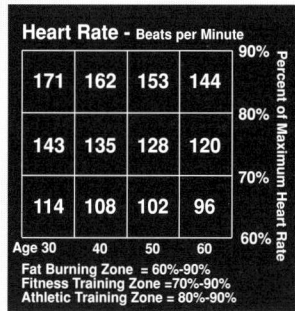

Heart Rate - Beats per Minute

171	162	153	144
143	135	128	120
114	108	102	96

Percent of Maximum Heart Rate
90% / 80% / 70% / 60%

Age 30 / 40 / 50 / 60

Fat Burning Zone = 60%-90%
Fitness Training Zone =70%-90%
Athletic Training Zone = 80%-90%

3

- By helping you to keep your heart rate within a training zone appropriate for your age and weight, CardioTouch helps to produce a more effective workout.

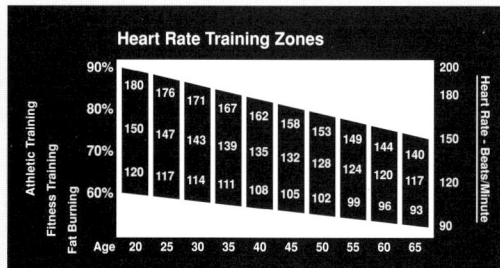

Heart Rate Training Zones

Athletic Training / Fitness Training / Fat Burning

Heart Rate - Beats/Minute

90%	80%	70%	60%						
180	176	171	167	162	158	153	149	144	140
150	147	143	139	135	132	128	124	120	117
120	117	114	111	108	105	102	99	96	93

Age 20 25 30 35 40 45 50 55 60 65

200 / 180 / 150 / 120 / 90

One of the drawbacks of exercising on machines is that it can be boring. The very latest exercise machines use virtual reality to combat this, as shown below. The user can choose from a whole range of exercise worlds, available on CD-ROM. Most of these are fantasy environments in which it would be impossible to exercise – in mid-air or underwater, for example.

Making keep fit interesting through virtual reality. You can cycle underwater and in mid air!

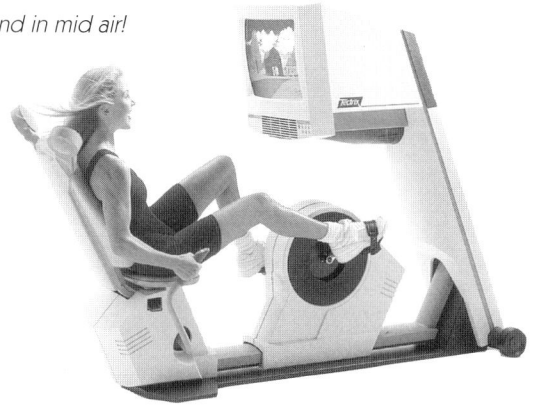

Questions

1 Discuss the following with a partner and then write a brief summary of your findings.

What are the advantages and disadvantages of exercising 'indoors' as opposed to the 'real thing'?

Research activity

Visit a local leisure centre, health club or gymnasium and check out the equipment available for keep fit activities. Ask the attendants how the equipment has changed over the past five years. Ask them to predict what equipment will be like in the future.

Electronic novelties - 'soft', noise-making toys

The UK market for toys for babies and very young children has grown enormously over recent years. There is now a wide product range of traditional soft toys, devices which automatically amuse young children and even toys which they can control themselves. The marketing of these toys often includes the suggestion that healthy child development, through stimulation and learning, is encouraged by these toys. The designers of such toys use the results of research into child development to make sure that the toy is suitable for the target age group. Television and magazine advertising is widely used to market these toys and major UK distributors offer customer help lines and product brochures.

Most of the toys for babies and very young children that are on sale in the UK are manufactured abroad and imported but they all have to conform to very strict safety laws. Babies and young children are very vulnerable to injury from any of the following:

The Tomy musical cot kaleidoscope is voice activated and lights up as well as playing a lullaby

- choking from swallowing small, detached parts or fluff;
- cuts from sharp edges or corners;
- strangling from cords;
- illness from poor hygiene.

Babies have poor motor control and it is easy for them to poke themselves quite hard in the eye. They explore all objects by putting them in their mouth so it is important for toys to be washable.

P Pause for thought

How were babies amused before such toys were available?

Tomy Toys First Fun Lullaby Teddy Bear

The Tomy Lullaby Teddy Bear was designed for babies from birth onwards so it has to meet particularly high safety standards. It is manufactured in China and comes complete, ready for distribution, to Tomy in the UK.

The bear is designed to soothe babies when they wake and to send them back to sleep by playing a lullaby tune. The cheeks on the bear glow to provide visual comfort in the dark, and the bear itself is made from soft, cuddly fur fabric which provides tactile comfort.

The Lullaby Bear can be sponge cleaned and its clothes machine washed at a low temperature. Following washing, any loose threads need to be trimmed.

The Tomy Lullaby Bear

Tomy provide information about toy safety

The Lion Mark

P

Pause for thought

Why do you think Tomy produce information about toy safety?

Under the bear's bottom is a zipped cotton fabric compartment which holds a plastic box containing the batteries and main circuit. Wiring leads from the case to other components within the bear. Just above the nose there is a sound sensor embedded in the filling and inside the cheeks there are red LEDs. In the left paw is a push-button on/off switch. The battery compartment cover is fixed in place by a screw and the circuitry is also secured in the compartment by screws. The bear needs to be switched off after use in order to prolong battery life.

The overall structure of the toy is shown in the panel.

The lullaby tune and glowing cheek lights are sound activated. The sound sensor responds to the baby crying and also to other loud noises, such as the telephone ringing, someone coughing, etc. However, the sensor is set to ensure that the lullaby does not play in response to every household noise and it is at its most sensitive when placed 2.5 metres from the baby, in a completely quiet room.

The instructions to operate the bear are as follows.

1 Press the on/off switch.

2 Make a noise loud enough to be detected by the sound sensor.

3 The tune plays and repeats for about five minutes, reducing in volume until it becomes quiet.

4 At the same time the cheeks glow, but the glowing becomes dimmer.

5 Further noise reactivates the cycle.

6 To switch off, press the on/off switch.

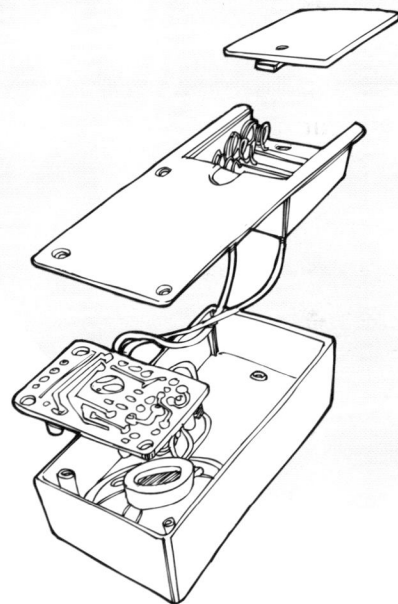

Questions

1 How would you find out whether a baby liked the Tomy Lullaby Bear?

2 What might happen if the toy made the baby cry?

3 What might happen if there were other noises in the baby's room?

The panel below shows a systems diagram for the Tomy Lullaby Bear.
The annotations describe how the system works.

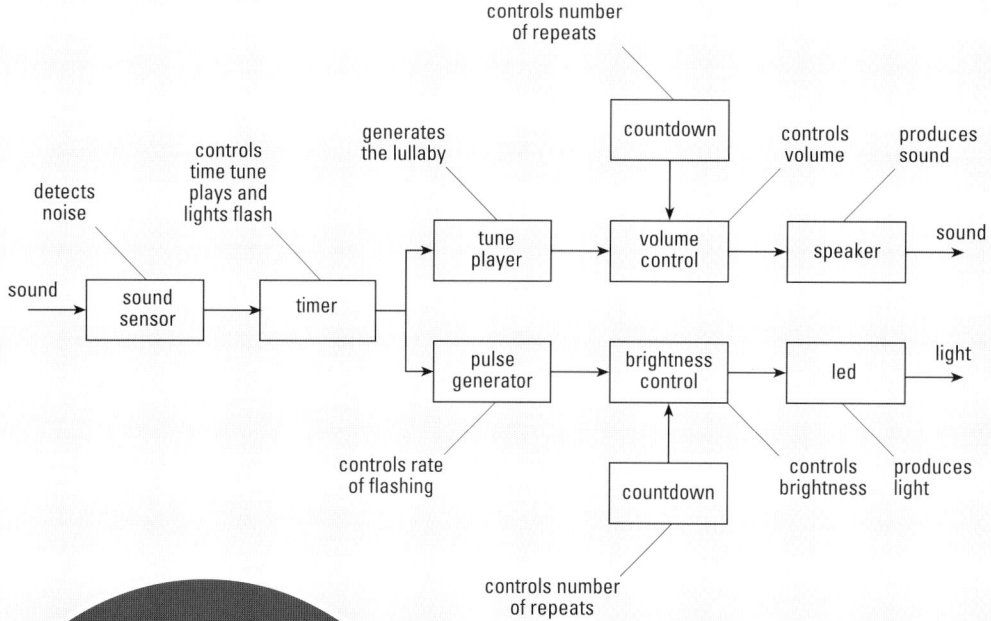

controls number
of repeats

generates
the lullaby

controls volume

produces sound

controls
time tune
plays and
lights flash

countdown

detects
noise

sound → sound sensor → timer → tune player → volume control → speaker → sound

pulse generator → brightness control → led → light

controls rate
of flashing

controls brightness

produces light

countdown

controls number
of repeats

R

Research activity

1 Find out about British Standard 5665. Make a list of the main requirements in your notebook.

2 Find another electronic toy and answer the following questions, using notes and diagrams.

- What age group is the toy for?

- What does the toy do?

- How does the toy work?

- Does it conform to the requirements of BS 5665?

Security devices - intruder alarms for cars

Thefts of vehicles and thefts from vehicles are a big problem in our society not only because they are criminal acts but also because they infringe the feelings of personal safety and well-being of victims of such crime. They have a further impact in that they are costly in terms of police time and insurance. The panel below gives information about vehicle crime.

Vehicle crime statistics

The Home Office reports that, of the 5.1 million offences reported in the period January 1995–December 1995, vehicle crime accounted for 26 per cent, that is 1.3 million crimes. However, vehicle crime was decreasing.

England & Wales				
	Jan. 94–Dec. 94	Jan. 95–Dec. 95	Change –number	Change %
Theft of a vehicle	533 683	509 104	-24 579	-4.61
Thefts from a vehicle	842 707	814 398	-28 309	-3.36
Total vehicle crime	1 376 390	1 323 502	-52 888	-3.8

Insurance claims

The Association of British Insurers' reports on motor theft claims (1995) – private car:

Claims settled: 370 000
Total cost of claims: £434 000 000
Average amount: £1173

- Around 90 per cent of car thieves are males under 25. In contrast, nearly 80 per cent of people who have their cars stolen are aged over 25.
- One in five stolen cheque and credit cards are taken from cars.

The types of vehicle crime may be summarised as follows.

- **Opportunism**
  The vehicle is left open and unattended and the thief takes advantage of the situation to steal either the vehicle or valuables in the vehicle.

- **Unlocking the vehicle and hot-wiring**
  Some vehicle locks are easily picked, the engine is not disabled and the intruder starts the car without an ignition key (hot-wiring).

- **Breaking in and hot-wiring**
  Some vehicle locks are hard or impossible to pick so the intruder breaks in (often by breaking a window) and then hot-wires the ignition.

- **Breaking in and stealing valuables**
  The intruder breaks in, not to steal the car, but to steal valuables. These may be car accessories (radio, phone) or other items left visible in the car.

- **Stripping**
  Stealing parts of the car which can then be sold, for example hub caps, wheels, tyres.

- **Vandalism**
  Causing damage for no obvious gain, for example breaking off wing mirrors or aerials, scratching paint work, smashing windscreens. Sometimes a thief turns to vandalism when frustrated in attempts to gain entry to a vehicle.

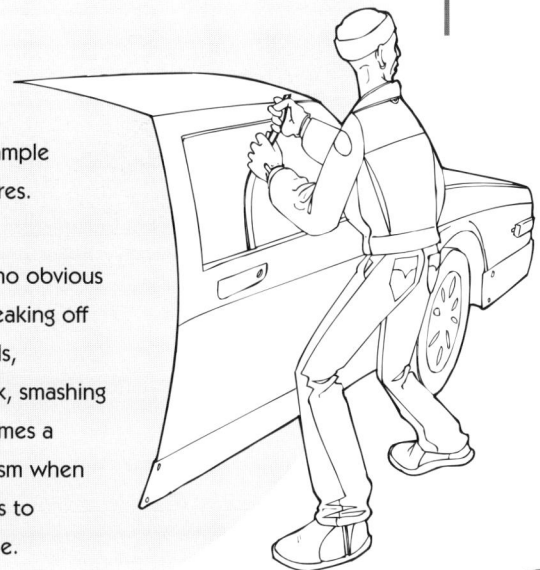

Pause for thought

Has any member of your family suffered vehicle crime?

Protecting against crime

The opportunist criminal can be defeated by taking simple precautions, such as always closing and locking all openings; not leaving wallets or cheque books visible in the car; not leaving vehicle documents in the vehicle; security marking stereos; removing ignition keys and engaging the steering lock; parking in well-lit, open locations; putting the aerial down. The presence of a security system, as shown by a sticker, is believed to have a strong deterrent effect even if the security system has not been installed!

🄳 *Immobilising a vehicle without electronics*

Immobilising the vehicle

The degree of theft can be limited by immobilising the vehicle. This can be done with mechanical products like steering wheel locks but also by disabling the engine in the following ways.

1 Disabling the starter circuit. This prevents the vehicle from being started by using the starter motor. It will not prevent 'bump' starting following 'hot wiring'.

2 Disabling the fuel supply. This isolates the fuel pump on a petrol injected engine or the solenoid valve on the fuel line of a diesel vehicle.

3 Disabling the ignition. Ignition sparking can be prevented by isolating the ignition coil or the electronic ignition circuitry.

Vehicle alarms

A vehicle alarm system senses an attack and sounds audible warnings.

Intruder alarms can be divided into two groups.

1 Hard-wired logic circuits which can be brought into operation by direct switching e.g. a simple toggle switch or a key switch. Once the system is wired into the car it is fixed and cannot be adjusted.

2 Microprocessor controlled alarms which have a greater range of functions, and are operated by radio transmission of a coded signal from a small handset usually carried on a key ring. Transmission may be by radio frequency or infra-red. These systems can be used more flexibly as they can be programmed according to a user's requirements.

Ⓠ

Questions

1 How might you disable a push bike so that it cannot be ridden away?

Make a list and comment on the feasibility of each suggestion.

Sensing the intrusion

1 Contact breaking

If the switch contacts are broken then the change in voltage is detected by either the logic gates or the microprocessor system.

2 Impact sensing

A piezo-electric crystal generates a voltage when subject to impact so this can be used to detect the vibrations caused when a vehicle is disturbed. This voltage is amplified to the point where it will operate a switching transistor. The gain of the amplifier is variable to provide sensitivity adjustment.

3 Movement sensing

Interior movement sensors are of two types:

a ultrasonic sensors

A pair of ultrasonic transducers operating at 40 kHz detect air movement caused by entry to the interior of the vehicle.

b microwave doppler, operating at 2.5 GHz

It is directly sensitive to an increase in mass occupying the space within the vehicle.

Processing the information

Logic circuits

The hard wired circuits of simpler alarms, and the auxiliary circuits of microprocessor alarms, consist of combinations of simple logic gates. These are principally NOR and NAND gates. Once the vehicle is alarmed, the status of the logic gates is set and any changes in this status (as caused by intrusion) result in the alarm being sounded.

Microprocessors

GT radio-operated microprocessor alarms contain a standard circuit of 5-volt power supply, two control oriented processors (COPs), an EPROM memory i.c. and a radio signal receiver module. Each COP operates on a stored internal program and each has its own crystal clock generator. One of the two COPs decodes the received radio signal and stores the identifying code in the EPROM during coding. During operation it compares the received code to that stored. If they match, it generates the arming and disarming signals for the second COP which controls the operation of the alarm in response to various inputs from the vehicle.

A simple block diagram of the GT autoalarms system is shown below.

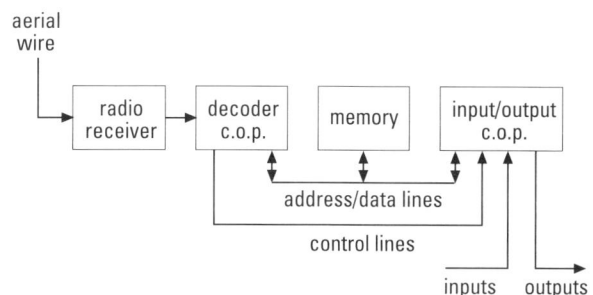

Block schematic diagram of control system

Questions

2 Use brief notes to explain the function of each block in the block diagram.

Sounding the alarm

1 Audible

The loudspeaker requires a large, modulated astable signal to produce a siren sound. Field effect transistors provide the amplification necessary to drive the loudspeaker.

2 Visual

  a Indication of the 'armed' state is provided in some models by means of a dashboard-mounted flashing LED. This LED is also used to signal, by a flashing sequence, the input to which the alarm has responded.

  b The vehicle direction indicators are flashed by means of a relay. The relay coil is pulsed to give the flashing operation.

▶ *A complete alarm system*

Encryption

In microprocessor controlled alarms the handset transmits an operational code which is received and stored by the alarm. The alarm software then permutates this code to obtain a range of future codes to which it will respond on reception of subsequent transmissions. The same permutation is generated within the handset. On subsequent transmissions the handset selects one of the acceptable codes at random, and transmits it to the alarm. The alarm responds to this code once only, therefore the codes transmitted need to change each time. The number of possible different codes can vary from a few hundred to literally trillions. The system used to generate these codes is called **encryption**.

Recording the incidents

In the case of vehicle crime, as with all crime, it is crucial to record and report exactly both what has happened and when it happened. Witness statements are particularly useful. These records are needed for the police and for insurance purposes. Keeping a record of stereo or car-phone serial numbers and vehicle documents separate from the vehicle will help.

® Research activity

Find out about the vehicle crime in your area. You could survey reports in the local press over the past year or you could talk to the local crime prevention officer. Present your findings as a report and make suggestions as to how vehicle crime might be reduced.

Communicating devices – clockwork radio

In order for people to make informed decisions, they need access to information and radio is an important means of communicating information. In some situations the messages broadcast can be a life-line – for example, the shipping forecast, weather reports, news, or programmes about health. In developing countries, and particularly in the more rural areas of these countries or in townships without widespread access to mains power, receiving radio programmes is a problem because batteries are expensive and difficult to obtain.

Look, no batteries! The Freeplay Radio power-source works on the principle of a wind-up spring that turns an internal generator

A main use of a spring is to store energy. When a spring is compressed or stretched, energy is used to make it move. If the energy is not released straightaway, it is stored.

An unwinding spring releases this energy. This energy can drive something else.

The generator uses magnetism to make electricity. The power released by the unwinding spring spins the coil between the magnet poles. The coil cuts through the lines of force, generating an electric current in the coil

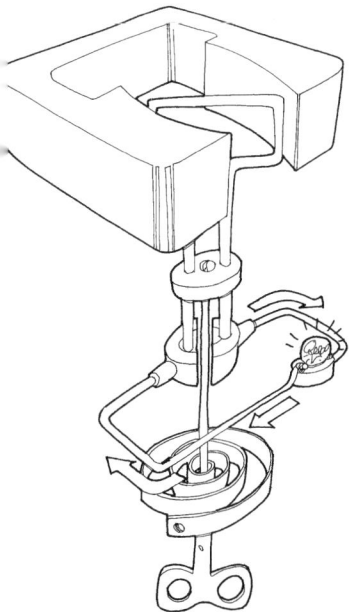

P

Pause for thought

When your portable radio battery runs out what do you do? Why might this not be possible in a developing country?

The clockwork radio idea

Trevor Baylis is an inventor. His workshop is at Eel Pie Island on the River Thames. In 1992 he became concerned about the difficulties in communicating information that could prevent the spread of HIV in Africa. Radio broadcasts transmitted the information, but people weren't hearing it because they couldn't afford to buy batteries for portable radios. So he 'invented' the clockwork radio – a radio that doesn't need batteries or mains electricity.

The basic idea

Trevor Baylis developed the idea of his radio by trying out a very simple idea. He used a small electric motor as a generator and a hand drill to turn the shaft, and found that this system would power a portable radio. All that he needed now was a clockwork wind-up motor to operate a generator! He demonstrated a prototype system on the Tomorrow's World television programme, which gave just ten seconds of play time from a complete wind up.

A business plan

Chris Staines, an accountant, saw the programme and was impressed. He had good connections in Africa, particularly in the Cape, and he saw the potential of the technology. He contacted Trevor and, within days, he had negotiated the product development rights. He put together a consortium of British universities and companies who were prepared to develop the product and approached the ODA (Overseas Development Agency) for support. The ODA does not usually get involved with manufacturing but in this case it did, through the Head of Information and Emergency Aid – Andy Bearpark. The ODA put £200 000 into the project.

Technical specification – Freeplay Radio	
Power source	Internal – B-Motor carbon steel spring, driving a generator through a transmission; External – AC Adaptor jack plug socket
Frequency	FM – 88 – 108 (Mhz) AM – 520 – 1700 (Khz) SW – 3.3 – 12 (Mhz) Model A – 5.8 – 18 (Mhz) Model B
Speaker	3.5 inch, 8 OHM, 4 Watt
Antenna system	FM – Telescopic antenna SW – Telescopic antenna AM – Built in ferrite bar antenna
Operating specifications	Wind-up 60 turns (approx. 20 seconds) Playtime per full wind – 30 minutes
Generator life	About 10 000 winds
Dimensions and weight	Width 13 $\frac{1}{2}$ in
Height	9 $\frac{1}{2}$ in
Depth	5 $\frac{1}{2}$ in
Weight	6 $\frac{3}{4}$ lb
Optional accessories	External SW antenna 9V – AC adaptor
Warranty	Six month warranty against defective workmanship or materials
Environmental benefit	A comparable AM/FM radio would require over 400 'D' cells to match the Freeplay's minimum rated generator performance of 6600 hours.

The product was to be assembled in South Africa by disabled workers and, because the project now had the support of the ODA, Chris Staines was able to attract investment from South African investors. In October 1994 a South African company, BayGen, was set up by the shareholders. The final specification for the Freeplay radio is shown here.

Not just any old spring

There were considerable difficulties with the design of the spring. In order to get sufficient power storage the spring had to be large and made of just the right material. University electrical engineers and materials technologists worked at developing this and eventually were able to get about 30 minutes of playing time from every 20 seconds of winding.

The image and style of the radio

CLK, a specialist branding research company, investigated the image and styling of the radio. The radio had to satisfy a broad range of potential consumers. This was because BayGen would distribute the radio to aid agencies and market the radio in Africa and Western countries. The radio had to be quick to assemble on a low-technology production line; appeal to a range of tastes; and be very strong and robust.

CLK brought in TKO, a product design consultancy. The TKO partners, Andy Davey and Anne Gardener, had to find out what would appeal in Africa. They had to put aside their own preconceptions of current Western image and style. A rugged, fairly large set seemed to be preferred. TKO produced a number of different prototypes as the shape and size of the radio components changed, while taking into account CLK's and BayGen's ideas on what would be most marketable in both Africa and the West.

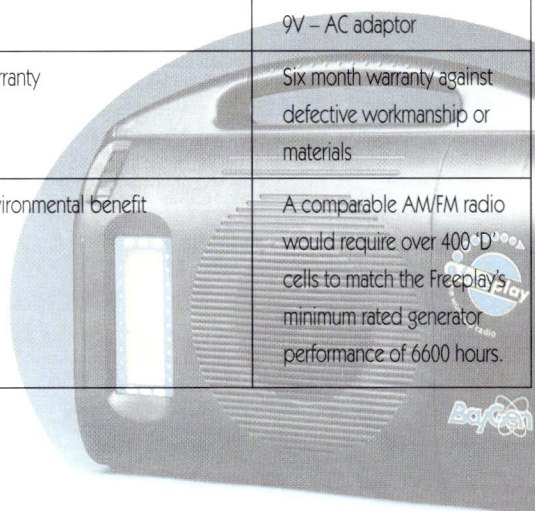

The final design of the Freeplay radio is quite bulky, partly because of the need to enclose the large spring. The buttons and dials are recessed for protection. The radio looks tough and rugged, but with a smoothness in its curves and a utilitarian look which also appeal to current Western taste.

Questions

1 Calculate the following:

- the rotational input speed in rpm if 60 turns take 20 seconds;

- the rotational output speed in rpm if 60 turns now take 30 minutes.

2 Design a compound gear train that would provide this gearing down.

Production

The Freeplay is assembled by workers on the BayGen assembly lines near Cape Town – where a third of the workers are disabled. It uses British-made generator units and Far Eastern electronics. The casings are moulded in South Africa. Over a million radios are produced each year. Marketing distribution stretches across south-east Asia, South America and the UK.

In the UK Friends of the Earth, among others, market the Freeplay. A percentage of all sales of Freeplay in the West is used to provide radios to needy areas in the developing world. Also, for every ten radios sold, one radio is donated to World Child, a British non-government organisation [NGO], for health education projects in Africa

BayGen now have plans to extend their product range to include wind-up flashlights, a wind-up Walkman style radio, and cellular phones.

President Nelson Mandela with the Freeplay's inventor Trevor Baylis

Research activity

Use notes and diagrams to answer the following points.

1 Describe three different sorts of spring.

2 Give examples of a use for each sort of spring.

3 Explain how the structure of each spring enables it to be used in this way.

Questions

Currently, in the UK the Freeplay retails at an RRP of £69.99, and in the USA at around $149.00. It is advertised on the Internet as well as in newspapers and magazines.

3 What sort of consumer is being targeted?

4 Is it justifiable to charge more in some countries in order to subsidise the costs in other countries?

5 Could an increased access to radio have any harmful effects?

Communicating devices – bus arrival times system, the countdown service

In cities there is a growing trend to encourage the use of public transport as a means of dealing with traffic congestion and pollution. Some people enjoy travelling by bus; others don't.

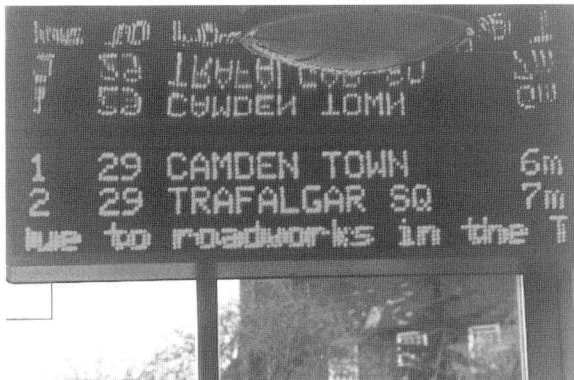

P **Pause for thought**

Have you ever had to wait on your own for a bus on a cold, dark night? What did it feel like?

Bus time-tables provide schedule and route information but traffic congestion, large numbers of people using the bus and the re-routing of buses due to roadworks often cause variations from the schedule. Countdown is a service system introduced by London Transport Buses to combat these problems.

The Countdown displays at main bus stops give passengers the information they need – when they can expect the first bus, and its destination. The display also provides information on further buses. Countdown displays can also be used to show special messages from a service controller at the garage – about traffic delays or other problems. It can also include next stop displays on-board the bus.

How Countdown works

Countdown uses a network of roadside microwave beacons to pinpoint the location of buses. These are quite small (200 × 200 × 100 mm) and are fixed on lamp-posts along the bus routes. Each one has a unique identity. These beacons are only activated when a bus passes them and they then transmit their identity to the bus [this is the automatic vehicle location system – AVL].

The beacons only pick up buses which are passing in a certain direction. They are battery operated. The bus receiving system recognises when the beacon battery is running low. This is then relayed to the central system.

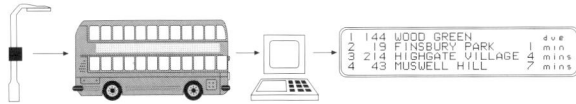

An overview of the system

On-line information appears on screen

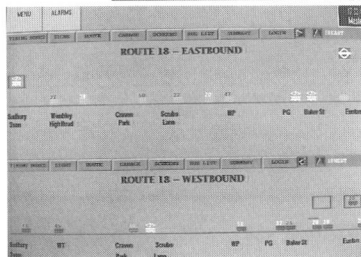

On board each bus there is a **microwave transponder**, modem and **odomoter** (wheel revolution counter). The transponder, installed on the nearside of the bus, picks up the identity of the beacon it passes and resets the odometer count. Both the beacon identity and odometer count are stored in the modem, along with bus route data, which communicates through the London Transport Buses radio system to the central computer. A polling mechanism requests each bus location every 30 seconds.

P

Pause for thought

Have you ever been stuck in a traffic jam? What did it feel like?

The central computer system includes a database of route and schedule information. This system does not rely for operation on scheduled information, but can take account of changing conditions automatically.

Predicting arrival times

The central computer estimates how long it will take to reach the stop from where the bus is now. The precise position of each bus at any time is known from the AVL and route data. The central computer predicts the time through a calculation based on the time it has taken the three previous buses to cover the same distance. This enables traffic congestion and other variable factors to be taken into account. Equipment on board the bus can also be used to operate a 'next stop' display for passengers.

Q

Questions

1 What happens to the bus stops and bus shelters in your area. Make a list of all the physical factors which affect them. Comment on how well, in your experience, they stand up to these.

The bus stop

The way that passengers normally wait for a bus, and what passengers want, was taken into account in the design of the Countdown system. It was discovered that passengers want to be able to view the display without changing the way they wait for a bus – for example, while sitting under a shelter. Passengers also want clear, simple information which will both help and reassure them.

Countdown at bus stops

Evaluating the Countdown system

The information supplied by the Countdown system is shown in the panel below.

Countdown bus-stop display information

The display provides the following information.

- The order of arrival at the stop, destination and minutes to arrival – shown for each bus approaching the stop.

- At busy stops – between three and ten buses can be shown on one or several routes.

- Standard messages – such as 'All buses go to Kings Cross'.

- Special messages – such as 'Delays expected in Highbury due to football match'.

- Messages can be scrolled across the screen every 90 seconds.

- Audio information: this is a design improvement and enables passengers to hear all the information displayed at a stop. The information is drawn from a computer-held stock of audio messages.

- Fail-safe control: if the bus driver fails to enter, or enters incorrectly, the destination code, then the display will simply tell waiting passengers in which direction the bus is travelling.

Countdown have used market research to find out how useful people find this information. Here are some of the findings.

Passenger view

On the pilot Countdown route (18)

- About 96 per cent of passengers felt that Countdown information was clear and easy to see and that they had no problems with the system.

- About 70 per cent of passengers referred to the display when they arrived at the stop and about 90 per cent looked at the sign while they waited. About 60 pr cent said they looked at the sign at least once a minute.

- About 65 per cent of passengers felt they had waited a shorter time for their buses after the introduction of the system.

- About 64 per cent thought that the service was now more reliable (although it hadn't actually changed).

- Most people said that the waiting time passed more quickly.

- About 50 per cent of late-evening bus travellers felt safer with the Countdown system in operation.

- Passengers found that the main information displayed was easy to understand. Some base-line messages were not so well understood.

- In general, people became much more positive about travelling by bus:

  68 per cent said they now had a higher opinion of bus travel;

  54 per cent said they now had a higher opinion of the operator;

  45 per cent said they now had a higher opinion of London Transport.

Videos taken at bus stops with and without Countdown show that passengers are a lot more relaxed when they know how long their wait will be. Some even use the time they have to visit nearby shops.

Operator view

There were initial doubts about the introduction of the system among the bus transport workers. Some were concerned that it was like 'Big Brother' or 'a spy in the cab'. On the positive side, a driver can now be told, before he or she even leaves the garage, that the journey will be subject to delays and is therefore much less likely to face passenger displeasure as waiting times are known in advance. Also, from an operator's point of view, a whole day's bus and driver movements can be logged and displayed on the computer screen.

In the future

Overall, the evaluation showed that the system has brought benefits to both workers and passengers. The success of the trials has led to the AVL system being expanded to the whole of the London Transport Buses network. This means that Countdown signs will be fitted to the main bus stops in London, about 6500 bus stops! Note that London Transport Buses (LTB) are not bus operators. LTB define, regulate and set fares across the London wide network (the 33 London boroughs). There are just over 30 individual bus operating companies working in London and LTB provides a London wide service by cooperating with these service providers.

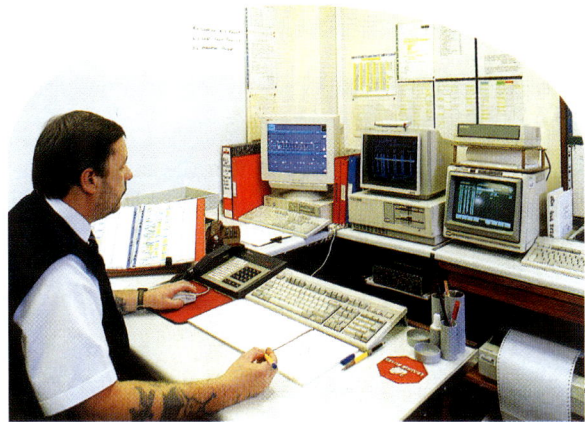

Q Questions

2 LTB can't afford to fit Countdown to all bus stops so they have to decide at which stops it would be most useful. How could they do this – maximum number of boarders, outside schools, outside factories, outside train stations? Discuss this with others in your group and prepare a list of guidance points.

R Research activity

1 Find out how one of the following transport information services works:

   a London Underground tube trains;

   b UK rail overground trains;

   c in-flight aeroplane journey progress.

2 Use notes and diagrams to explain how each of the following works:

   a transponders;

   b odometers;

   c modem.

Electronic load controllers for micro hydro power

Ghandruk is a small village in the Annapurna mountain range in the country of Nepal.

It is far away from roads and the power lines of the national grid, so the village has its own (very small) hydro electric power station. The station is so small it is known as a 'micro' hydro power station, and it harnesses the power of the local river.

The water from the river is diverted into a pipe which carries it down the hill to a water turbine.

Micro hydro schemes usually produce less than 100 kW of output power. The scheme in Ghandruk produces only 50 kW, which is enough to power the whole village.

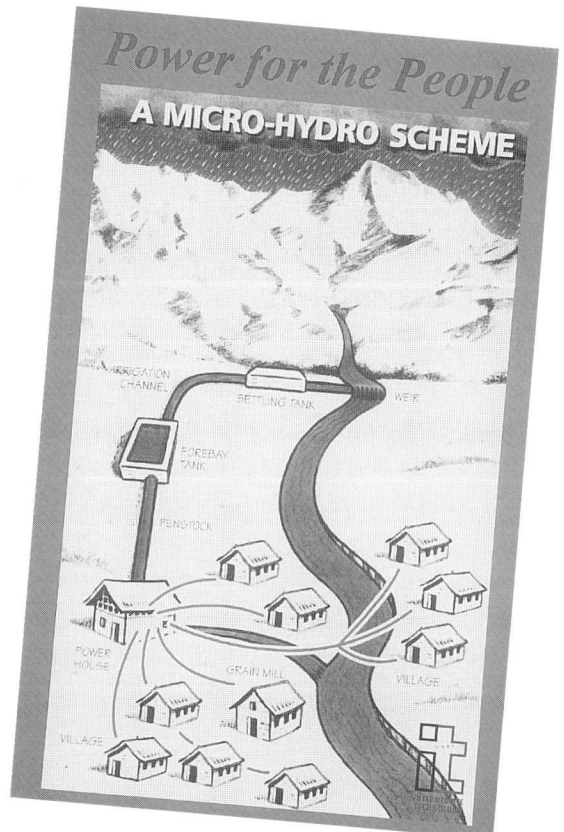

Turbines have been used for centuries all over Nepal to turn mechanically the drive shaft of food-processing appliances, to mill grain or squeeze out oil. Nowadays, in Ghandruk, turbines are also often connected with drive belts to small generators (or alternators) to produce electricity.

P

Pause for thought

How much electricity does the average house consume in the UK? (A electric cooker is rated at 9 kW peak power, a microwave oven is rated at 750 kW and hair dryers at 1 kW.)

Focused case studies

Meeting the demand for electric power

Calculating the demand

The demand for electric power varies with the time of day, and sometimes the time of year. For instance, in a village such as Ghandruk there will be a demand for electricity for lighting during the evening, but none during daylight hours.

In countries where electricity is used for cooking, there will be a demand from people while evening meals are being cooked, but not during the middle of the night.

If the demand for electricity in a village like Ghandruk was measured, it might look something like this.

Installing the right capacity

Once the demand has been calculated, micro hydro scheme engineers measure the water flow in the river and calculate how much they must use to meet the demand. They install the scheme turbines and generators with these factors in mind.

Excess power

In the UK, most power stations are connected to the national grid. This acts as a 'pool' which soaks up any power that isn't used by consumers close to the power station. When UK power stations are not grid-connected, they change the amount of power produced by regulating the water flow through the station turbines so that they can match their output to the demand for power. If this isn't done, the scheme will produce too much power which will burn out the system very quickly.

In Ghandruk, the micro hydro scheme is far from the national grid so any excess power has nowhere to go.

While the village was planning electrification, they found that they could afford the cost of the basic micro hydro scheme, but that the equipment they needed to change the flow of water into the turbine was too expensive. Instead of abandoning the scheme, they decided to use an electronic load controller.

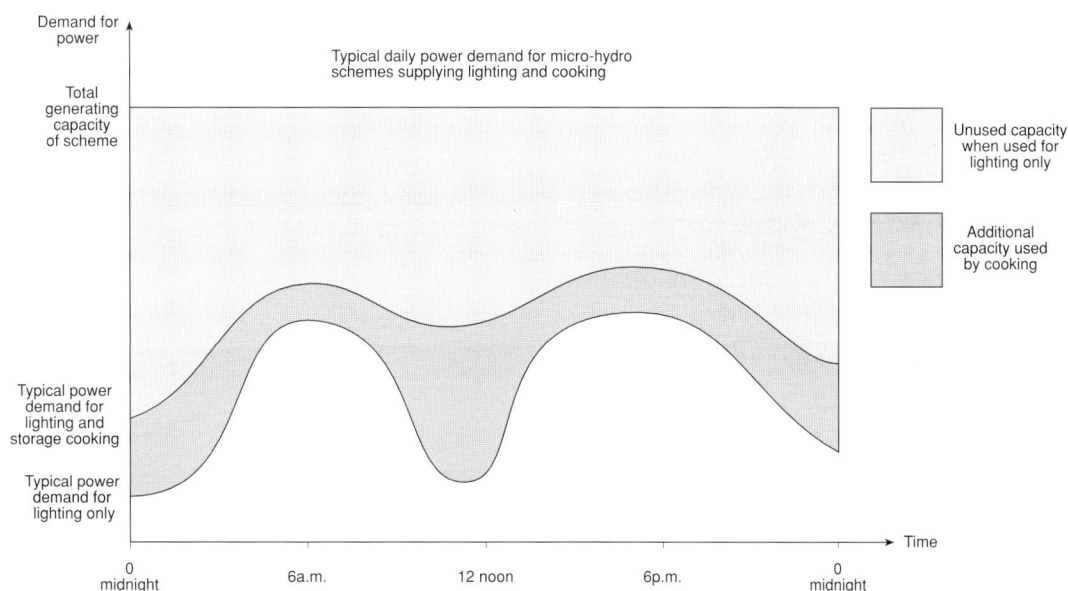

Typical daily power demand for micro-hydro schemes supplying lighting and cooking

Demand for power

Total generating capacity of scheme

Typical power demand for lighting and storage cooking

Typical power demand for lighting only

Time

0 midnight — 6a.m. — 12 noon — 6p.m. — 0 midnight

Unused capacity when used for lighting only

Additional capacity used by cooking

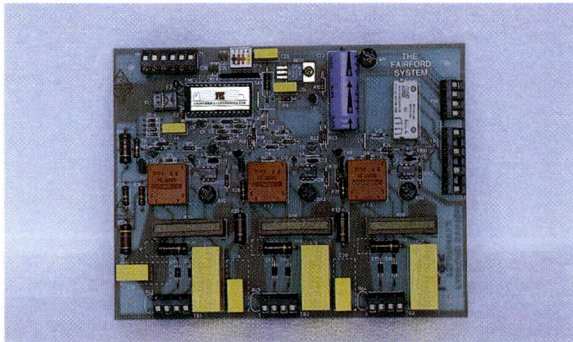

Electronic load controllers for micro hydro power

Electronic load controllers

Intermediate Technology (IT), an international organisation, commissioned an electronic engineer based in Cornwall to design an electronic load controller (ELC) to address this problem. IT's office in Nepal was involved in specifying the original design. Once this was worked out and tested, IT worked with local manufacturers to modify the ELC to make it suitable for manufacture and use in Nepal.

The ELC ensures that a stand-alone generator can be run at full output, 24 hours a day, without the need for expensive equipment to govern the input of water. An ELC does this by matching the amount of electricity sent to the village with the demand for power.

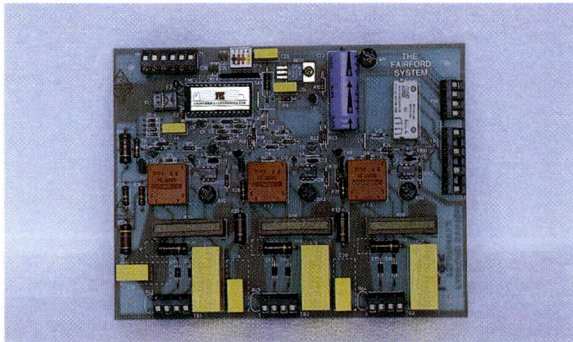

The electronic load controller circuit board

How does an ELC work?

All the electric power produced by the generator goes to the ELC. The ELC senses the demand level from the village and sends exactly the right amount of power to the village to meet the demand. Any remaining power is 'dumped' to a bank of resistors known as the 'ballast load', which can be any type of resistive load, such as water heating or space heating elements.

The resistor bank varies in size, according the ELC, to make sure that it can completely soak up the leftover energy. Where there is no demand from the village, for example, the ELC sends all the power to the ballast load. If, however, someone switches on a light in their house, the ELC detects this almost immediately and sends the required amount of electricity to the village.

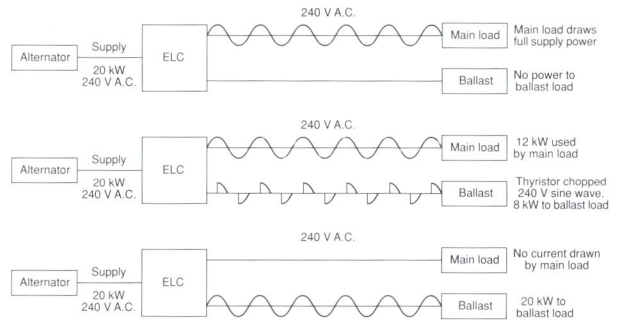

The ELC makes sure that: Total Energy Demand + Total Energy Dumped = Total Energy Supplied

Micro hydro schemes *with* supply/demand matching controlled by ELCs cost about *half as much* per installed kW as those with conventional governing systems (which control the input of water).

60

Hot showers in Ghandruk

The power which is soaked up by the ELC ballast load isn't usually wasted.

In Ghandruk, for example, the ballast load is a bank of nine 6 kW water heating elements in a 400 litre water tank.

Every year Ghandruk is visited by almost 7000 tourists from all over the world on trekking expeditions. The tourists are keen to take hot showers after their treks. Trekkers' lodges have, in the past, used firewood to heat water for washing, but the demand for firewood became so great that it was having a damaging effect on local forests. The water heated by the micro hydro scheme ballast load currently supplies three hot showers in the village. Trekkers pay a price of around 35 Nepali rupees for a five-minute shower, generating much-needed income for the village.

Micro hydro schemes in Nepal are appropriate technology because:

- once the schemes are set up, they are affordable to run;
- they are manufactured and maintained within Nepal;
- they allow communities to manage their own power supplies;
- they save thousands of women from the drudgery of milling grain by hand;
- they generate electricity for lighting which improves the quality of life for people;
- they enable electric cookers to be used which saves trees and time previously spent in collecting firewood.

Questions

Discuss these questions with a partner.

1 Are there any negative affects on people or the environment from installing a micro hydro scheme?

2 What other resistive loads might be suitable as 'ballast' for an ELC?

Research activity

An ELC contains an electronic component called a thyristor. Find out what thyristors do and what they are used for.

Improved transit facilities

Focused case studies

Helping to keep air breathable

The air we breathe

Protecting the air we breathe is important. If it becomes polluted and causes breathing difficulties, then the quality of life of many people will be affected. The Environmental Pollution Act, introduced in 1990, controls the amounts of harmful substances that industries can discharge into the atmosphere. Industrial emissions are monitored jointly by HMIP (Her Majesties Inspectorate of Pollution) and local authorities. They have powers to impose heavy fines on companies who break the law and, ultimately, to close factories that cause too much pollution.

Air across Europe

The member states of the EC (European Community) have set up a variety of organisations to help to ensure that our air becomes cleaner. One of these is Eureka-EuroEnviron. It provides financial support and advice on the development of environmental technology projects across Europe. Hytec is one British company which has received support from Eureka-EuroEnviron and, through this funding, Hytec has been able to research and develop a project called IPAS.

R

Research activity

There appears to be an increase in the incidence of asthma. Could this be due to increased air pollution?

The IPAS Project

IPAS stands for 'in situ pollution analysis' using solid state sensors. This system is designed to be used in incineration plants. These are plants which burn waste material. The heat energy produced can be used to power a variety of activities such as water heating or generating electricity, but it is important that the emissions from the smokestack do not cause pollution. The overall structure of the system is shown below.

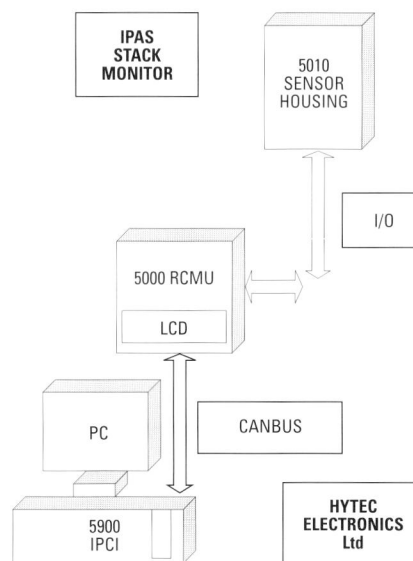

The sensor system (5010 Sensor Housing), which is placed in the smokestack, is linked via an input/output (I/0) board to a RCMU (remote control and monitoring unit). The RCMU is then connected to a PC, using a CANbus interface which acquires measurement data and transmits control information via the 5900 IPCI (intelligent PC interface) to the screen. The advantage of this interface is its ease of programming in a Windows computer environment.

The system allows the emissions of harmful gases to be controlled because it operates in real time. As soon as the concentration of a harmful material is seen to increase, the incineration plant can be controlled to prevent this taking place. This is usually done by adjusting the temperature of incineration and the air flow rate into the incineration chamber. The information from the sensor is providing the feedback necessary to control the process and eliminate the pollution. An important feature of IPAS is that it uses fuzzy logic to enable the system to learn. Initially, when the feedback from IPAS indicates pollution, adjustments are made by skilled operators. The system learns how to do this for itself so that when similar conditions arise again, IPAS can make the changes necessary all by itself, without the need for human intervention. At the moment IPAS is still undergoing trials to ensure that it can work properly in the harsh and demanding environment of an incineration plant smokestack.

P

Pause for thought

Is it wise to give IPAS total control of emissions?

The overview

An important way of looking at the impact of a product on the environment is product life cycle analysis (PLCA). PLCA is sometimes called 'cradle to grave analysis' because the intention is to cover the following:

- all primary inputs of raw materials and energy;
- all the emissions to the environment and solid residues;
- all the inputs and wastes associated with the reuse, recycling and ultimate disposal.

The life cycle of a product is summarised below. You can see that environmental impact is minimised if the inputs and outputs labelled* are minimised and the efficiency of the feedback loop** is maximised. IPAS and systems like it can help to keep emissions to a minimum.

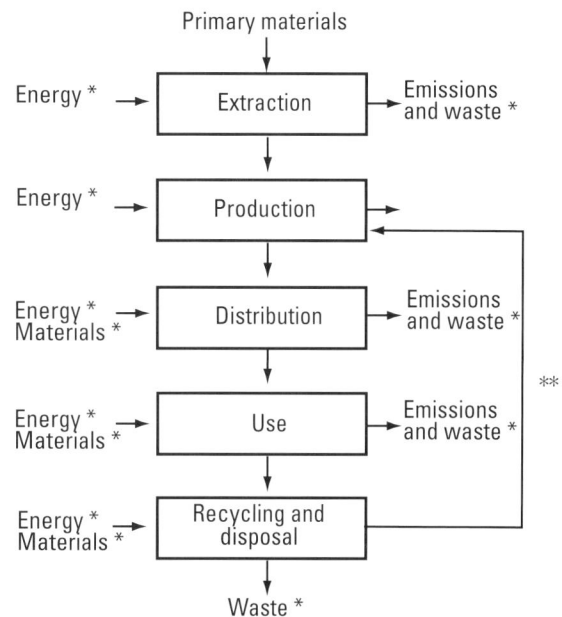

The life cycle of a product

R

Research activity

Carry out a PLCA on an electronic product such as a small radio. You will need to find out about the materials and components it is made from, how these are produced and what happens to them when the radio reaches the end of its useful life.

Focused case studies

A radio revolution

Radio broadcasting is going digital. This started in 1995 when the BBC set up digital broadcasting transmitters. Since then it has been spreading, as shown below.

The problem of interference between stations has been overcome so there is 'room' for lots more radio stations to broadcast. This is summarised below.

end of 1996

summer 1997

spring 1998

▶ *The spread of digital broadcasting*

In analogue broadcasting each radio station both transmits and receives on its own frequency. The frequencies cannot be too close together otherwise they interfere with each other. This puts a limit on the number of radio stations that can broadcast. In digital broadcasting the signals from each radio station are combined and carried as a single block of frequencies by a process called multiplexing. At the radio receivers this multiplex signal is divided up into the various signals for each radio station.

How much will it cost?

The change to digital broadcasting requires radio receivers to be more complex, as this block diagram comparison of analogue and digital radio receivers shows. DAB will be introduced first to hi-fi systems and then to in-car radios. Initially, a hi-fi system with DAB reception might cost as much as £5000. However, as with compact disc technology, it will become cheaper as more people buy into the technology.

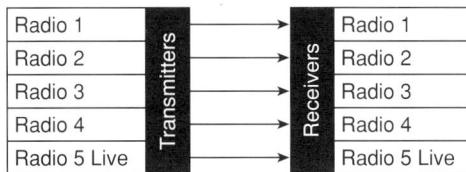

Analogue Radio Broadcasting

Each service is carried on its own frequency

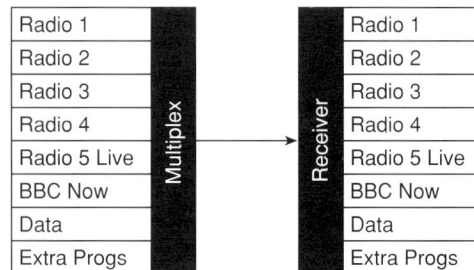

Digital Audio Broadcasting

Services combined and carried on a single frequency block

P

Pause for thought

How much would you pay for improved radio?

▶ *Digital broadcasting means more choice*

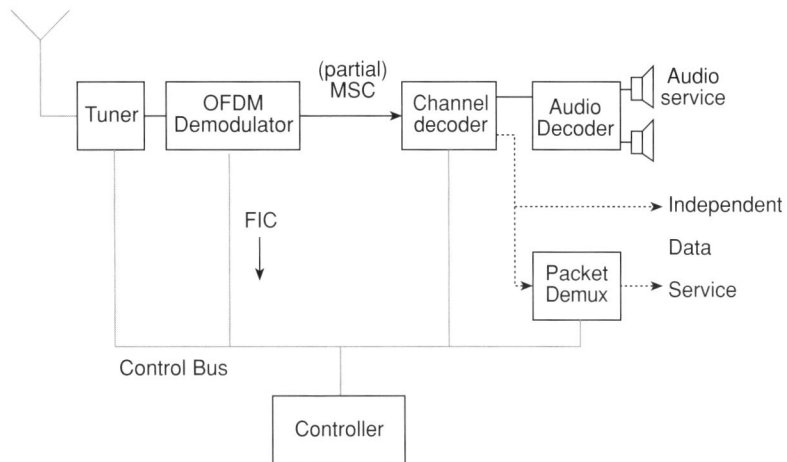

Digital reception requires more complicated technology

Questions

Discuss with a partner
what improvements
you would like to see
in radio broadcasting.

What extra services?

DAB offers the following improvements
immediately:

- high quality sound;
- interference-free reception;
- automatic tuning;
- increased choice of programmes and stations.

However, the DAB radio will also have a
small screen and be able to be linked to a
range of peripheral devices – personal
computer, fax machines and printers. So, in
the future, listeners and users of DAB will
have access to the following:

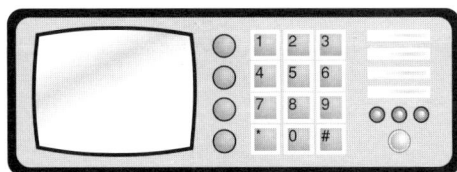

- programme-related text – phone-in telephone
  numbers and further information mailing
  addresses;
- printing of text, graphics and data from a DAB
  service via computer, fax and printer links;
- picture transmission – still and moving pictures will
  accompany news reports and documentaries.
  Album covers and pictures of recording artists will
  accompany music broadcasts. It may even be
  possible to carry a service like karaoke;
- electronic newspapers – there will be immediate,
  on-air delivery of publications and the option
  to store such information on portable PCs;
- traffic and travel information, including digitised
  maps, traffic problems, weather reports, car
  parking availability and accommodation;
- satellite-based navigation data for motorists
  and the emergency services.

User interface

Is this what a digital radio will look like?

Research activity

Visit your local hi-fi store and find out what
they know about digital broadcasting. Use
the answers they give you to estimate
when it will become affordable.

Identifying needs and likes

You can revise strategies for identifying needs and likes from previous work by thinking about these people at a busy shopping centre on a Saturday morning. They are all using electronic products.

Thinking about what people might need

The people out shopping will have different needs and likes. You can try thinking about these by using the PIES approach. PIES stands for Physical, Intellectual, Emotional and Social. Each of these words describes a type of need that can be met by products that have been designed and made.

Observing people

You can find out a lot about people's needs and likes by watching them. It is important to record your observations in a way that doesn't affect what the people are doing. The illustration shows several different recording methods. Can you explain which ones are suitable for use in a shopping centre?

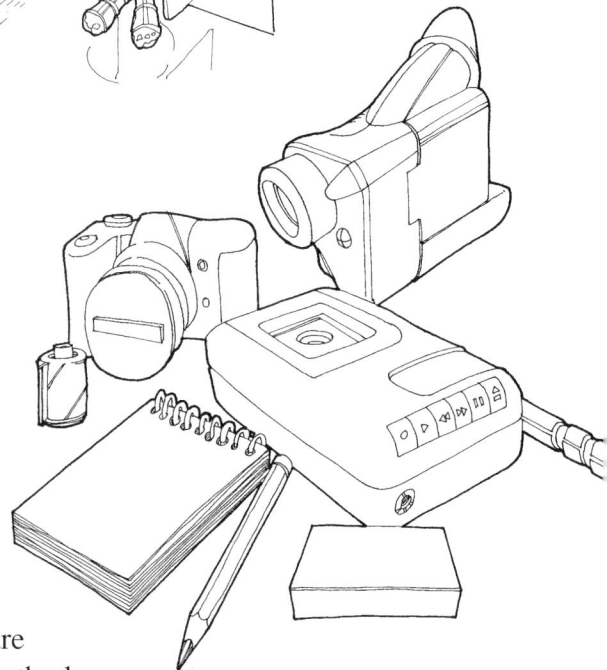

SRT1, SRT2, SRT4, PART1, PART2, HSRT1

Asking questions

You can find out about people's preferences by talking to them and asking questions. This is sometimes called **interviewing**. It is different to using a questionnaire as you will only interview a few people. It is important to ask the right sorts of questions. To find out what each of the people shown want from the electronic products they use, you would probably need to ask them different questions.

Using books and magazines

Sometimes you need to find out something by looking things up in books and magazines. Some magazines would tell you about the latest electronic products. Others would tell you about the preferences of the people using electronic products. Where would you find these magazines? Some books and magazines would tell you about the way electronic products work and how you can make them for yourself. Where would you find these books and magazines?

Image boards

You can make a collection of pictures of things that a group of people might like, places they might go, activities they might do. This is called an image board. An image board for Georgie will look very different to one for Maisie. Making image boards will help you to understand what different people might like. It may also help you to understand the style of products that will appeal to the different people. For example, Jo and Dot may both wear a wristwatch but their watches will almost certainly look very different.

Questions

Here is the beginning of an image board for Jo.

1 What does it tell you about her?

2 What other images could be added to give a fuller picture?

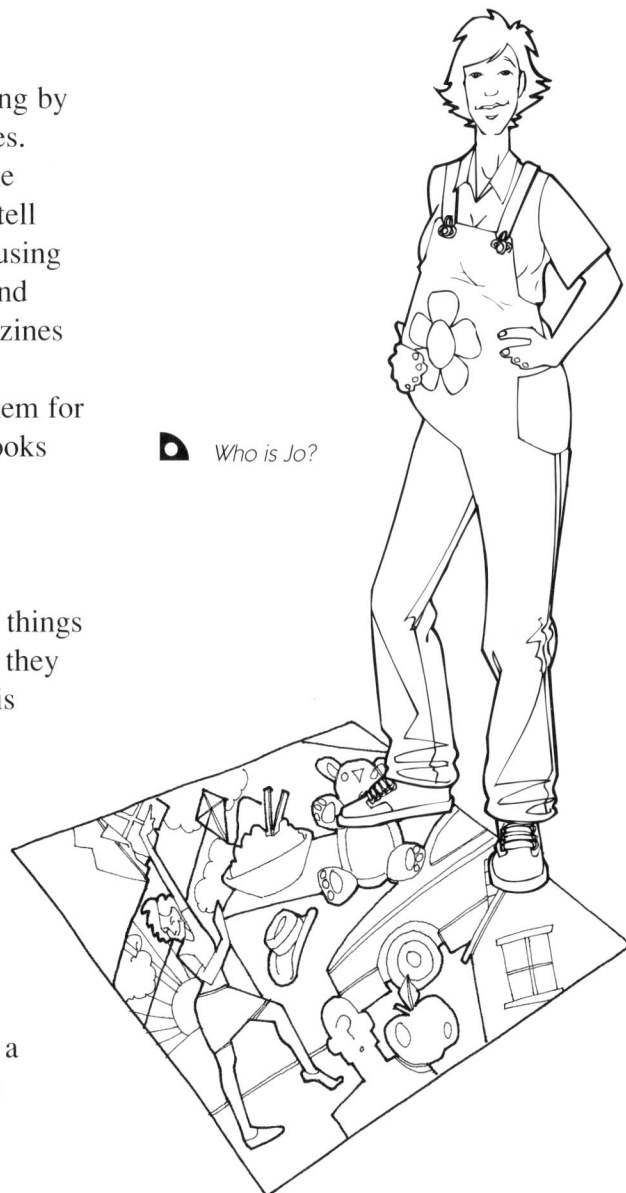

Who is Jo?

Strategies – needs and likes

Using questionnaires

A questionnaire is a carefully designed set of questions. It is often used by businesses to find out what different groups of people like or would buy. A questionnaire will usually try to get information about the sort of person who is answering it – their occupation, how much they earn, and so on. This information enables businesses to provide goods and services that people want at a price they are prepared to pay. It also shows where and when these products could be sold and how best they might be advertised.

Designing your own questionnaire

You need to be clear about what you are trying to find out. Target your questions to obtain the information you want. Avoid leading questions that suggest the answer. Avoid questions that don't discriminate, such as 'Do you like sunny days?' Everyone always answers yes!

Sometimes you will use the questionnaire in face-to-face questioning when you record people's answers. At other times people will fill it in on their own and return it to you. In this second case it is particularly important that the meanings of the questions are clear as you won't be there to explain.

Advice on writing questionnaire questions is given on the right.

Who should I ask?

It is important that you use questionnaires with the right people. If you want to find out which electronic products are bought by the elderly, it is important to use the questionnaire with elderly people. If you want to find out about the electronic products used by toddlers, then ask their parents.

Questions

Note how newspapers and magazines use so-called questionnaires to attract the readers' interest rather than to provide useful information.

1 What sort of information do these questionnaires reveal to the readers?

Questionnaire question guide

- Use closed questions. These require a yes or no answer or give people a choice of answers.

- Make it easy to fill in the answers. Use tick boxes where possible.

- Each question should be short and simple.

- Use words that people will understand.

- Write questions which have only one meaning.

- Each question should ask only one thing at a time.

- A scaled choice of answers is a good way to find out people's attitudes

What sample size should I use?

It is important to present your questionnaire to as many people as possible. This will give you a large number of responses from which you can draw reasonable conclusions. A hundred responses would be an ideal number, but this would be a major task for one researcher. If the research is shared among a group of people, the task becomes manageable, both in terms of collecting responses and in collating data. If each member of a class of 20 students took responsibility for five questionnaires, the sample size would be 100.

Collating the results

Once you have the returned questionnaires, you will need to analyse the information. Here's how to do it.

- Draw up a summary results table or tally sheet of the possible answers to each question.
- Count how many of each possible answer you got for each question and write this in the table or tally sheet.

When you have done this for each question on each questionnaire, the table is complete and you can begin to think about what the results mean. You will find that putting this information into a database or spreadsheet may help you to collate it quicker.

Using spreadsheets and databases

The database will organise the information so that it is easily accessible and can be displayed clearly. The database can be 'interrogated' for statistical information and thus provide a picture of user needs and likes.

Statistical information from the database can be put into a spreadsheet. The spreadsheet displays the information as rows and columns of numbers. You can analyse the information in a variety of ways and present your findings in graphical forms like pie charts and bar graphs.

Here is an example of a survey of electronic toys. The completed questionnaires provided information on the use of electronic toys by children and young people in students' families.

This information was recorded on a tally sheet. It was then analysed using a spreadsheet to identify user preferences. The results were presented visually.

Total number of people surveyed = 149	
Male	72
Female	77
Ages	
Age 0 - 5	37
Age 6 - 10	39
Age 11 - 15	39
Age 16 - 20	34

This questionnaire was used by pupils who were designing electronic toys suitable for use by those with impaired vision

Electronic toy questionnaire

Please tick the appropriate box for each child or young person who owns an electronic based toy in your

Male ☐   Female ☐

Which of the following sorts of toy does the person own?

Age 0 - 5 ☐   Age 6 - 10 ☐   Age 11 - 15 ☐   Age 16 - 20 ☐

hand held game ☐

noise making toy ☐

speech making toy ☐

play station ☐

musical instrument ☐

controllable model vehicle ☐

How much was spent on the toy?

hand held game
under £1.00 ☐   £1.00 - £5.00 ☐   £5.00 - £10.00 ☐   £10.00 - £20.00 ☐   £20.00 - £5

noise making toy
under £1.00 ☐   £1.00 - £5.00 ☐   £5.00 - £10.00 ☐   £10.00 - £20.00 ☐

Design briefs

A design brief is a short statement which describes some or all of the following:

- the sort of product to be made and its purpose;
- who will use it;
- where it will be used;
- where it might be sold.

An **open** brief provides general guidelines and offers the opportunity for a wide range of possible outcomes. A **closed** brief is more specific and detailed in its requirements. Here are examples of open and closed briefs for two lines of interest.

Sensing devices

Open design brief:

Design and make a range of items that utilise simple sensing devices.

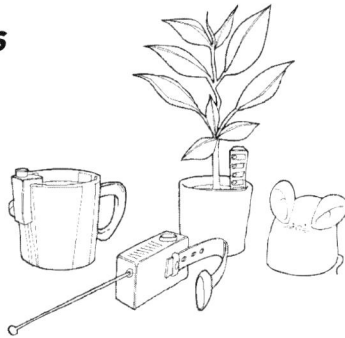

Closed design brief:

Design and make a sensing device that can be used to sense the temperature in a hen coop and sound an alarm should the temperature fall below 4°C.

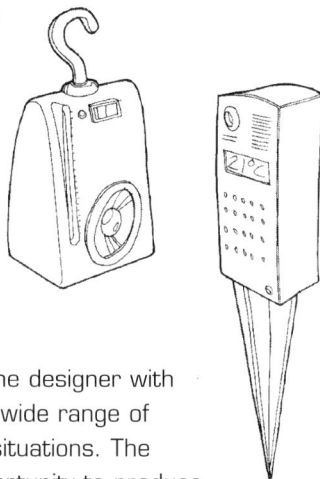

The open brief provides the designer with the freedom to explore a wide range of sensing possibilities and situations. The closed brief provides opportunity to produce different solutions, but the nature of the sensing device required is more clearly defined so the range of possible outcomes is limited.

Control systems

Open design brief:

Design and make a product that uses timing technology.

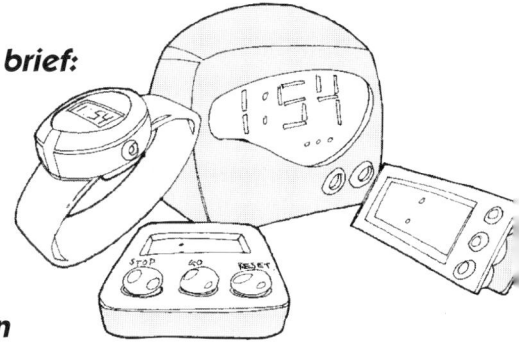

Closed design brief:

Design and make an electronic wristwatch with alarm facilities suitable for young people in the 15–19 age range.

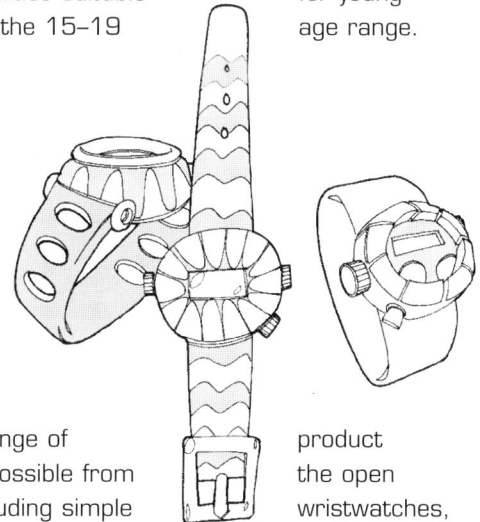

A wide range of types is possible from the open brief, including simple wristwatches, simple clocks, simple stop watches, and timer units for microwave ovens. In the closed brief the nature of the product and the end user are more clearly identified. This provides a more detailed picture of what is required.

The closed brief provides the opportunity to produce different solutions, but the limited ability of the users, the size, water-resistance requirement, and probable limits to the purchasing price constrain the range of possible outcomes.

Specifying the product

You will need to develop the design brief into a performance specification. This will provide a list of criteria against which you can assess your design as it develops.

The performance specification will always:

- describe what the product has to do;
- describe what the product should look like;
- state any other requirements that need to be met.

For example:

- how it should work;
- how much it should cost to manufacture;
- possible production levels, one off or batch production;
- what materials it should be made from;
- what energy source should be used if it needs to be powered;
- ergonomic requirements related to end user;
- legal requirements to be met in its development and use;
- environmental considerations and requirements.

Here are two examples of performance specifications and products that meet their requirements.

Intruder alarm specification

What it has to do:

- detect break-ins through doors or windows;
- sound a loud alarm;
- show on a display panel where the break in has occurred.

What it should look like:

- its presence should be obvious and not hidden;
- its visible parts should look hidden;
- the display panel should be easy to read.

Other requirements:

- it should be impossible to deactivate from outside the building;
- it should be suitable for batch production.

Remote system for controlling roller-blinds on high-level windows specification

What it has to do:

- control the smooth opening, closing and part-closure of roller blinds;
- control blinds in high-level angled, horizontal and vertical windows;
- ensure the chosen position of the blind is maintained for as long as is required.

What it should look like:

- the casing of the control unit should look appropriate in a range of windowed environments.

Other requirements:

- be a portable control device;
- a wall-mounted storage unit should be included in the design;
- the portable unit should feel comfortable to use;
- the system should be easily usable by a wide range of users;
- the system should have a very high degree of reliability.

Generating design ideas

Brainstorming

You probably did some brainstorming in previous work. Here is a reminder.

Brainstorming is:

- a process for getting ideas out of your head!

- a process for getting ideas you didn't know you had!

- a process which uses questions and associations and links ideas to actions;

- a process you can use on your own, but it is usually better in a group.

Brainstorming an idea can help you to identify a wider range of options for your designing and making and to work out how best to develop these ideas.

How to brainstorm

- First state the problem or need.

- Record every idea suggested as words, phrases or pictures.

- Produce as many ideas as possible.

- Don't make judgements until the brainstorming pattern is complete.

- Allow enough time for new and diverse ideas to emerge, but agree a time limit so that ideas remain fresh.

- Sort out ideas by considering which are unrealistic, inappropriate and unachievable and removing them. What is left will give you a focus for action.

What can I use for this?

By asking this question you can identify design options. You can give each possibility a yes/no verdict based on specific criteria – availability, cost, effectiveness, feasibility. You can refine the remaining options using similar criteria until you are left with a 'best' solution:

Here is an example.

This brainstorming session gave full details of the overall style, materials, basic circuit and user interface for the radio. Note that the brainstormers used images, design guide information, plus Chooser Charts to answer the questions.

What can I use this for?

This is the sort of brainstorming that you use when you have some technical capabilities and aren't sure what to do with them.

Imagine that you have access to a sensor plus circuitry that can be used to measure weight. You can use brainstorming to find something useful to do with all this knowledge.

Here is an example. Note how the brainstormers have used the PIES approach within their brainstorming.

Where?
home, garden, zoo, museum, laboratory, industrial site, building site

What?
heavy things, light things, small things, large things, live things, e.g. babies, pets

SENSOR PLUS CIRCUITRY FOR MEASURING WEIGHT

Who?
adults, young adults, children, the elderly, trained, untrained

Why?
Physical, Intellectual, Emotional, Social needs

When?
leisure time, work time, domestic time

Who?	What?	Where?	When?	Why?
adults	babies	at home	domestic time	Physical – monitoring babies development Intellectual – intrigue of growth and weight gain Social – relationship with baby Emotional – security in knowledge of weight gain

Attribute analysis

You may have used attribute analysis in previous work. Designers and engineers use it to help them to produce new designs for familiar products.

Here is an attribute analysis table for sensing systems. The headings of the table describe attributes which will affect the final design. You can read across the columns and combine different words from each column to create new designs. Some combinations will be totally inappropriate, while others will offer viable design ideas. In the examples shown both combinations give interesting and worthwhile designs. One combination leads to a device that continuously monitors the temperature of a patient in hospital. The other combination leads to a safe noise level monitor for a disco.

What does it sense?	Where does it sense?	Style	User	Response and display
presence of smoke	home	plain and unobtrusive	*untrained adults*	**alarm noise**
change in temperature	office	*distinct and prominent*	**trained adults**	*alarm lights*
change in light level	*leisure environment*	**functional**	impaired hearing	digital readout
change in noise level	**medical environment**	decorative	impaired vision	dial readouts
change in moisture content	gentle industrial environment	period	impaired manipulation	**monitor readout**
change in magnetic field	harsh industrial environment			printed readout
change in pH	outdoors			**memorised data**

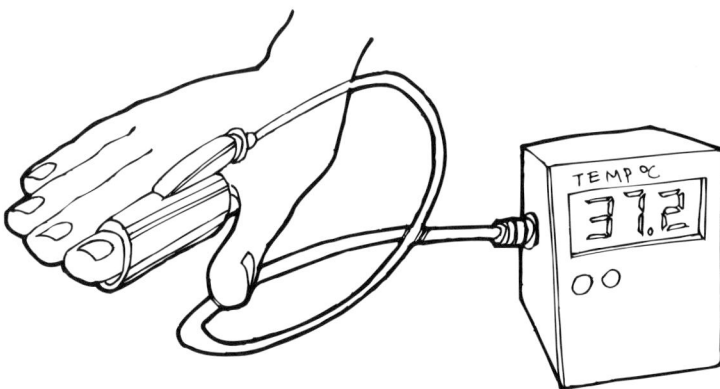

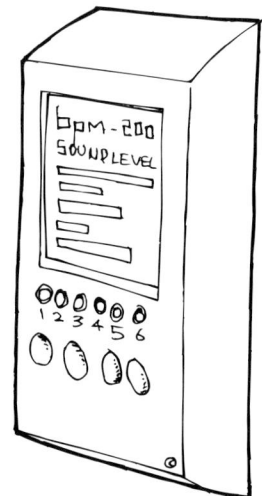

Observational drawing

You can use observational drawing to give you a reference as to what things look like and to help you get ideas. Here are some examples showing where observational drawing has been used to help with designing.

Observational drawing	The resulting design	Observational drawing	The resulting design
These drawings of flower shapes helped with the design of a soil moisture detector		These drawings of the bones in arms and hands helped to provide ideas for a pick and place robot	
These drawings of fish helped to provide ideas for the appearance of an electronic weighing machine used at a fishmongers		These drawings of sweets helped with the design of radios for children in hospital	
These drawings of circus clowns helped with the design of a talking toy		These drawings of bicycles helped to provide ideas for exercise machines with continuous performance readout	
These drawings of keys and keyholes helped to provide ideas for a range of personal possession security devices			

Investigative drawing

You can investigate the way something works by doing careful drawings that try to explain how it works. Here's how to do it.

- First find out how the thing works by using it and looking at it quickly.

- Write down what you have to do to make it work and what you think might be happening when it works.

- Then investigate how it works by looking more closely. Use a hand-lens for close-up views. Look inside and, if necessary, undo parts to get a good view.

- Draw the parts you can see and add notes and other drawings to show what the different parts do.

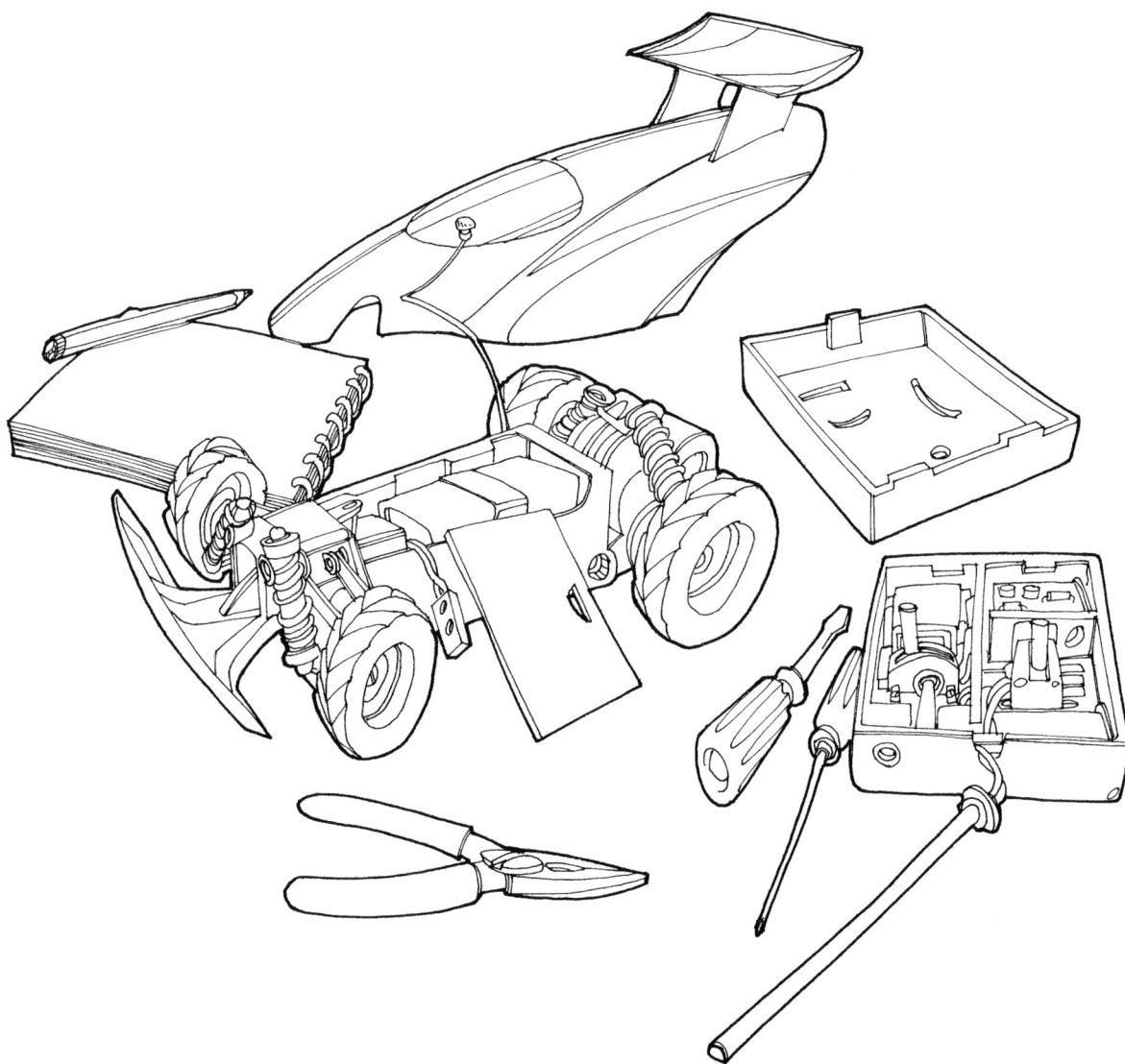

Modelling

It is often difficult to imagine what a design idea will look like or how it will work. Modelling your design ideas gives you something to look at, think about and test. Modelling will help you to:

- clarify and develop your design ideas;
- evaluate your design ideas;
- share your design ideas with others.

Modelling appearance

There are many modelling techniques, some of which you will have used previously. Here are examples of the way modelling techniques have been used to develop the designs for electronic jewellery.

② Using a source of ideas

Zoe looked at pictures of differen style collars.

③ Thumb-nail sketches

Zoe made lots of small, quick sketches. This is a quick way of getting your ideas into a visual form. You can also make notes to explain things which you cannot draw.

① Talk through

Talking to people who might wear the jewellery helped Zoe to realise that she needed to find out about collars.

④ Annotated sketches will provide details of
the design. Zoe used these for both the electronic
system and the appearance of the product.

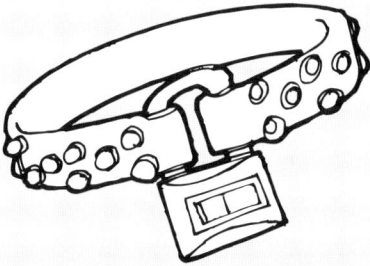

⑤ A foam model can be shaped and finished to
provide you with a model which looks just like the
finished product.

⑥ Using a net
helped Zoe to ensure that the
circuitry would fit into the available space.

▶ *Modelling appearance is a useful process for
assessing design ideas to develop into real products*

▶ *Modelling how electronic
products will work*

Modelling product performance

Modelling not only describes the way a product will look, it can also describe the way it will fit together and how it will work. You can use a range of modelling techniques to develop design ideas about product performance. Talking about the design, thumbnail sketches and detailed drawings will help you to model how a product might work.

However, you will need a more sophisticated approach for products that involve some form of movement or control. There are three ways to model how the electronic part of your product might work. These are shown below.

The investigations board approach is probably the quickest, providing there is a board which deals with the electronic systems you need.

The systems board approach will take slightly longer but, as a wide range of sub-system boards is available, it is likely that you will be able to model the electronic performance of your product.

The breadboard approach takes the longest but has the advantage that you will be working with the actual components you will use in the final product. This may not be the case for the investigations board or systems board approaches.

Whenever you design products that people will use, you will need to think about sizes and shapes (**anthropometrics**) and movements (**ergonomics**). Tables of data are available and you can use this information to make your product easier to use. All user interface designs shown need to be informed by anthropometric and ergonomic information.

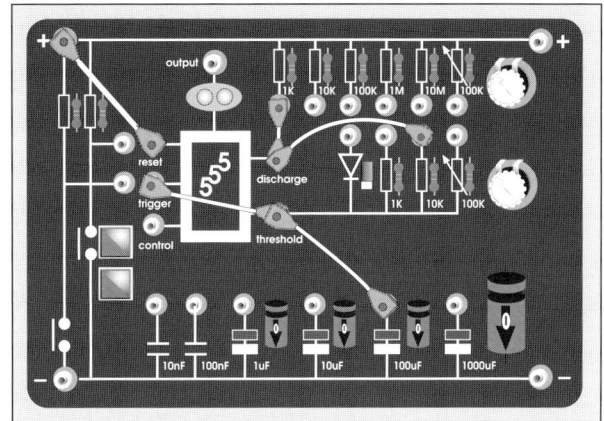

Modelling with an investigation board

Modelling with system boards

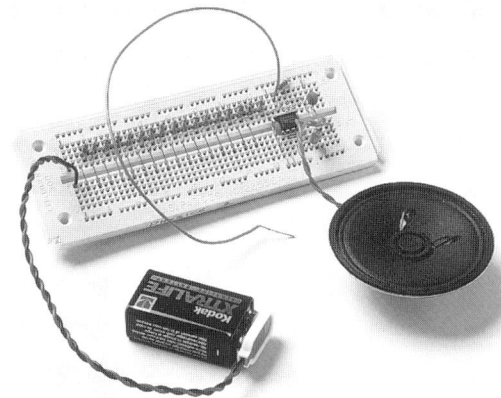

Modelling on a breadboard

Modelling how electronic products work

Modelling appearance and form with computers

If you use computers properly, they can help you to model your design ideas so that you will be able to explore many more possibilities than if you were working just with pencil and paper. There are several ways to start using the computer, as these examples of measurement instrument design show.

I like to draw it on paper first, then I scan it into the computer and manipulate the image.

I like to start with an existing image I've grabbed from a library and then I manipulate it.

I like to draw straight onto the screen and manipulate the images as I go.

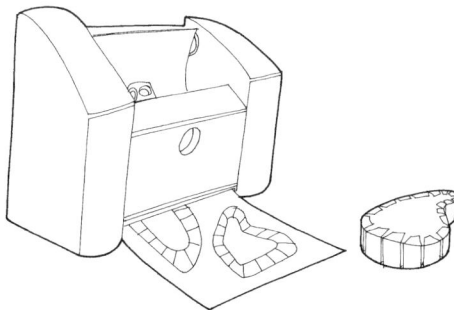

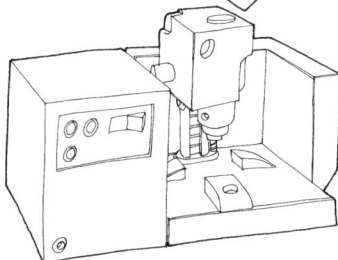

Once we've got the images we like we can do any of the following:
- *Print it out as a single copy or in multiple copies and in different colours*
- *Cut it out from card or thin plastic sheet; as a one off or in multiple copies*
- *Produce it as a 3D item using a CNC lathe or milling machine*

Modelling function with computers

You can use a computer to model the way the electronic circuits in your product might work. You can make changes to the design 'on screen' and see how this affects the performance.

The design for the circuitry of simple sensing systems is being explored to find the values of the resistors needed for a range of potential dividers. The software enables the circuit designer to find out what happens with different resistor values and different sensors in the potential divider arrangements. Modelling different arrangements enables the designer to choose the one most suited to the sensing requirement of the situation.

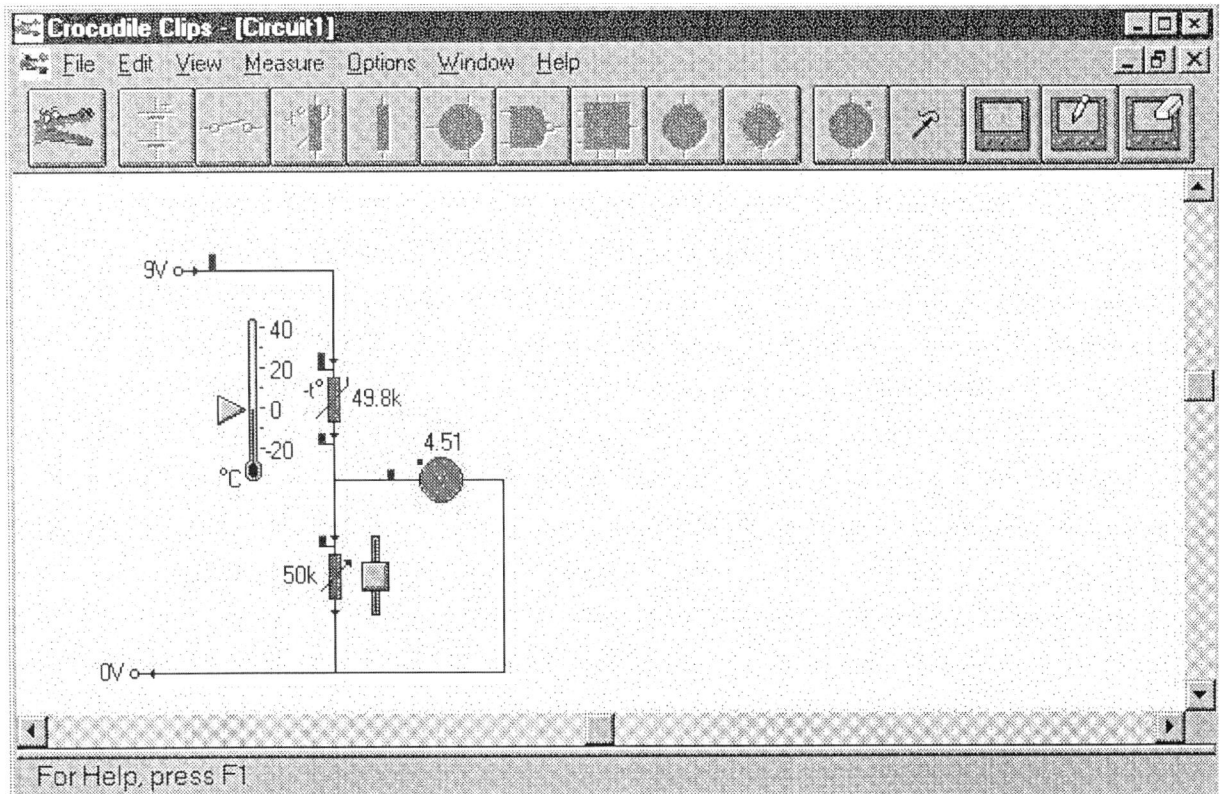

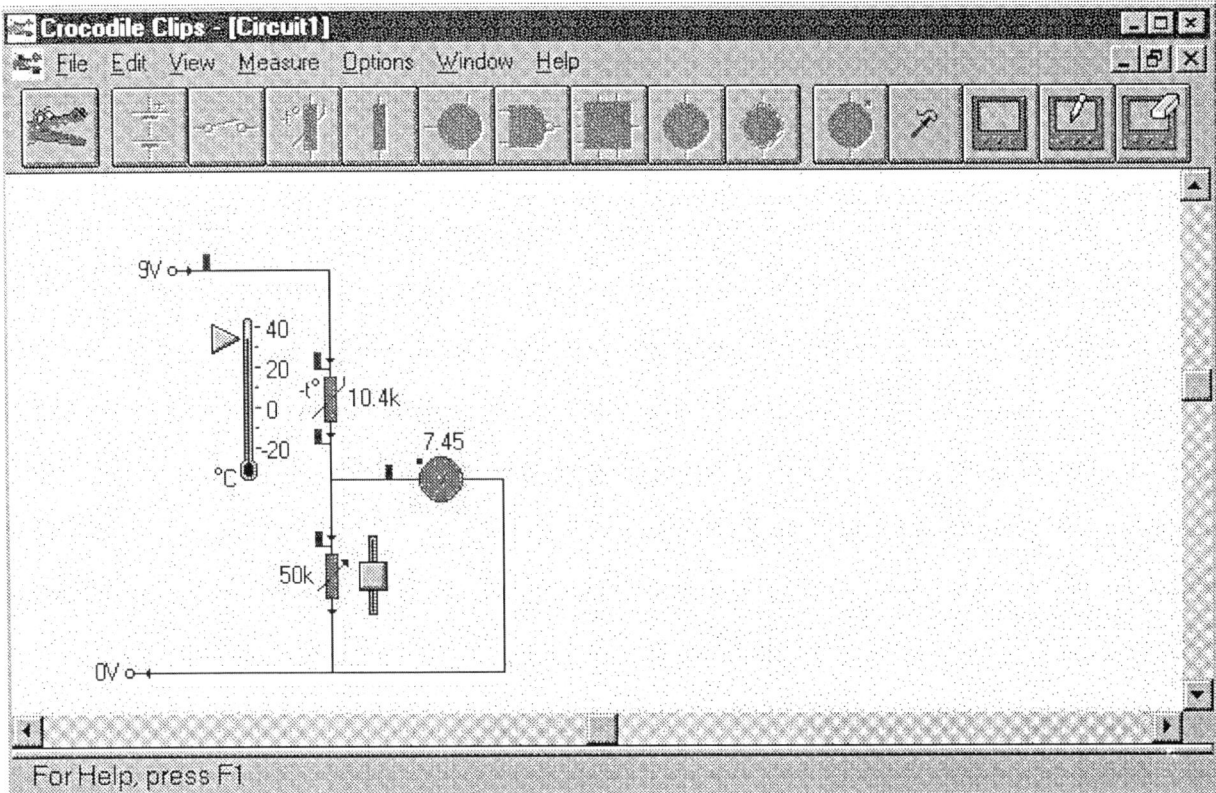

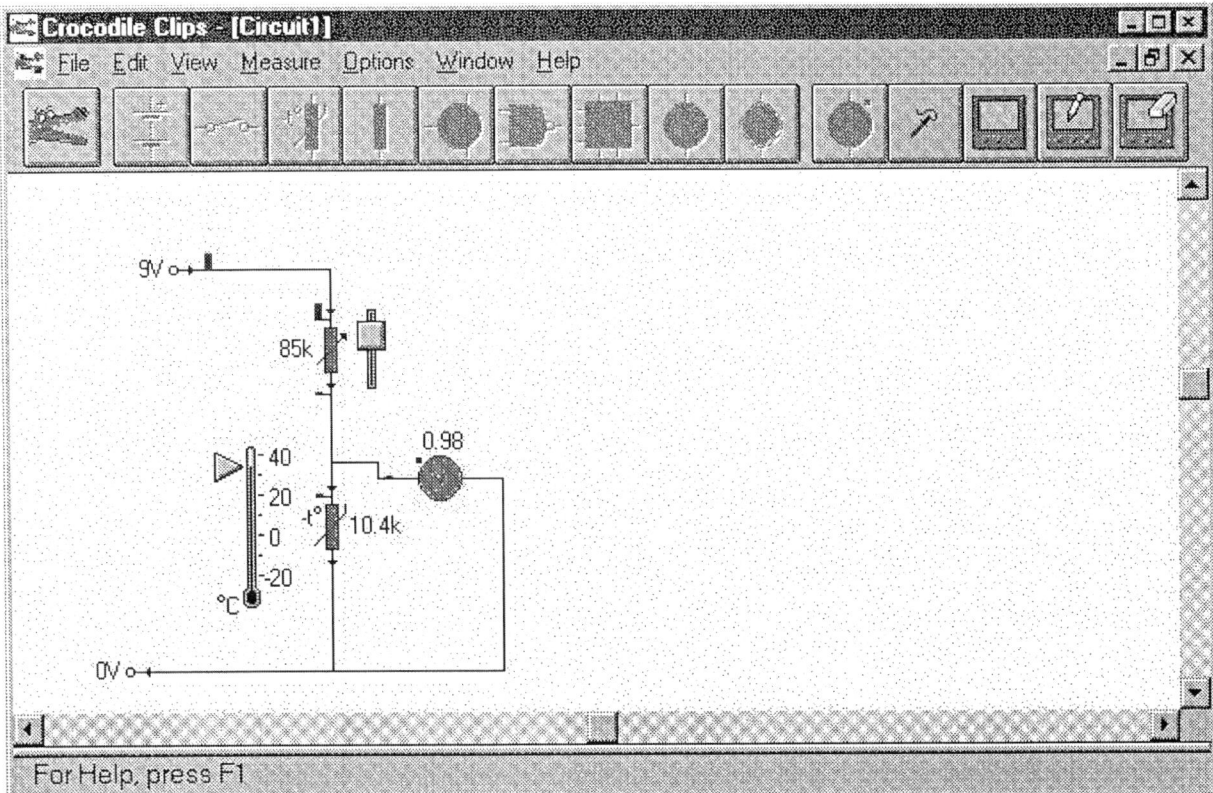

Applying science

Checking on your choice of material

You may learn about the properties of materials in science lessons. The strength of a material tells you how much force we need to break it. It is important that the material in a product can bear its load. The load may try to squash the structure or pull it apart. If the material is not strong enough, then parts of the product will break. If you know about the strength of materials, you can choose those that are strong. Here is an example.

A thin rope is fine for towing a car but not a lorry; for that you need a steel cable. Although it is the same thickness as the rope, it is much stronger.

You can find out how strong some materials are by looking them up in the Materials Chooser Chart on pages 178–179. The chart will tell you about the tensile strength of the materials; that is, how hard you have to pull on them before they break. The chart will help you to list materials in order of strength.

If a part of your design isn't strong enough, you can do one of two things:

- change the design so that the cross-sectional area of the part is greater – if there is more material there, it will be stronger;
- make the part out of a stronger material.

The elasticity of a material tells us how much force we need to stretch, squash or bend it. It is important that the material in a structure is stiff enough to resist the stretching, squashing and bending caused by the load. If the material is not stiff enough then parts of the product will deflect so much that the product will be unsafe. Here is an example.

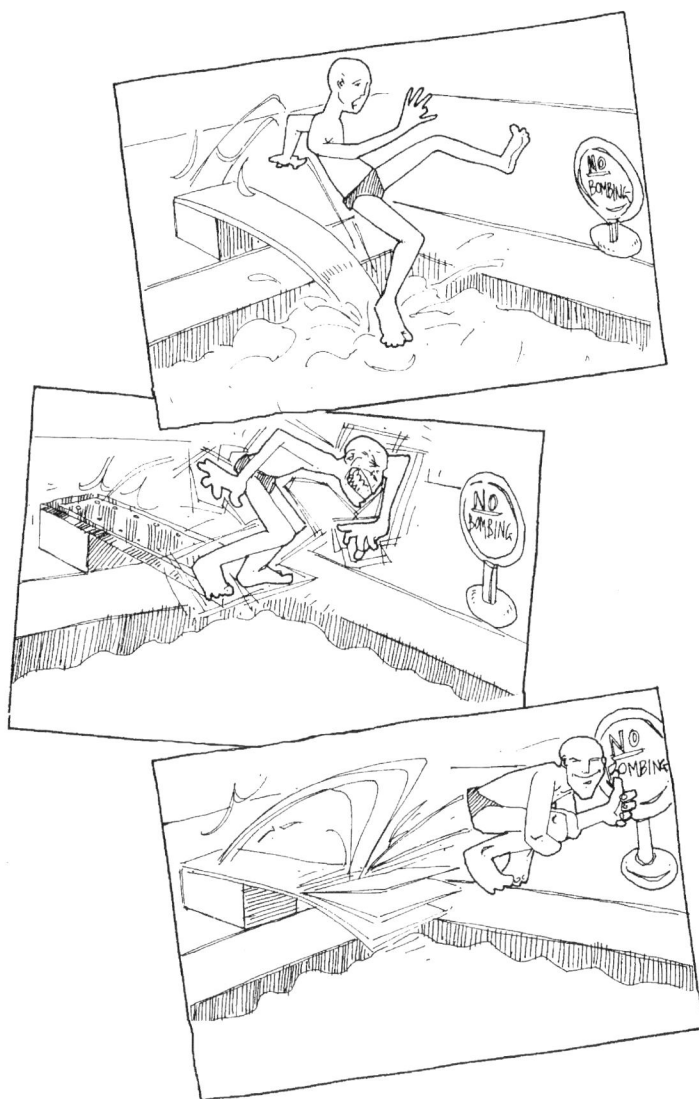

A diving board made from polythene would bend so much that the diver couldn't walk to the end. A diving board of the same shape and size, made from steel, would be so stiff that when the diver jumped on it he would get no spring. The same shape and size of diving board made from pinewood would have just the right stiffness.

You may find that a material is strong enough but too elastic; it doesn't break under the load but it does bend. This elastic property of a material is often measured as Young's modulus of elasticity. You can find out how elastic materials are by looking them up in the Materials Chooser Chart.

If a part of your design bends too much you can do one of two things:

● change the design so that the part has a cross sectional shape that is less bendy;

● use a material that is less elastic.

Most materials will react with their surroundings in some way. Some will react only slightly and it will take a long time for them to corrode or rot. Others will decay quite rapidly. The time taken will depend on the material and the severity of the conditions. You can check on the durability of materials by looking them up in the Materials Chooser Chart. You can improve the durability of your design in two ways. Use a finish on the material, which protects it from the surroundings, or choose a more durable material.

You may learn about centre of gravity in science lessons. Objects that are difficult to topple over often have a low centre of gravity. It is easy to push over the figure on the left, but when she crouches into a martial arts stance she is much more stable. Can you work out why she now has a lower centre of gravity?

Systems thinking

During your earlier work you may have been introduced to systems thinking. You can use this to help you to understand complex products. Here is a summary of the important ideas, using a music centre as an example.

This music centre can be thought about in terms of the subsystems that make it up. You can show the subsystems by drawing a systems diagram. It doesn't look like the music centre but it does help you to understand how it works. Information from the record deck, the CD player and the tuner subsystems are inputs into the amplifier subsystem. The amplifier subsystem processes this information and it becomes an output from the amplifier and an input into the speaker subsystem which turns the signal into sounds we can hear. Why does the cassette deck subsystem have an output and an input from the amplifier sub-system?

The system boundary will depend on what you want to think about. If you are concerned only with the internal workings, it will not include the casings. If you are interested in the appearance and style, it will include the casings. If you are designing it for a particular room, the boundary will include this as well.

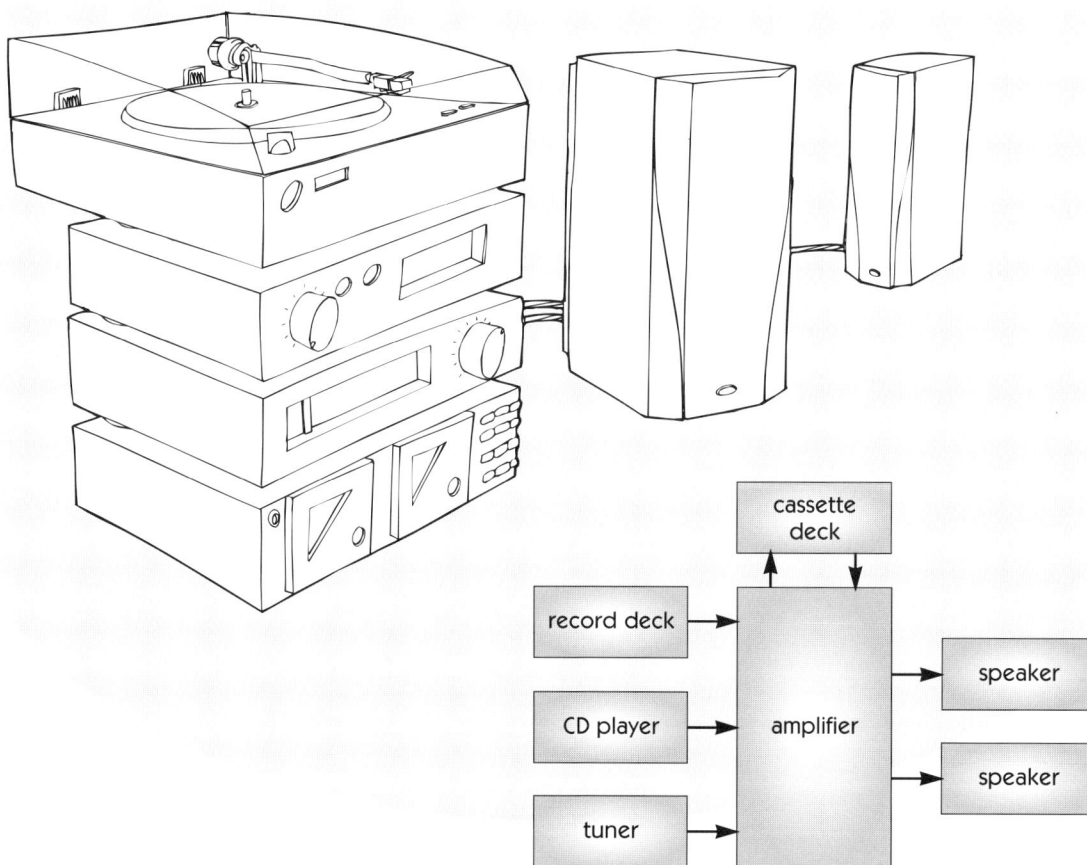

You can find out more about using systems thinking in designing electronic products on pages 132–150 (the Systems Boards approach section and the Investigation Boards approach section).

User and operator interfaces

The parts of a system used by people are called **user interfaces**. For the customers of railway stations the user interface may be a counter where they buy their tickets and ask for travel information. This interface is a **human interface** but **machine interfaces** are becoming increasingly common. These include ticket machines which take money and, more recently, 'queue buster' machines which take credit cards. Human interfaces are more friendly and can explain things and answer queries. However, they require special training and are not usually available 24 hours a day. A machine interface has the advantage of always being available, but it can appear unfriendly and difficult to use. Machine interfaces should be designed to be self-explanatory and user friendly. All electronics products have a user interface and it is important that these are as self-explanatory as possible.

The parts of a system operated by the people who run and control a system are called **operator interfaces**. They are usually more complicated than user interfaces because operators need more information and have to be able to do more things than the users. Operators are usually trained to operate the system, while users are not. The operator must be able to put information into the system through easy-to-use controls. The operator interface should be as easy to use as possible. The information systems used by railway staff selling tickets with reservations are a good example of an operator interface. They give the seller access to up-to-date information on availability of seats and allow accurate reservations to be made in the minimum of time.

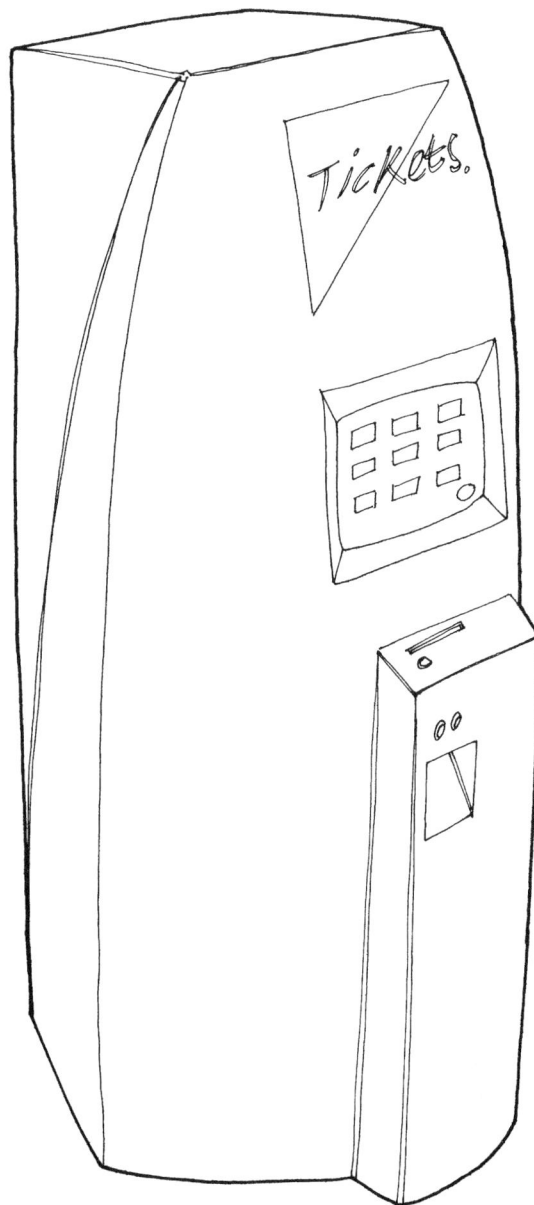

◣ *A machine interface for users*

Feedback and control

Control systems need information so that they can respond to changes. This information is called feedback. Systems with feedback are called closed-loop systems. A system without feedback is called an open-loop system. The situation in which a tap fills a bath for a set time and then turns off automatically is an example of an open-loop system. There is no feedback to tell the system that the bath is full. So if the bath was half-full when the tap was turned on, it would just add water for the set time, causing an overflow and flood before it turned itself off. A better system checks the level of the bath water. It switches off the water when the required depth is reached. To do this the system has to take (or feedback) the information from its output (the water level) and use it as another input. Systems diagrams for both of these situations are shown on the right.

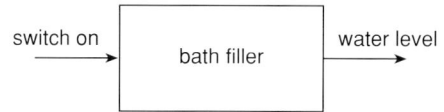

Open loop control of bath water may lead to problems

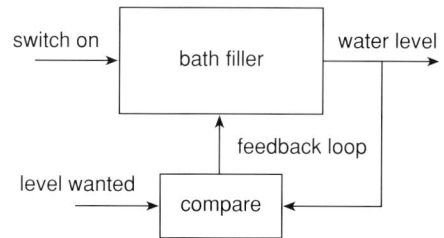

A closed loop system with feedback is must better

Planning

Flow charts and Gantt charts

You can use flow charts and Gantt charts to help you to plan your way through a Capability Task. In year 11 you may spend two whole terms on a single Capability Task as part of your GCSE assessment. It will be important to ensure that school holidays, public holidays, sports days, etc. don't spoil your plans.

You can use the headings in the flow chart to get the order of the task right. Once you

```
                      Decide on line
                        of interest
                            ↓
                      Justify your
                        decision
         ┌──────────────────┼──────────────────┐
         ↓                                      ↓
   Sort out extra                        Identify useful
  learning necessary ──────────┐   ┌──── case studies
                               ↓   ↓
                          Draw up other
                        subjects check list
         ┌──────────────────┼──────────────────┐
         ↓                                      ↓
   Working with                          Write design brief
   other people ─────────────┐   ┌──── and specification
                             ↓   ↓
                         Generate
                        design ideas
         ┌──────────────────┼──────────────────┐
         ↓                                      ↓
     Develop                              Make presentation
   design ideas ───────────┐    ┌──── and working drawings
                           ↓    ↓
                        Plan the
                         making
                            ↓
                       Make the
                        product
                            ↓
                       Evaluate
                      the product
                            ↓
                       Put on a
                        display
```

have the order right, you can use a Gantt chart to think about how long each part should take and to make sure that you get the task done on time. A Gantt chart will give you an overview of the whole task, showing both what needs to be done and when it should be done.

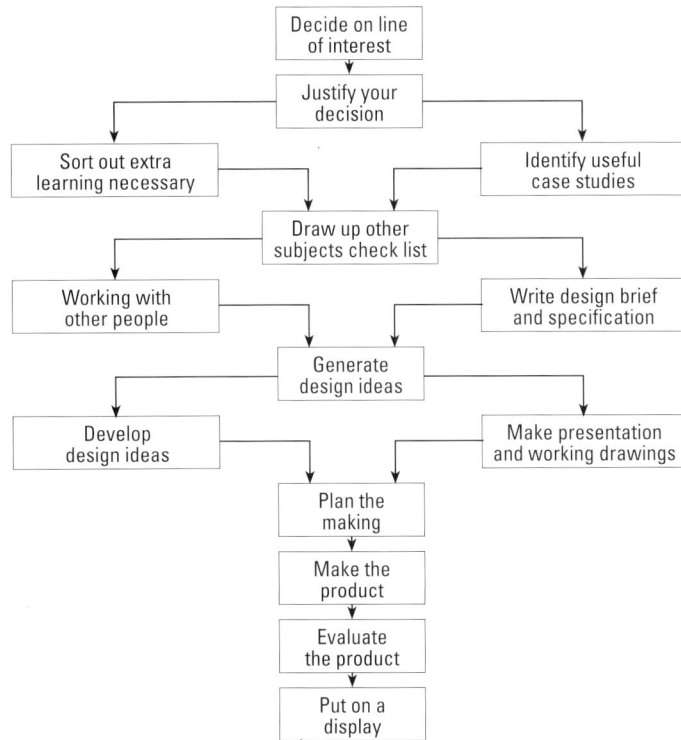

Week 1	Week 2	Week 3	Week 4	Week 5	Week 6	Week 7	Week 8	Week 9	Week 10	Week 11	Week 12
Decide line of interest Justify decision Extra learning Case studies											
		Other subjects Other people Brief & Spec									
		Generating design ideas									
			Developing design ideas Presentation and working drawings								
				Planning the making							
					Making the product						
										Evaluating the product	
										Display	
	11 weeks to go	10 weeks to go	9 weeks to go	8 weeks to go	7 weeks to go	6 weeks to go	5 weeks to go	4 weeks to go	3 weeks to go	2 weeks to go	1 week to go

Evaluating

User trip

The simplest way to evaluate a product is to take a user trip. This involves using the product and asking a few basic questions.

- Is it easy or convenient to use?
- Does it do what it is supposed to do?
- Do I like it?
- Would I want to own or continue to use it?

The owner of a large apartment block has decided to modify the security system so that, rather than having a security guard, the user simply speaks into the receiver which recognises their voice and then lets them in. Will the occupants support this change? Our user group, Georgie aged 3, Maisie aged 13, Jo aged 28, Jack aged 39 and Dot aged 70, have been asked for their views and are taking a user trip.

Their thoughts about the new system will be expressed when they respond to the user trip questions. How do you think they will respond to the change?

Winners and losers

The outcomes of design and technology will provide benefits for some and disadvantages for others. Designing and making a product will affect lots of people both directly and indirectly.

Maisie's brother, Wayne, works hard, doing odd jobs around the house for his parents, to raise enough money to buy himself a small radio-controlled car. Within four weeks he has raised enough money. Wayne is excited that all his hard work will allow him to buy the toy and provide the opportunity to have lots of fun. His parents are pleased because, for the first time, Wayne has helped to keep the house tidy. The toy shop owner is pleased because he will sell another toy. Maisie is not sure. Wayne has been too busy to bother her for the last four weeks and that has been good, but now she is concerned. He monopolises the living room for hours setting out complex race courses and he sometimes uses the car to chase the cat. She is not sure that this toy encourages Wayne to be considerate or kind.

This Winners and Losers Chart identifies some of those people directly and indirectly affected by Wayne's purchase of the radio-controlled car. Who do you think are winners and who are losers? Who else will be affected?

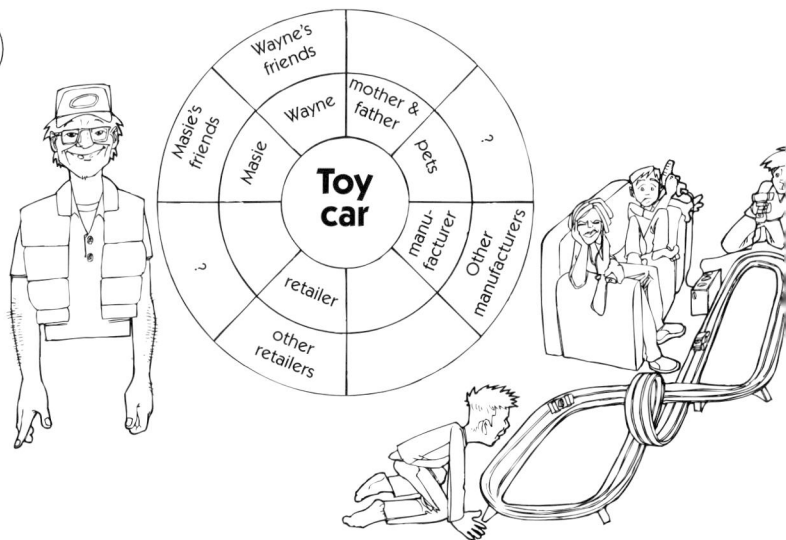

'Will I be able to reach the microphone?'

'What if someone imitates my voice?'

'This way puts the doorman out of work'

'What happens if I speak too fast?'

'Will it work when I've got a cold?'

Wayne's friends

Maisie's friends

Maisie

Wayne

mother & father

pets

?

Toy car

manufacturer

Other manufacturers

retailer

other retailers

?

Performance testing

Evaluating a product will involve comparing how well it works against its performance specification. You have to ask: does it do what it was designed to do? Here is an example.

Young children need almost constant looking after. One of the few times that they don't need to be watched is when they are asleep, but even then parents like to 'keep an ear out' for them. Knowing whether a child is sleeping or awake, happy or upset, is very important. A baby listener allows someone to listen to a child without having to be in the same room.

Here is the design specification for a baby listener.

What it has to do:

- detect the sounds made by both a sleeping child and an awake child;
- transmit those sounds to another location where they can be heard by listening adults.

What it should look like:

- either unobtrusive or in keeping with the likely style of such a room;
- the unit in the other location should be unobtrusive but, if noticed, have the appearance of a stylish electronic product.

Other requirements:

- it must be highly reliable and not prone to failure;
- it must use communication through wires;
- the listener should be able to control the following features:
  – on/off;
  – volume of received signal;
  – sensitivity of detection.

These questions will help you to compare the performance against the specification.

- Does it detect the sounds made by both a sleeping child and an awake child?
- Does it transmit those sounds to another location where they can be heard by listening adults?
- Is it unobtrusive?
- Is it in keeping with the likely style of a child's room?
- Does it have the appearance of a stylish electronic product?
- Is the product highly reliable?
- Does it use communication through wires?
- Can the listener control on/off, volume of received signal and sensitivity of detection?

You can find the answers to some of these questions by investigating the product for yourself. For others, you will need to observe the reactions of different people who might use the product.

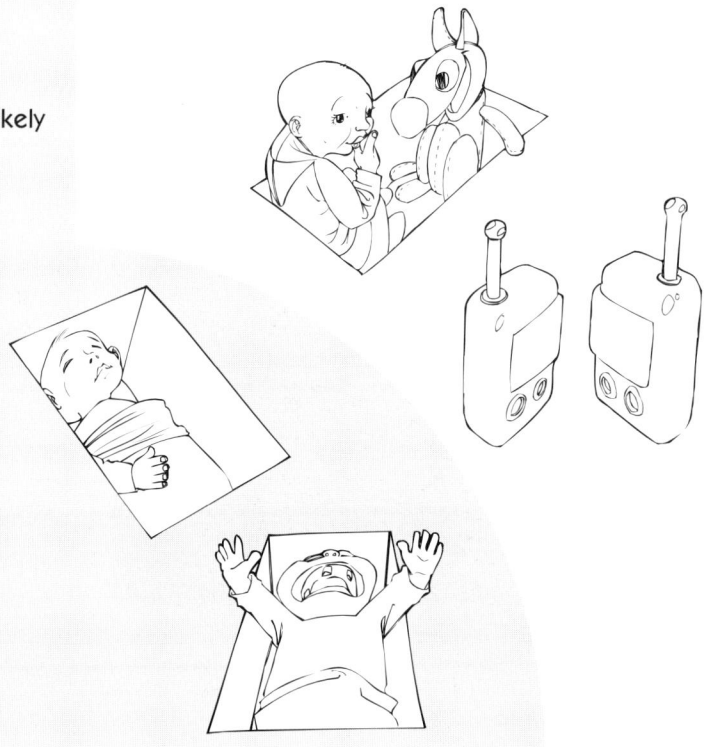

Is it appropriate?

Appropriate technology is suitable technology. You can use these questions to find out if a product or technology is appropriate.

- Does it suit the needs of the people who use it?
- Does it use local materials?
- Does it use local means of production?
- Is it too expensive?
- Does it generate income?
- Does it increase self-reliance?
- Does it use renewable sources of energy?
- Is it culturally acceptable?
- Is it environmentally friendly?
- Is it controlled by users?

It is unlikely that any product or technology will score highly against all of these questions. Many will seem appropriate in one context and inappropriate in another. Here is an example.

The assembly of the circuit boards for electronic products requires the placing of components in the correct location and orientation on the board, followed by soldering the component in place. Until recently, these operations have been carried out by skilled workers, usually women. Now changes in manufacturing technology are altering the situation. First, pick-and-place robots can be used to place the components in the holes in the printed circuit board. Second, once placed, the components can be soldered into place automatically by the use of a soldering bath which sends a wave of molten solder across the bottom of the board, soldering all the components in place simultaneously. Third, some components are now designed for surface mounting, so they simply need to be placed on top of the printed circuit board by a pick-and-place robot, into pools of already liquid solder, which quickly solidify. From the manufacturer's view point, although expensive in terms of initial capital investment, the introduction of this technology is worthwhile in terms of increased reliability and reduced labour costs.

But if a local community depends on the manufacture of electronic products for most of its employment, then the introduction of more automated production is likely to put people out of work and this will have a profound effect on the quality of people's lives if they are unable to find alternative employment. In the long term, such changes can lead to an area becoming depressed and impoverished.

Whether a product or technology is appropriate will be dependent upon the situation in which it is used.

Strategies Chooser Chart

This Chooser Chart gives you information about strategies:

- when to use a strategy in a Capability Task;
- how long the strategy will take;
- how complex it is;
- whether it involves other people.

Use the key to find out what the icons mean.

Strategy	Comments				
PIES	beginning		short	simple	
Observing people	beginning		short	simple	
Asking questions	beginning		short	simple	
Using books and magazines	beginning		short	simple	
Image boards	beginning		short	simple	
Questionnaires	beginning		medium	complex	many
Writing design briefs	beginning		short	simple	
Writing specifications	beginning		short	complex	
Brainstorming	beginning	middle	medium	simple	two
Observational drawing	beginning	middle	medium	simple	
Investigative drawing	beginning	middle	medium	complex	
Attribute analysis	beginning	middle	short	simple	
Modelling appearance	middle		medium	complex	
Modelling performance	middle		medium	complex	
Using science	middle		short	simple	
Modelling with computers	middle		long	complex	
Using a systems approach	middle		medium	complex	
Planning tools	middle	middle	short	simple	
Evaluating by user trip	beginning	end	short	simple	one
Evaluating by winners and losers	beginning	end	short	complex	one
Evaluating by performance specification	beginning	end	short	simple	one
Evaluating by appropriateness	beginning	end	short	simple	one

Key to icons:

When: beginning middle end

Time: short to long

Complexity: simple to complex

Other people: one other to many

Communicating to the client

In the world of business and industry, design proposals can only be turned into products which can be sold if the designers communicate their proposals effectively. Designers have to communicate their ideas to clients and to manufacturers as shown below.

The designer
I work for a large company which specialises in electronic-based products such as sound systems, portable radios, and electronic-based toys. I am part of the in-house team of designers who develop new products. It is the client who decides whether the design will be produced or not, so we need to present our ideas as effectively as possible.

The client
I am the manager of the electronic products company. I and the rest of the management team are always looking to enlarge our product range. We employ a team of in-house designers. We have to be sure that the new products which the design team present to us are what people will buy.

The manufacturer
When a new product is proposed, I have to be involved at an early stage in planning the manufacturing process. I need to be sure that the factory can make the product quickly and efficiently to the required quality standard. I also need to make sure that we can buy the electronic components needed.

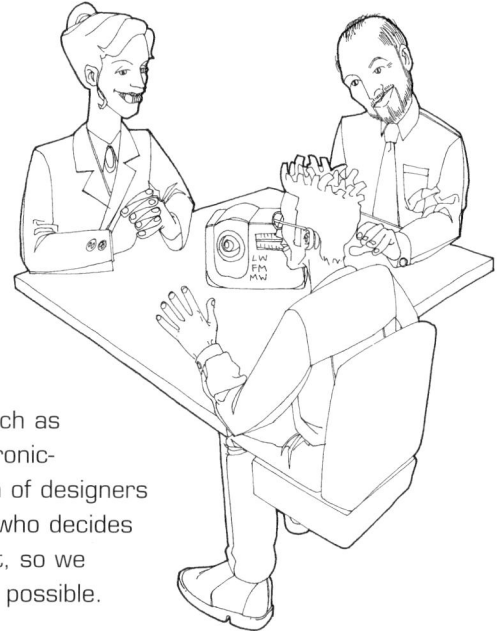

In your work you may be both the designer and the manufacturer. You might even be the client too. Do not fall into the trap of thinking you don't need to communicate your ideas just because you know what you are doing! You have to communicate your ideas so that they can be understood by other people. You can then ask them for their advice and opinions about your proposals. You will also be able to judge more clearly whether your design is exactly right, before you start making. You can use techniques in this chapter to help you communicate ideas.

Rendering

Designers use presentation drawings to show what a product will look like. They use a technique called rendering which shows surface textures. You can use a wide range of media to do this.

Metal and plastic

Electronic products are often enclosed in containers made from metal or plastic. Line shading is a good way of showing these materials. Use a black pen or pencil to draw a series of parallel lines on the surface. The spaces between the lines can be increased or decreased to give an impression of light or dark. It is usual to make the upward-facing surfaces lightest.

Felt marker rendering

To use markers well you will need to practise before working on a special piece of work.

Here are some tips which will help you.

1 Work quickly and evenly – don't rest the pen on the paper.
2 Don't worry about going over the edges of your drawing (see 3).
3 Cut out your finished drawing and remount it to obtain clear outlines.
4 Use coloured pencils to add details and white pencil for reflections.
5 Use white paint for highlights.
6 Use only a limited range of colours or a variety of shades of the same colour.

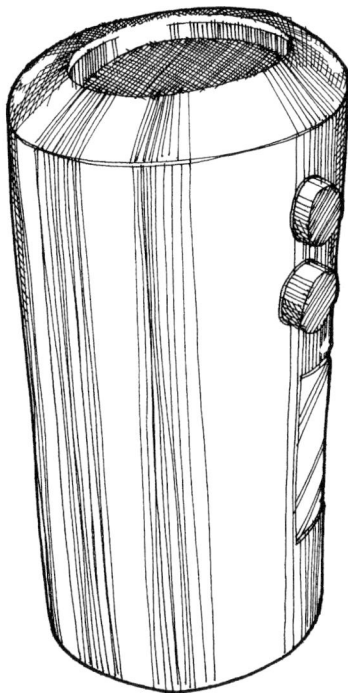

The shading shows that sides are curved and shiny metal while the top is flat and shiny plastic

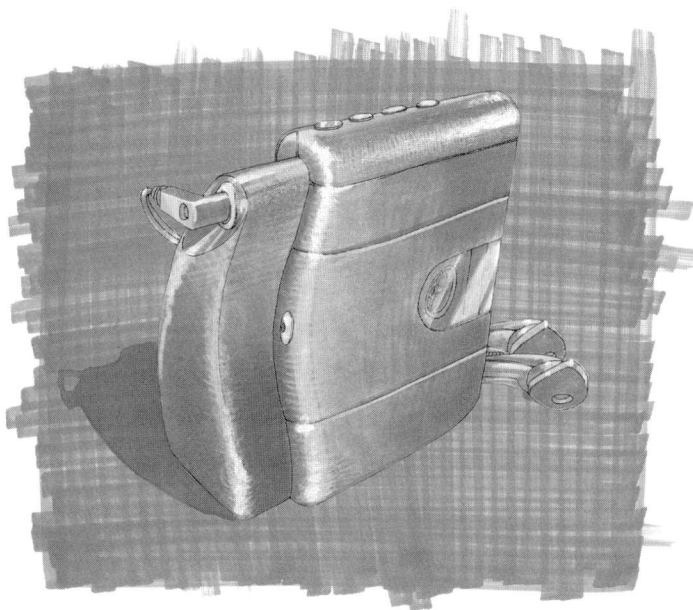

5 Crating

The circuitry for electronic products can be housed in containers of varying shapes. You can use crating to draw these shapes. You begin by imagining the container packed tightly in a box or crate. Then you draw this crate and add the details so that the form inside the crate becomes the container. The drawings below show how ideas for containers of a simple radio and a warning device circuit were developed by crating.

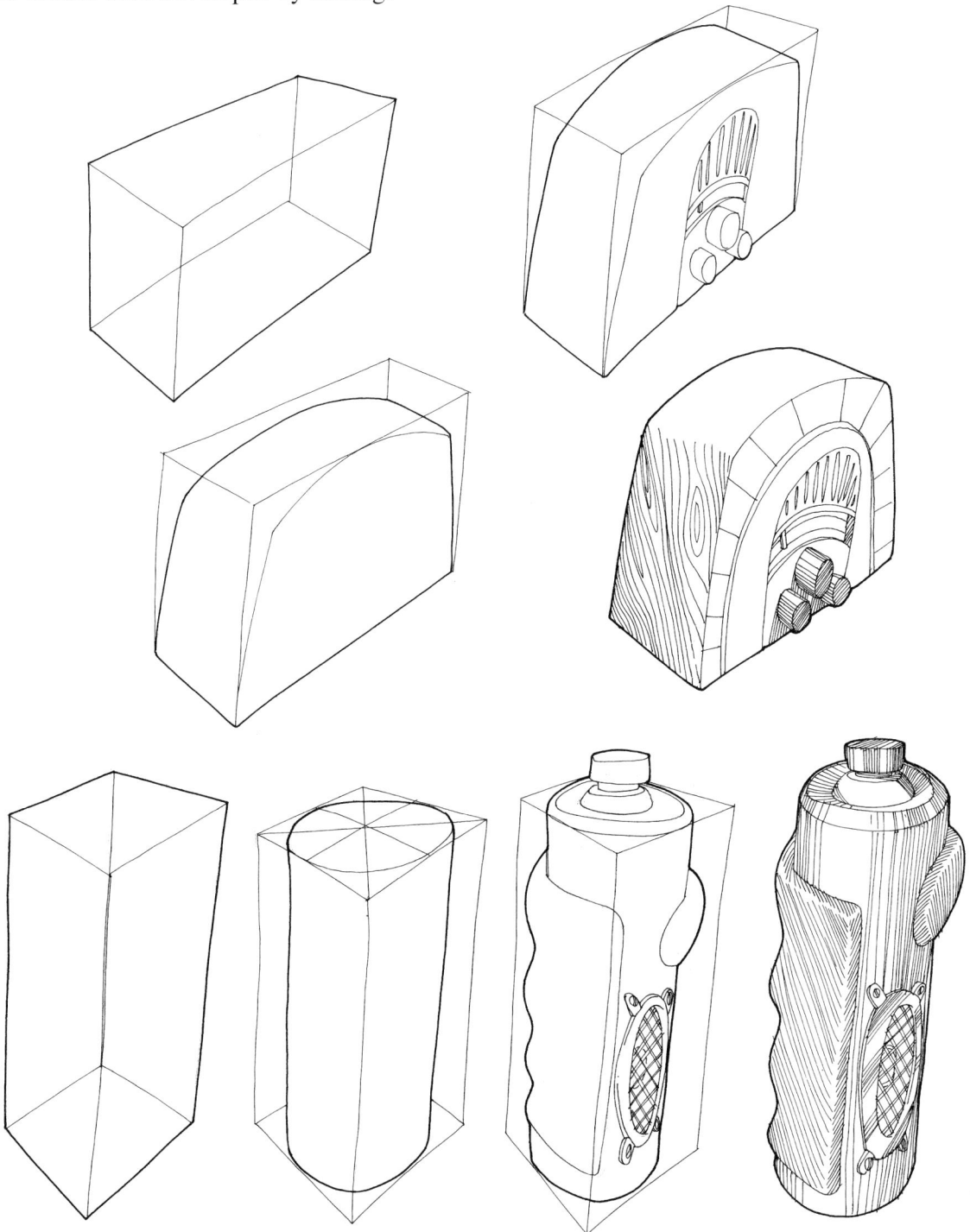

Isometric drawing

Isometric means 'equal measure'. In isometric drawings lines of equal length along the axes in the object being drawn appear as such in the drawing. This method of drawing is suitable for computer-aided design (CAD) where drawings are entered into the computer as a series of numbers or measurements.

You can draw this way by following the steps illustrated using a 60/30 set square.

1 Draw a base line and construct the nearest corner of the object at 30° to the base line.

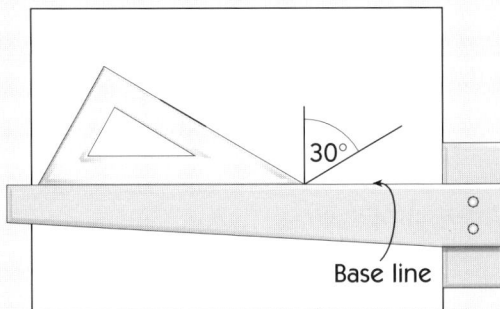

2 Construct the crate by drawing lines parallel to the three corner lines.

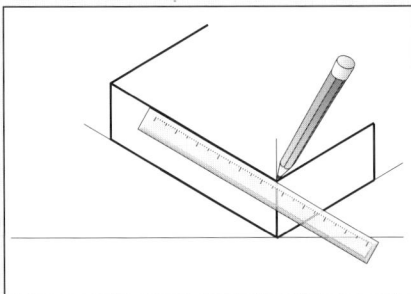

3 Use a ruler to mark off the correct measurements to construct your drawing.

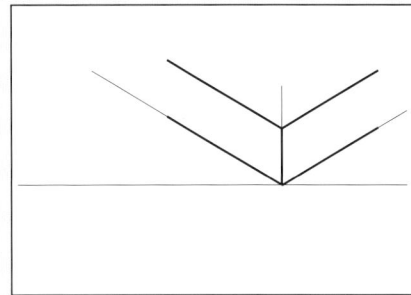

4 Adding final detail.

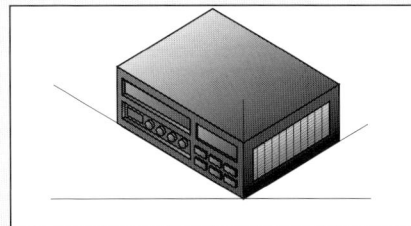

Communicating costs

You will need to show the costs of the components, the cost of producing a circuit board which holds the components, and the cost of the container for the product.

Costing electronic components and circuit construction

The chart below lists a range of components which you are likely to use, and their approximate costs. You can use this to estimate the cost of components.

Costing the container

The chart on the right lists some ways of making containers for electronic products in school, with information about cost and additional features you may need to consider when deciding on your container.

Method	Application	Costs	Comments
From flat sheets of polystyrene glued together	For single prototypes	Low	Rapid Easy to do Can be sprayed for extra realism Limited range of forms possible Not very robust
From sheets of acrylic glued together	For single prototypes	Medium	Rapid Quite easy to do Can be sprayed for extra realism Wider range of forms available through use of strip heating Robust
From polystyrene sheet vacuum formed	For short runs	Medium	Rapid but mould making is very time consuming Moderately easy to do Can be sprayed for extra realism Wide range of curved forms possible Quite robust
From aluminium sheet pop riveted together	For single prototypes	Low	Time consuming Difficult to do Can be sprayed for extra realism Limited range of forms possible Very robust
Using ready made tubing	For single prototypes	Low	Rapid Moderately easy to do Can be sprayed for extra realism Wide range of forms possible Very robust

Key: ▲ = less than £ 0.20,
       ◆ = between £ 0.30 and £ 0.70
       ● = between £ 0.80 and £ 1.30,
       ■ = between £ 1.40 and £ 2.00

Discrete components		Integrated circuits		Output devices		Circuit construction	
Resistor	▲	555 timer	◆	Relay	■	Perforated board 100 mm x 50 mm	◆
Thermistor	▲	741 op amp	◆	Low power motor	◆	Strip board 100 mm x 50 mm	●
Diode	▲	7404 AND gate	◆	Geared motor	■	Printed circuit board	
Low power transistor	▲	7402 NOR gate	◆	Buzzer	◆	100 mm x 50 mm (photo-resist)	■
High power transistor	◆	7493 binary counter	◆	Pico sounder	●	Printed circuit board	
Electrolytic capacitor	◆	7475 latch	◆	Low voltage lamp	▲	100 mm x 50 mm (copper clad)	◆
Polyester capacitor	▲	4056 7-segment driver	◆	LED	▲		
Tuning capacitor	◆						
LDR	◆						

CRT2, CRT3

Orthographic projection

You should use the drawing system called orthographic projection for accurate scale drawings of the casings for electronic products. These drawings are called **working drawings** and are based on square-on views of the object. As you can see, you can obtain six square-on views of a portable radio/tape player.

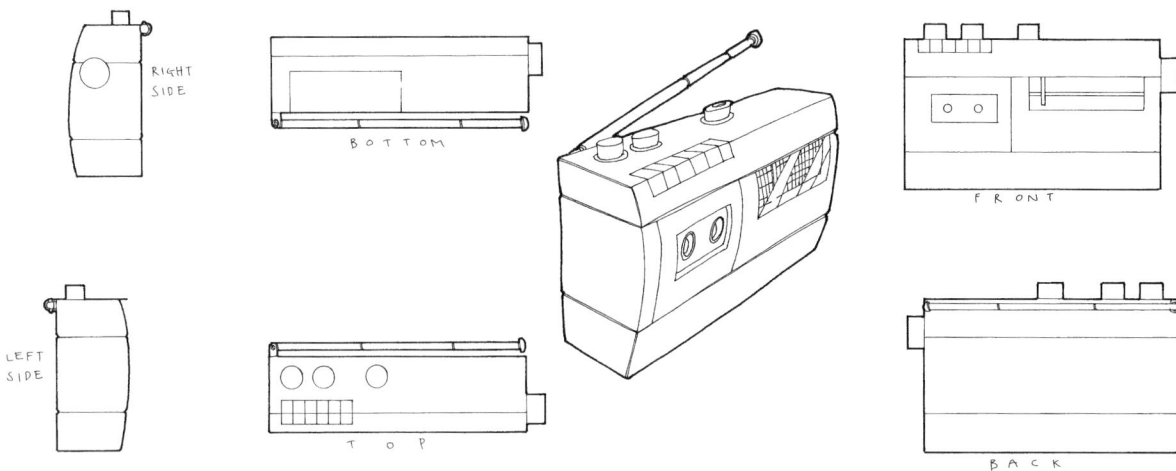

Usually you only need to draw three views to give enough detail about your design. There are two ways of arranging these views, as shown below. They are called **first-angle projection** and **third-angle projection**. Each has its own symbol, as shown. You must always show whether your plans are first- or third-angle projections.

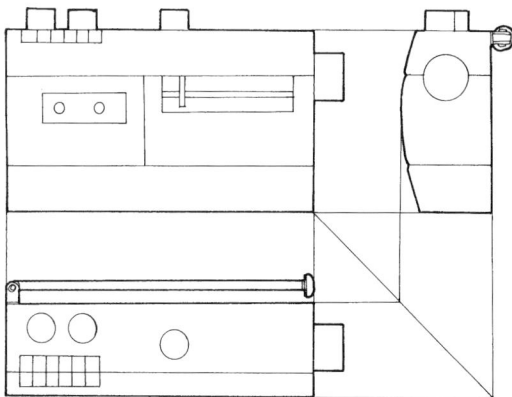

First angle projection

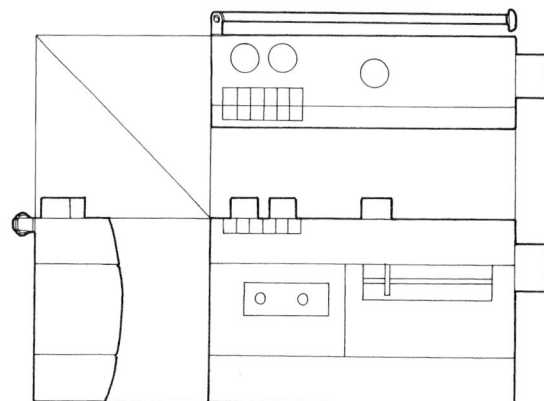

Third angle projection

Drawing a first-angle projection

You will need to use a drawing board with either a T-square or parallel motion for drawing parallel lines. You will also need set squares, a pair of compasses and a sharp pencil.

Here are the step-by-step instructions for drawing a first-angle orthographic projection of a bracket used to hold an electronic motor.

1 Draw the front elevation on a baseline.

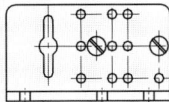

2 Draw in vertical and horizontal projection lines from important features.

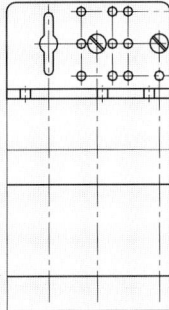

3 Draw in the plan view.

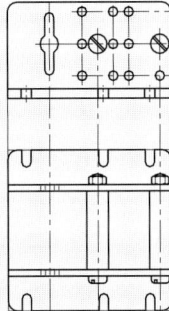

4 Draw in the horizontal projection lines from important features and a line at 45° from the front elevation across the horizontal projection lines from the plan view.

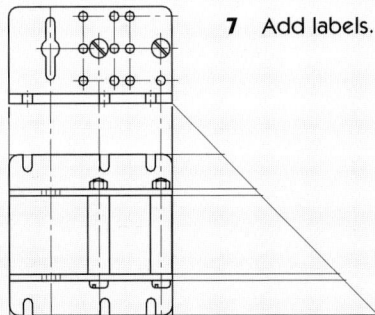

5 Draw in vertical projection lines from the points where the 45° line cuts the horizontal projection lines.

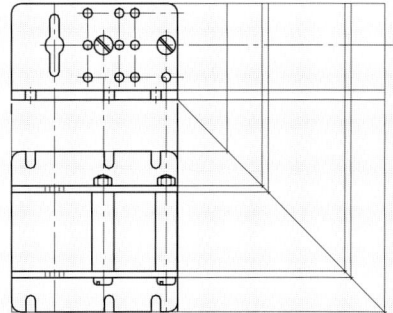

6 Use the crossing points of these vertical projection lines and the horizontal projection lines from the front elevation to construct the end elevation.

7 Add labels.

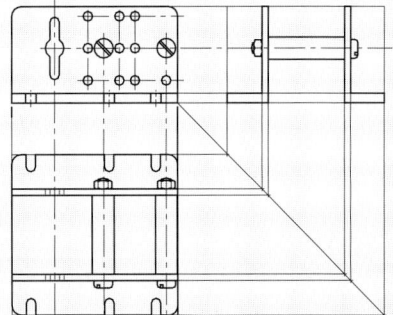

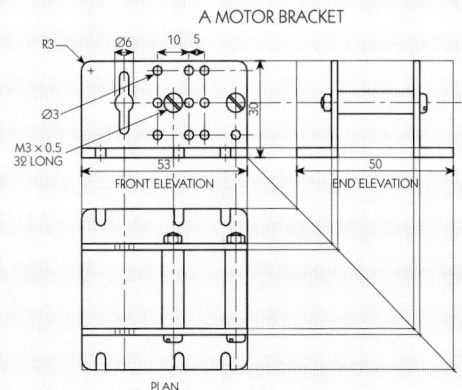

A MOTOR BRACKET

Using British Standards conventions

In industry it is unlikely that the person making a product is the same person who drew the designs, so it is important that the designer produces drawings which communicate his or her ideas clearly. These kinds of drawings are called **working drawings** and should be set out in a clear and organised manner. The British Standards Institution (BSI) gives a set of rules (conventions) for such drawings.

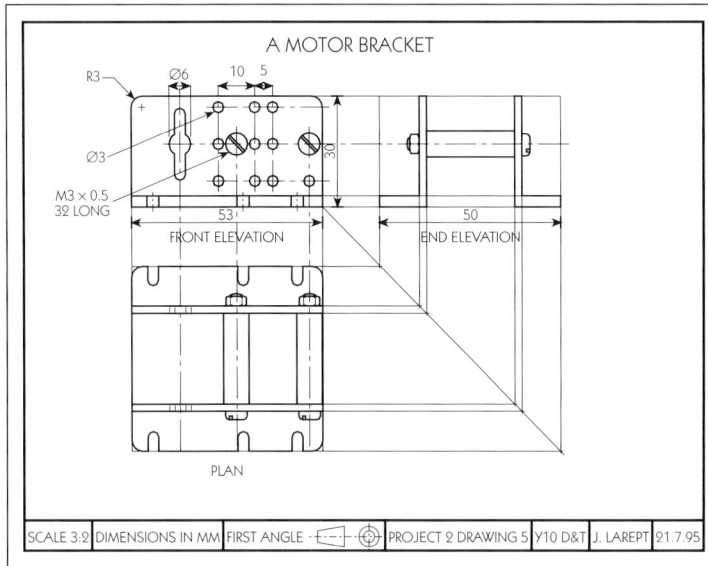

A MOTOR BRACKET

SCALE 3:2 | DIMENSIONS IN MM | FIRST ANGLE | PROJECT 2 DRAWING 5 | Y10 D&T | J. LAREPT | 21.7.95

Some common abbreviations	
Ø	Diameter
R	Radius
mm	Millimetre
cm	Centimetre
m	Metre
CSK	Countersunk
O/D	Outside diameter
I/D	Insider diameter
RDHD	Roundhead
DRG	Drawing
Matl	Material

Dimensioning

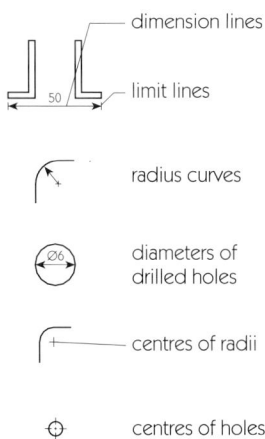

- dimension lines
- limit lines
- radius curves
- diameters of drilled holes
- centres of radii
- centres of holes

Some useful symbols

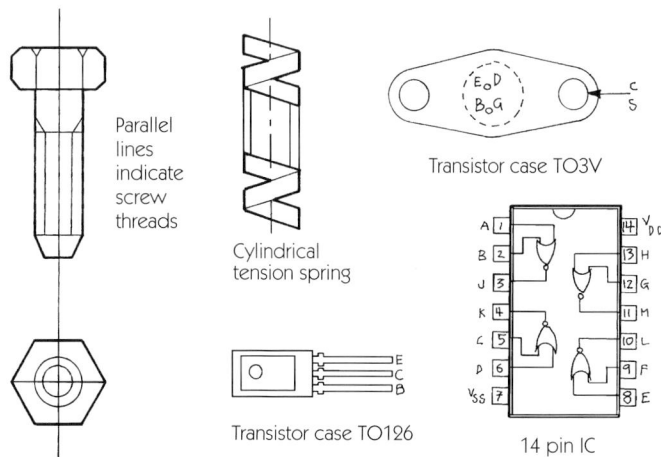

Parallel lines indicate screw threads

Cylindrical tension spring

Transistor case TO3V

Transistor case TO126

14 pin IC

Sectional views

Most electronic products are enclosed in some sort of container. It is important that the layout of the container and the way in which circuit boards and components fit is clear. You can use a sectional view to show this. In a sectional view an imaginary cut is made through the object, you then remove one half and draw what you can now see. Any surfaces which are 'cut' are cross-hatched with lines drawn at 45°. These lines change direction between different pieces of material.

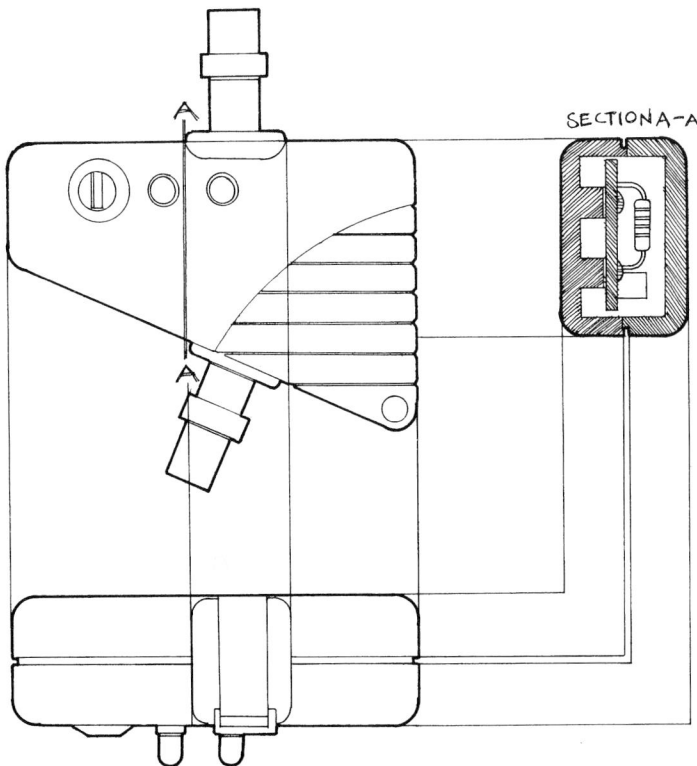

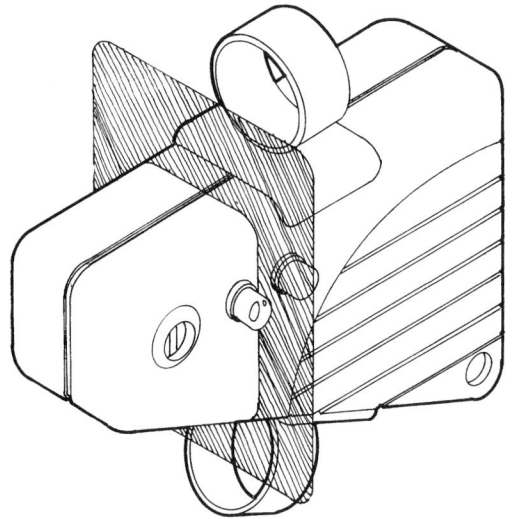

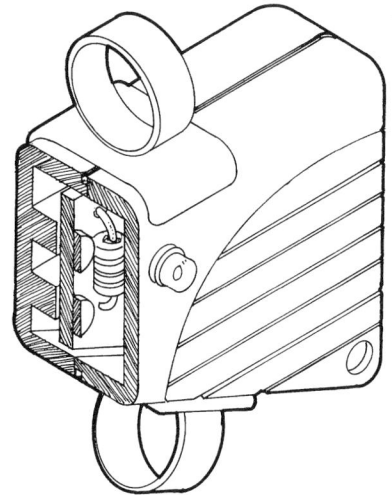

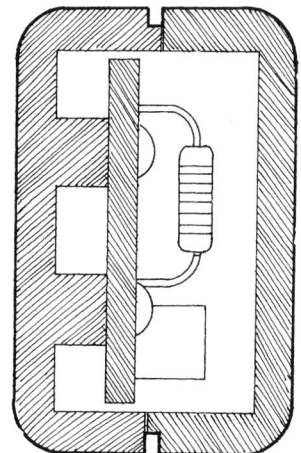

SECTION A-A

A

A

CRT2, CRT3

Assembly drawings

You can use an assembly drawing to show how the different components of an electronics product fit together. This type of illustration is sometimes called an exploded view. It is particularly useful for electronics-based products as the position of the components can be clearly seen.

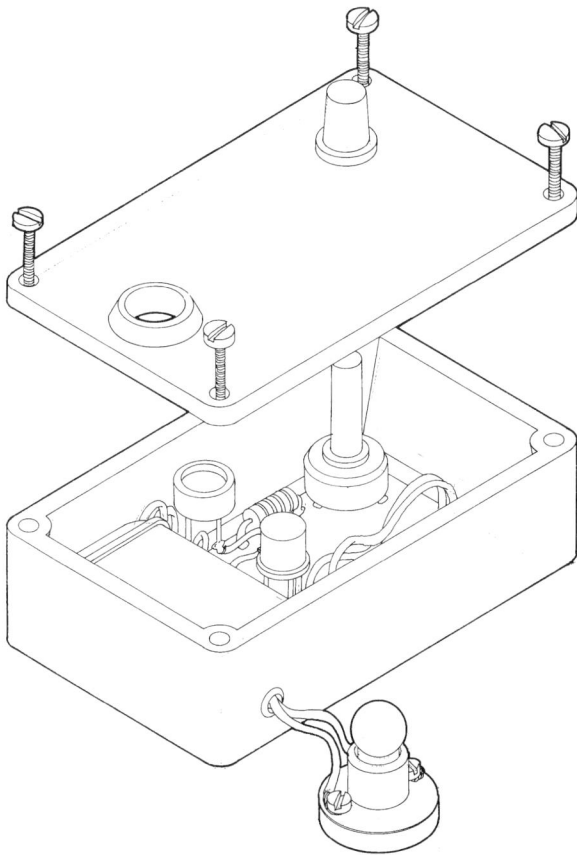

Hints for producing successful assembly drawings

- Use isometric paper to provide a guide grid.
- Keep parts on the same axis (in line with each other) when exploded.
- As far as possible, show each piece separately.
- Avoid overlaps.
- Keep all parts exploded along an axis in the order in which they fit together.
- Do a sketch first. It is easy to run out of room.

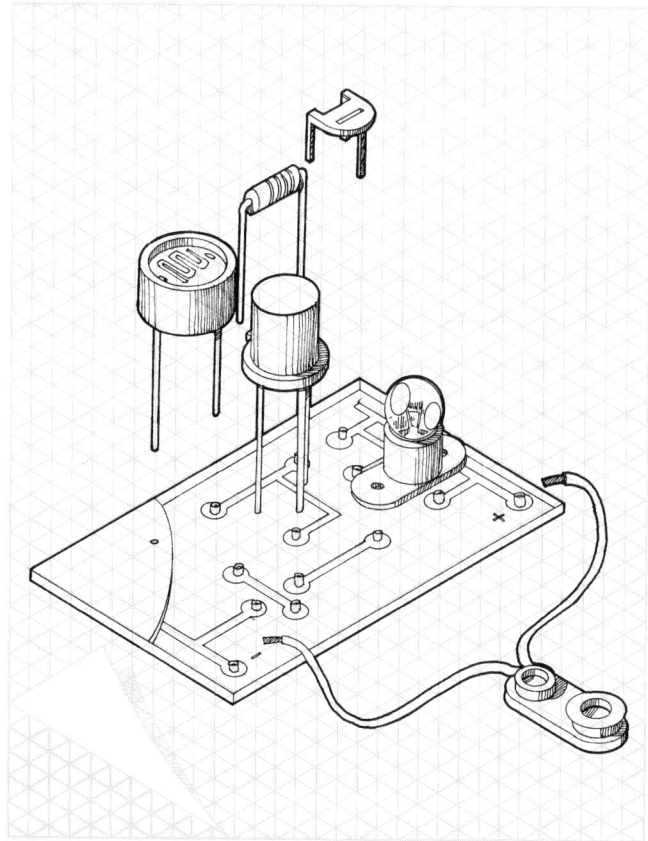

Process specification

When you make a product, you need to think about the order of work. The picture below shows a container for an electronic product made by vacuum forming. The base fits inside the plastic moulding and is held in place by four screws which pass through the cover and into threaded holes in the edge of the base. The vacuum forming has to be done first as the base must be made to fit inside.

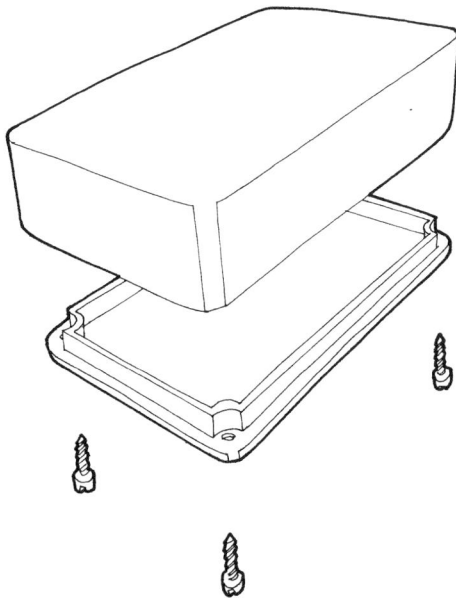

In other products various sub-assemblies may have to be made and tested before they can be tried together. A remote control vehicle that follows a white line has a drive system which requires an electric motor and gearbox. It would be sensible to make up the motor and gearbox assembly first and make sure that it works before fitting it into the vehicle and adding the control circuit.

The same idea can be applied to electronic circuits. The components which need protection from heat, such as transistors and ICs, should be fitted last so that they are not subject to heat when other components are being fitted. In complex circuits, try to build these as subsections which can be made and tested before being joined to other parts of the circuit. If you have a design which uses a sensing circuit, this can be built and tested for an output before fitting it to the process part of the circuit. Similarly, an output section, which might involve a power transistor, relay and a motor, can be tested before fitting it to the process part. This method of construction makes fault finding easier as any faults will be limited to a small part of the circuit.

In industry, the designer will usually specify the order of construction to the person who makes the product. In your work in school you can use flow charts to plan the order of your work.

CRT2, CRT3

Using jigs and fixtures

You can use a jig to help you to carry out difficult or tedious making operations. If you have to make a number of identical parts or work very accurately, then a jig will help. Here are two examples. To make 24 of the part shown here, each with four holes in exactly the right places, is both tedious and difficult. The drilling jig makes this a simple operation.

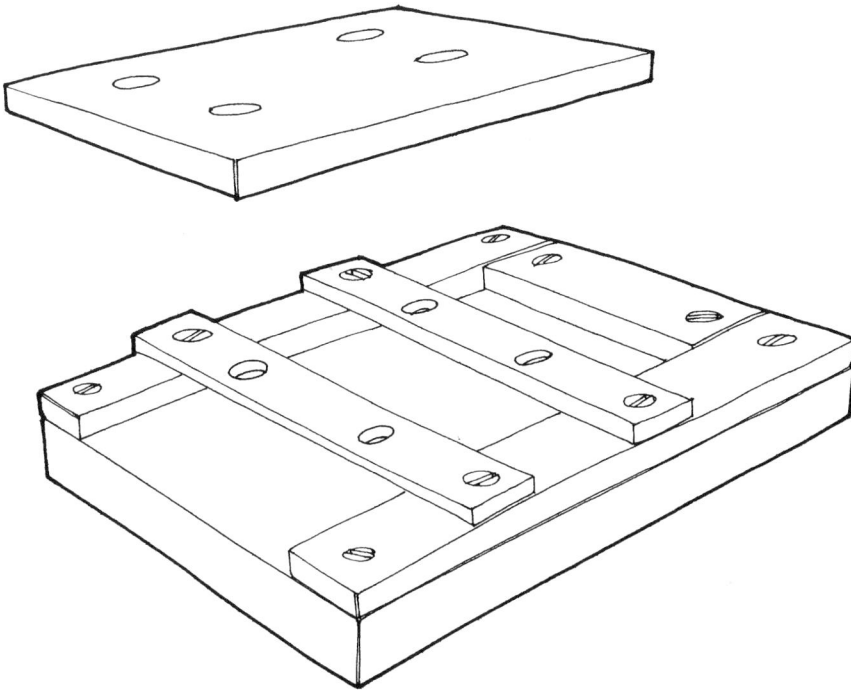

Producing a coil for a radio aerial or for a solenoid takes a long time and requires accuracy, so a coil-winding jig like the one shown is particularly useful. If you design and make this yourself, then this work can count towards your examination grade.

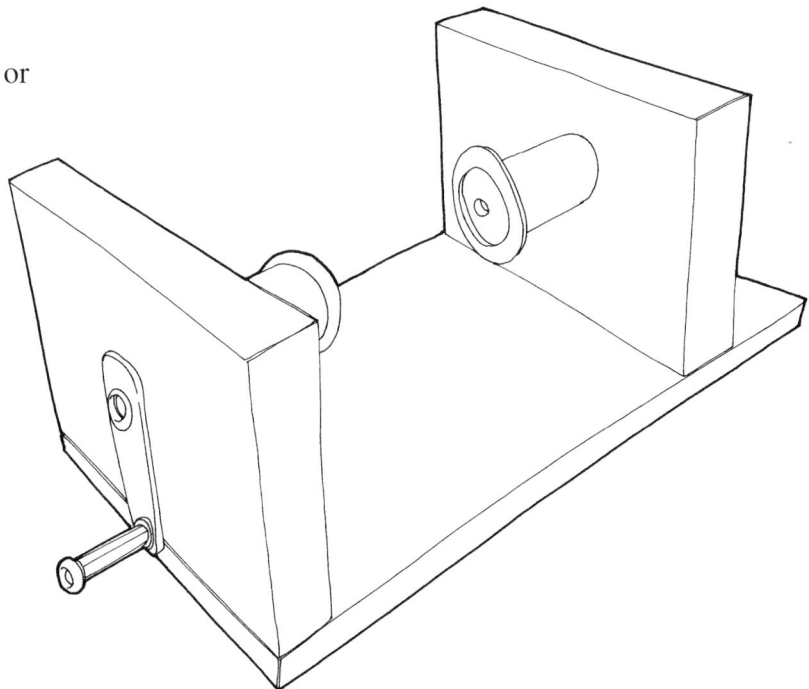

Communicating the circuit

Circuit diagrams

A circuit diagram for an electronic product shows the order in which the components are connected together. This sort of diagram is drawn with space between each component so that the connections can be seen clearly. Standard symbols are used to show the components and how the connections are made. When you draw a circuit diagram, make a free-hand sketch first and then draw the diagram neatly. You should use the standard symbols, some of which are shown below

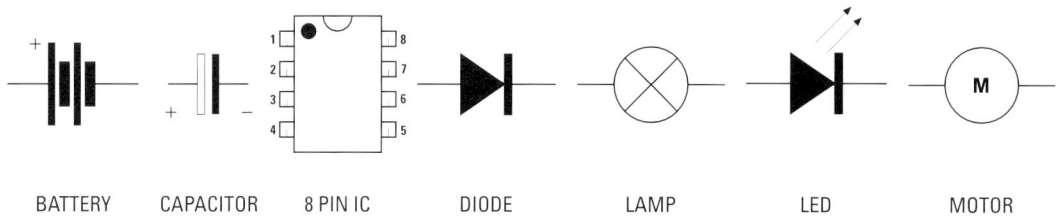

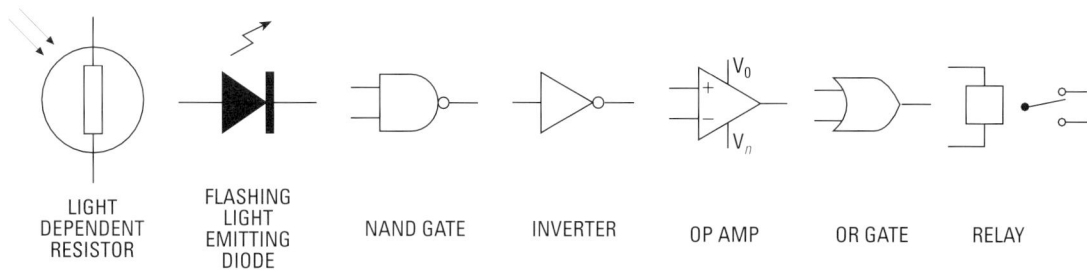

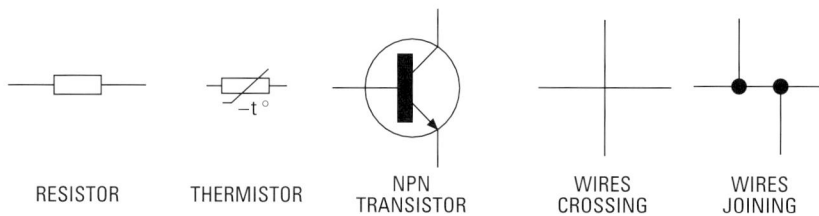

BATTERY	CAPACITOR	8 PIN IC	DIODE	LAMP	LED	MOTOR

LIGHT DEPENDENT RESISTOR	FLASHING LIGHT EMITTING DIODE	NAND GATE	INVERTER	OP AMP	OR GATE	RELAY

RESISTOR	THERMISTOR	NPN TRANSISTOR	WIRES CROSSING	WIRES JOINING

Layout diagrams

Once a circuit diagram has been worked out, it usually needs to be modified to show how the circuit can be set out on a circuit board. The layout of the circuit has to allow components to be fitted into the space available, and connections to be made. Switches need to be placed so that they can be operated. Input sensors will need to be placed so that they can sense the physical condition for which they were designed, and output devices will have to be seen or heard. Sometimes you will need to save space and place components as close together as possible. Often the layout diagram looks different from the circuit diagram but, of course, the way in which the components are connected together is the same in each, as shown below.

Examples of circuit board layout

The drawings below show a circuit diagram and the way in which it can be set out on a printed circuit board.

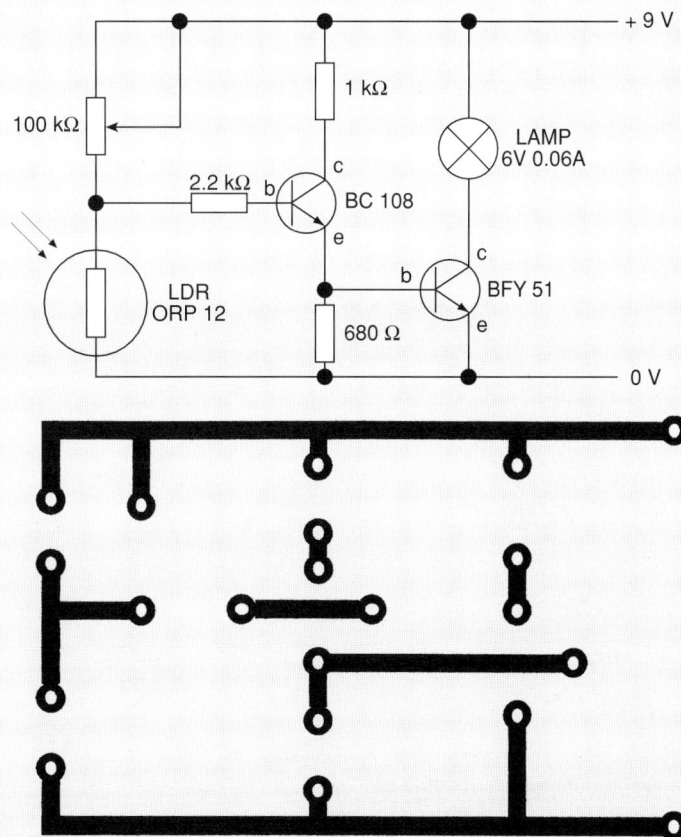

This is a simple sensing circuit that activates a lamp when it becomes dark

You can find out how to produce a printed circuit board on pages 174–175.

Communicating to the user

Many products are provided with an instruction book or user guide. These are used to describe simple operations, such as how to fit the various blades and beaters to a food processor, as well as complicated procedures, such as how to assemble an item of 'flatpack' furniture.

Some of the electronic products which you design and make will need user guides. If the product is simple, then the guide might just show how to replace batteries, indicator lamps or fuses. More complex products will require detailed instructions. For example, sensing instruments would need instructions on how to set up and connect the sensors; security devices would need a user guide to show how the sensors should be installed and how the device should be set and returned to a 'safe' condition. Control systems would need a user guide on setting up, testing and, if programmable, how the control sequence can be modified. A user guide may also contain a fault finding chart.

Producing a user guide is as much a design task as the making of a three-dimensional product and is an area where you can use your graphic skills to good effect. Use the following guidelines when producing a user guide.

- Keep body text to a minimum.
- Avoid over-technical language.
- Use illustrations plus annotations for the naming of parts.
- Use step-by-step drawings as instructions.
- Use graphics software and desktop publishing software for really professional-looking results.
- If you have access to word processing software, only use this for the text and leave space for illustrations which you can add to the print-out by hand.

When you have produced a guide, ask one of your friends to take a user trip and read it through to see that it makes sense!

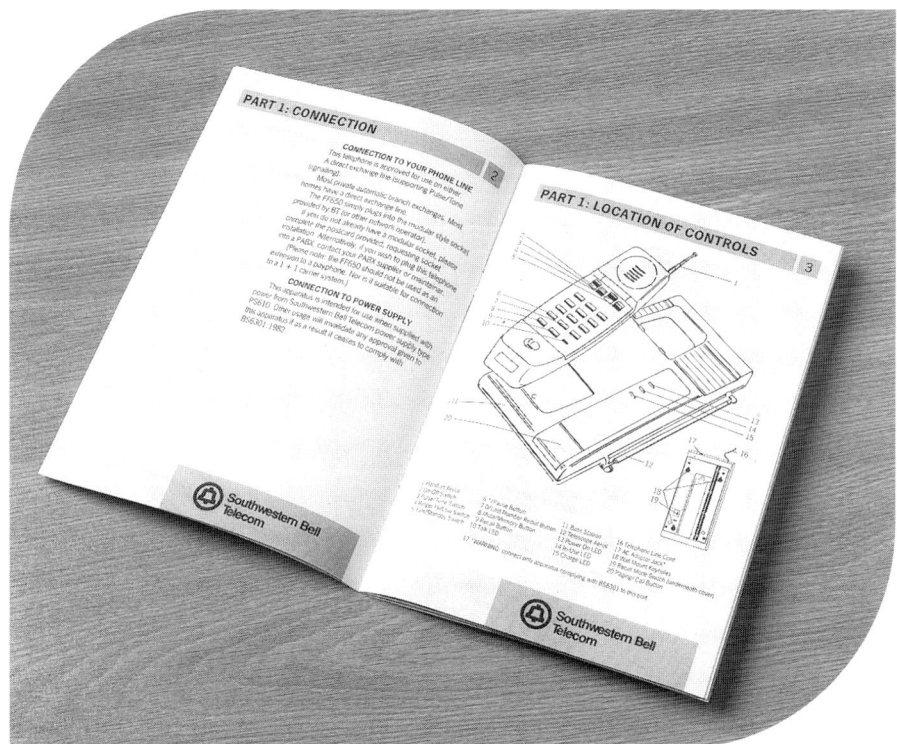

Communicating extra information

One system of drawing will rarely communicate all the information the designer wishes to convey to the maker, client or user. You will usually need to use a combination. Even then there will be times when additional information is necessary. Sometimes you will need to add written notes specifying a particular process of finish, such as sandblasting or dip coating. On other occasions you will need to add extra drawings. Here are some examples taken from the drawings of a radio-controlled car.

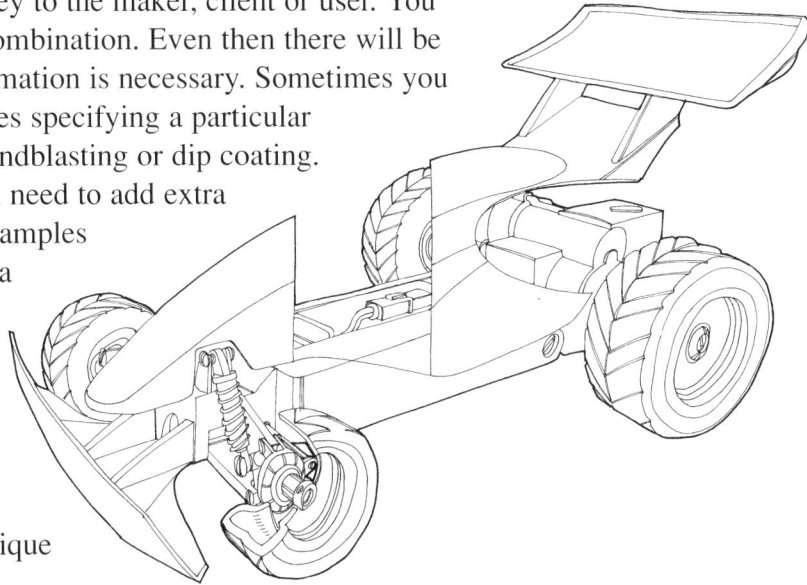

You can use this Chooser Chart to decide which technique or drawing system to use.

Which sort of drawing?

What you want to communicate	Techniques or drawing systems to use
Realistic appearance of a product	Rendering on perspective or isometric views
Overall appearance with correct proportion	Crating
Scale drawing suitable for CAD	Isometric drawing
Cost of materials and components	Costing chart
Details for making the container	Orthographic projection
Details of the circuit	Circuit diagram
Details of circuit construction	PCB layout diagram
Internal details	Sectional views
How parts fit together	Exploded views
Special features	Hidden detail Animation for moving parts Enlarged detail

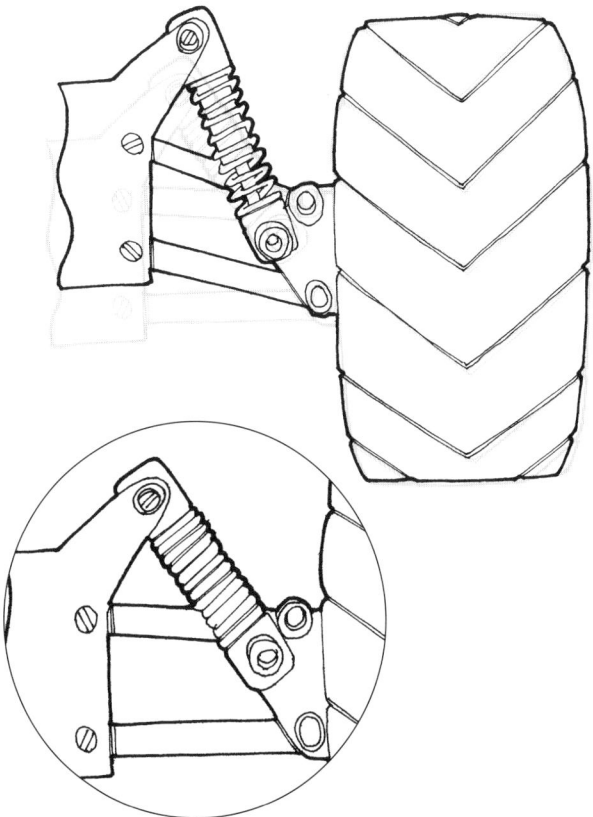

D *Enlarged details can draw attention to features which need additional explanation.*

Inputs

Sensing input signals

All electronic products make use of input signals and you will need to think about the way these signals are produced and sensed. Sometimes you will use a sensor and you will need to decide which one to use. There are electronic sensors to detect changes in a large number of variables:

- temperature;
- light level;
- sound level;
- moisture content;
- pH;
- magnetic field;
- force;
- movement.

The different sensors that are available are described on page 159.

Sensors are not the only input signals to think about. The product may also need:

- a switch to turn it on or off;
- a reset switch if the product latches or counts;
- an emergency or safety stop;
- a sensitivity adjustment (variable resistor);
- a selector to switch between different sensors;
- a selector to switch between output signals;
- a test button.

You can use these question to help you to decide on which sensor to use.

Technical questions

- What change does the sensor need to detect?
- Which sensors detect this change?
- Does the system require an analogue or digital signal from the sensor?
- How accurate does the sensor need to be?
- How reliable does the sensor need to be?
- Does the sensor need to be directional?
- Will the sensor be remote from the product?
- How much room is available for the sensor?
- What other signals might confuse the sensor?
- What environmental conditions will affect the sensor?

Non-technical questions

- How much do possible sensors cost?
- Will the sensor be seen or hidden?
- If seen, which sensors provide the right image for the product?

Note that it is possible to use one sensor for many applications and to meet the requirements of one application with different sensors, as shown below.

Measuring the light level on top of a street lamp

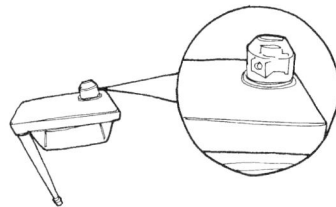

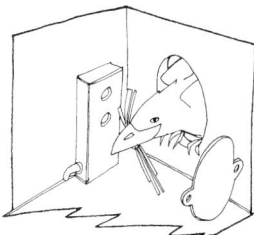

Detecting the use of a bird box

Using a microswitch

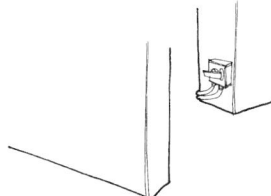

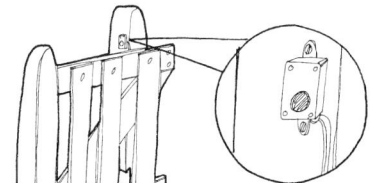

Using the shadow of the gate on a light sensor

▶ *Two applications using a light dependent resistor*

▶ *Two ways to detect a gate being opened*

Outputs

There is a huge range of different electronic output devices. It is easy to get confused, so the first step is to use the following list to decide exactly what sort of output you need. Is it:

- sound;
- movement;
- magnetism;
- force;
- a display;
- light for illumination;
- light for indication;
- radiation for signalling;
- electrical switching;
- fluid flow?

Once you have made this decision, you can use the Chooser Chart on page 160 to decide exactly which output device you need. Whichever one you choose, there will be other considerations to take into account. Use these points to help you.

Electrical considerations

Take care to ensure that the power requirements of your output device can be met by your power supply. You may need to calculate the power available ($I \times V$) and compare this with the power rating of possible output devices.

If the device is battery operated take care to ensure that the battery you are using will have a reasonable life. You will need to know the current drawn by the output device and the capacity of the battery (see page 155).

Structural and mechanical considerations

The output device must be an appropriate weight, size and shape to be fitted into the product. It must robust enough to deal with the environmental conditions in which the product will be used. In the case of motors, it is important that they are fastened in ways that do not cause undue vibration.

Communication considerations

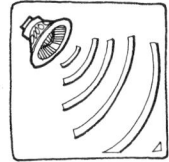

Some aspects of the choice of output components for a product may depend on how you want to communicate to the user. Here are some possibilities:

- a silent output to avoid disturbing or alerting others;
- a loud output to attract attention;
- an output that can be detected by those with a sensory handicap;
- a highly visible output suitable for public display.

Safety considerations

You will need to carry out a hazard analysis for the use of your design and identify any risks associated with its use. Your design should include ways to minimise these risks (see page 187). Here are some examples.

- Moving parts – make sure that users are warned of any dangers.
- Sound levels – don't produce sounds that could damage hearing or contravene environmental protection rules.
- Temperature – users should be protected from, or warned about, devices that get hot.

Design guides – outputs

Here are some ways of using common output devices to communicate information.

Device	Description	Device	Description
LED	Low power, easy to see in the dark, but more difficult in bright light. Different colours available. Can also be bought grouped either as 'bar graph' or square array.	Bell	Higher power and much louder noise than buzzer.
Flashing LED	As above, but the flashing draws attention to it.	Loudspeaker	For reproducing audio signals to be heard in an open space.
7-segment LED display	As LED above, for displaying LED display numbers or letters.	Earphone.	For reproducing audio signals to be heard by a single individual without causing annoyance to others.
7-segment liquid crystal display	As above but liquid crystal display (LCDS) use much less power than LEDs. Only visible in reasonable lighting.	Motor	Can be used to provide simple rotary movement or drive a mechanism to give a dynamic display.
Lamp	Higher power but more visible than LED, produces heat, can be used to illuminate a sign, different colours achieved using filters, flashing needs to be done electronically. ITS COLD IN THE GREENHOUSE	Solenoid	Can be used to switch a mechanism between two states.
Buzzer	Low power, intense monotone sound at short distance, pulsing improves ability to hear it over a distance.	Meter	Low power. For showing the size of an analogue signal. Particularly useful for showing slow change in a signal. May need to be calibrated.
Siren	Similar to buzzer but sound output is louder and frequency modulated. Requires a higher current.		

Enclosures

Deciding on an enclosure

The working parts of your product will be an assembly of PCBs, wires, components and accessories – almost impossible to use as they stand and unlikely to be items that are treasured and valued. In deciding on an enclosure or container for the working parts you have the task of turning an electronic system into an electronic product. Here are some questions to help you.

Thinking about questions **1–5** will help you to decide on the overall size and structure of the product.

1 Does your system need to be contained inside an enclosure or can it be located on the rear of a product without enclosing?

2 If it needs enclosing, will it need one container or several containers?

3 How much of the system needs to be contained on the inside of any enclosure? How much room will this need? How will it be located in position?

4 Will it be hand-held?

5 Will it be fixed to a surface or clipped onto something?

Thinking about question **6** will help you to decide on user interface details.

6 How much of the system needs to come to the surface or outside face of any enclosure? How will these parts be attached to the surface and connected to the rest of the system?

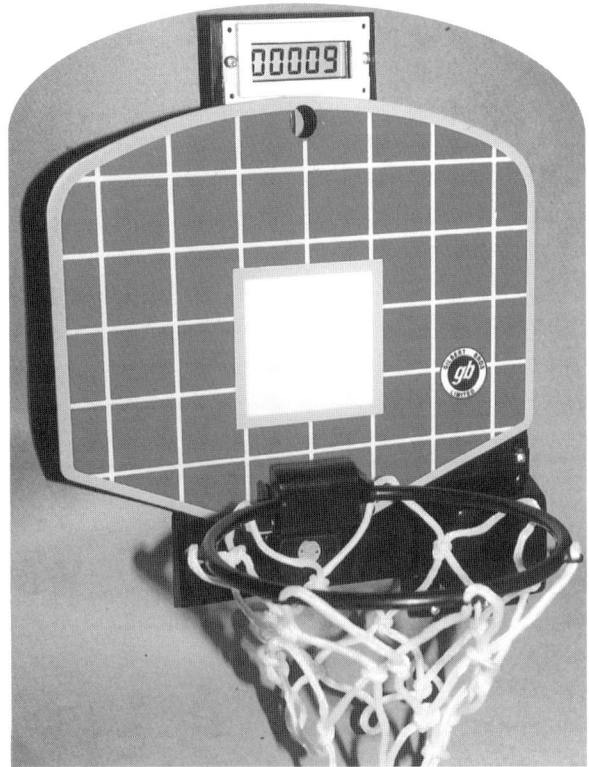

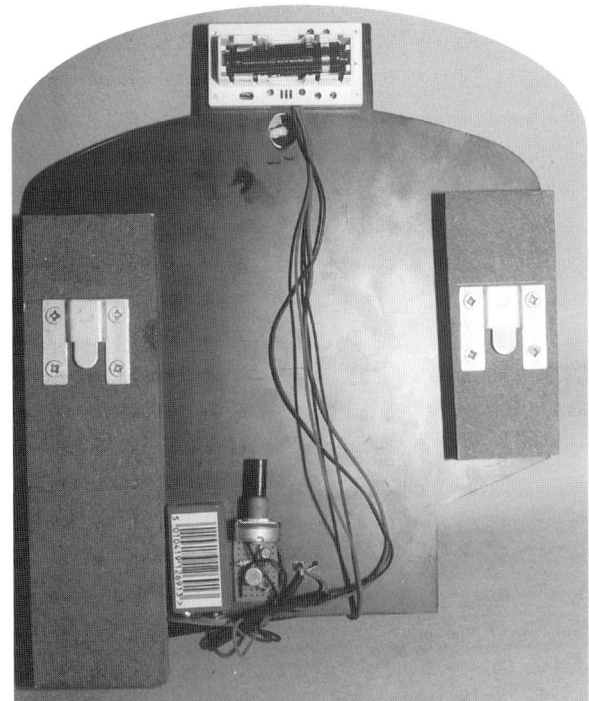

No enclosure is necessary for this electronic product

113

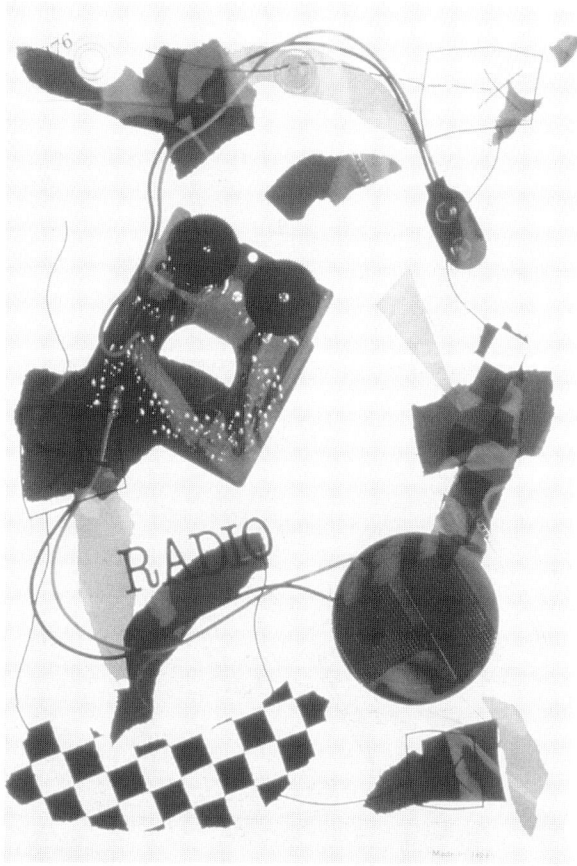

Bag radio designed by Daniel Weil in 1981

Thinking about question **7** will help you to decide on assembly and maintenance.

7 What sort of access will be required when putting the product together during manufacture and when maintaining the product in use?

Thinking about question **8** will help you to decide on the materials and structure to use for the product.

8 How will the product be used? In what conditions will it have to work?

Look at the photograph of the basketball game. A sensor detects each 'basket' and a counter displays the score. There is no need for an enclosure. The electronic system is clipped to the back of the board. The sensor, counter and reset button all need to come to the surface of the backboard. Access during making is straightforward as there is no enclosure. Changing the battery will be easy. A plywood sheet would provide a robust backboard. Compare this with the radical approach of the bag radio in which the electronic system for a radio is enclosed in a clear pvc bag!

Thinking about question **9–12** will help you to decide on the style of the product.

9 Who will use it?
10 What will make the product look appealing to the user?
11 Where will they use it?
12 Where will it be sold?

The same but different

The passive infrared detectors shown in the panel below both contain similar electronic systems but they look very different. Using the information in the panel and the questions on pages 113 and 114 will help you to understand why.

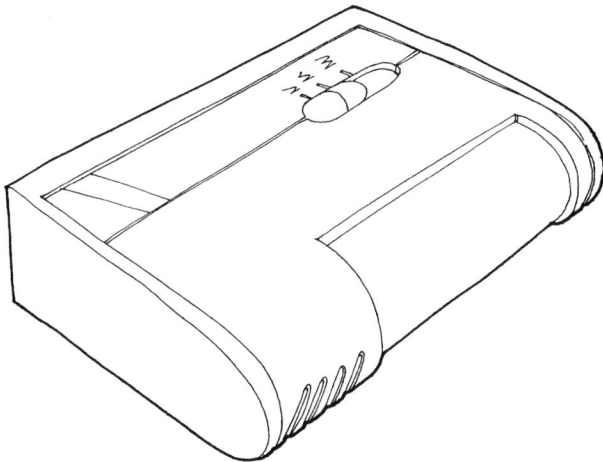

- Designed to be portable and with the ability to sound either a chime or an alarm when movement is sensed.

- Powered by a 9V PP3 battery, giving a standby life of six months.

- For use in a small shop or in the home so that an outside door can be left open and unattended.

- Casing made by injection moulding from polystyrene.

- Functional but smart style.

- Sold in specialist electronic shops and through mail order catalogues.

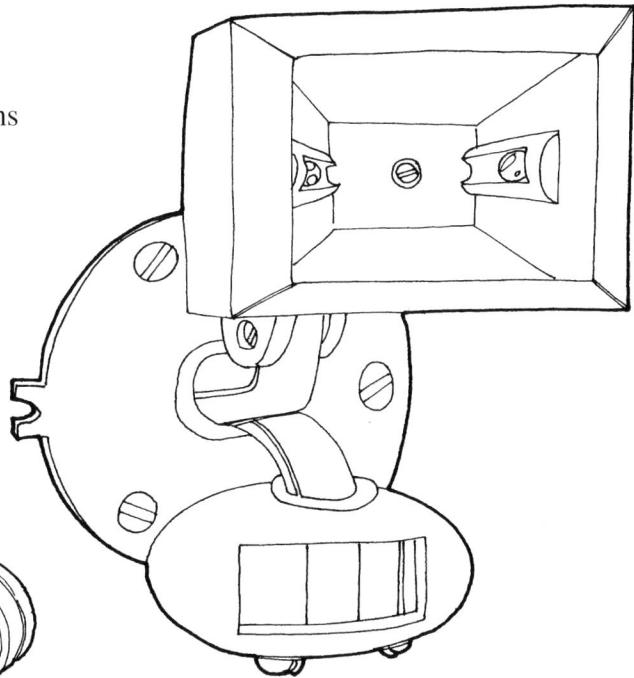

- Designed to provide lighting at night when movement is sensed.

- Powered by mains electricity.

- Used by home owners who like a light to come on as they approach their house in the dark.

- Can be fixed to an outside wall and is waterproof in all weather conditions.

- Casing made by injection moulding from tough abs plastic.

- Intended to be an attractive feature on the outside of a house.

- Sold in specialist electronic shops, through mail order and DIY stores.

The user interface

Reading the product

Your electronic product should explain itself to the user. The design should make the use obvious as many people do not read instructions. You can 'road test' the user interface by asking the kind of people for whom the product is designed to take a user trip.

Use this checklist to help with your design.

- List all the controls.
- Note what they do.
- List all the displays.
- Note what they show.

You can ensure that the purposes of controls and displays are made clear by their position and by adding lettering and/or symbols. Use widely accepted symbols if possible. If you design your own symbols, test them on others to ensure that they are understood. If you use word labels, make sure these are large enough and simple enough to be read by potential users.

- Make sure the output is appropriate and easily understood.

What does DSP mean?
What does SET/REMAIN mean?
What is P MODE?
What do the other buttons do?

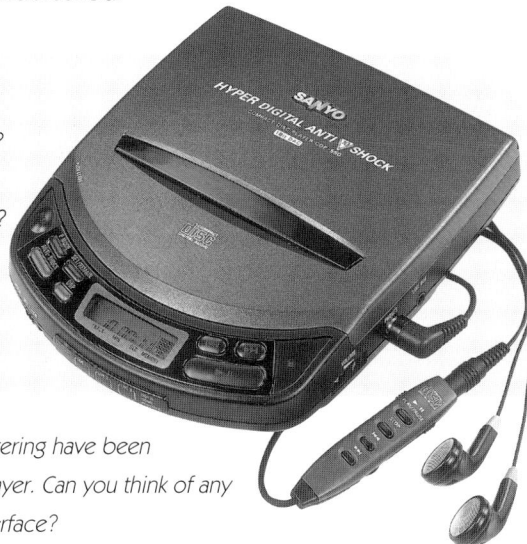

◖ *Positioning, symbols and lettering have been used on this personal CD player. Can you think of any way to improve the user interface?*

Using the controls

The controls should be easy to use. Different people will have different requirements, as shown below.

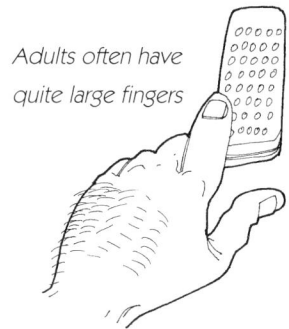

Adults often have quite large fingers

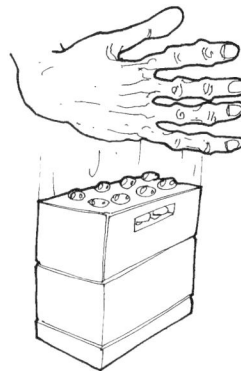

Older people may lose some strength in their hands and fingers

Portable devices should be able to be operated with the fingers of one hand

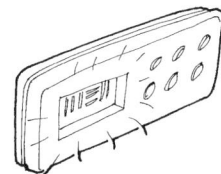

Sometimes controls need to be used in the dark

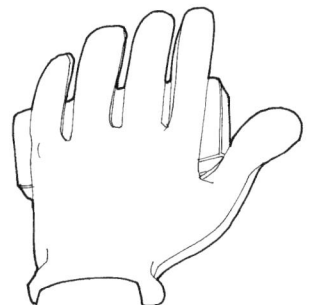

Sometimes users will be wearing gloves

Sensing devices

A sensing device gives a user information about some physical conditions in the real world. This information is detected somehow and then carried by a signal. These devices indicate whether a signal is above or below a particular level (the reference level). They often have a control to adjust the reference level.

Situations

In each situation decide what your device needs to detect and how this may be carried out.

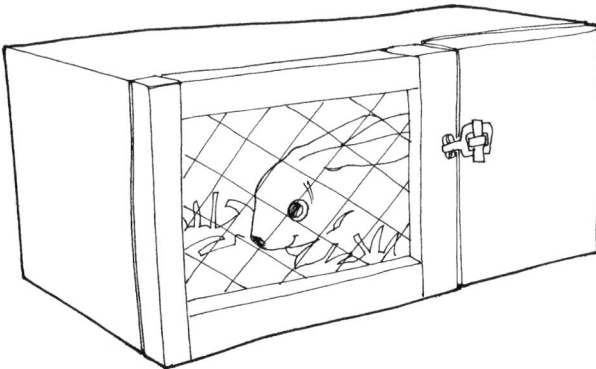

MUSTN'T GET TOO COLD

Sensing input signals

Usually very precise measurement of the physical signal isn't important as the device will be for situations that aren't critical. So, in some situations a digital sensor will be appropriate. Where an analogue sensor is used, cheaper non-linear devices would be suitable.

Producing output signals

The purpose of the main output is to indicate whether the physical signal is above or below the reference value.

Will your device will provide unintrusive information about the input signal level or will it provide a warning about the level by alerting the user?

Electronic processing

Your device may need some or all of the following features:

- **The ability to adjust the reference signal**

    Put an analogue sensor in a potential divider with a variable resistor. If this signal rarely needs adjusting, use a preset variable resistor.

    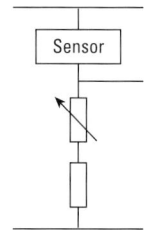
    Sensor

- **Amplification of the signal size**

    In most cases a transistor will amplify the signal enough. If the sensor provides a very small signal change use a comparator.

- **Amplification of the current to drive an output device**

    Use a transistor matched to the power requirements of the output device.

- **A latch to show that the signal has been above or below the reference signal**

    A thyristor will provide latching on an analogue input signal and also act as a driver for the output device.

    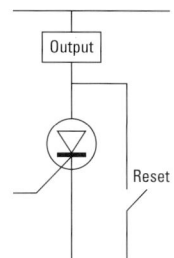
    Output
    Reset

Don't forget to include a reset. (This reset switch can also be used to check that the output device is working.)

Measuring devices

A measuring device gives the user information about either the level of a physical signal or a count rate of events or time. This information might be given as an actual value for the signal or count rate (quantitative) or as a relative level (qualitative).

Situations

In each situation decide exactly what it is that your device needs to measure. Then select the physical signal that can be used to represent this measurement.

Sensing input signals

To produce a measurement of a signal level use an analogue sensor. To provide a quantitative output, find a sensor with a linear response where the electronic signal is proportional to the physical signal.

For counting events, a digital or cheap analogue sensor will be sufficient.

An effective way to measure time is to produce (and count) regular electronic pulses.

Producing output signals

The measurement display might be qualitative (perhaps a set of lights or LEDs) or quantitative (for example a meter or a 7-segment display).

The display will, in all cases, need to provide information to the user about the values that it represents. To get these values, you may need to calibrate the display.

Electronic processing

Your instrument will need some of the following features:

- **Amplification of the signal size**
  An op-amp configured as an amplifier will give a linear analogue output. For event counting, a very small sensor signal change can be amplified with a comparator.

- **Analogue to digital conversion to provide a digital signal from an analogue signal.**
  Use a dedicated IC giving the accuracy of conversion that you need.

- **Counter to count events**
  A wide range of counter ICs is available, for example the '4029' is an IC that counts in tens.

- **display driver for 7-segment or bar graph display;**
  To drive 10 LEDS as a bar display use a '3914' IC. Each 7-segment display needs a driver to convert a set of four digital signals into signals for the displayed number. There are also ICs that combine counting and driving.

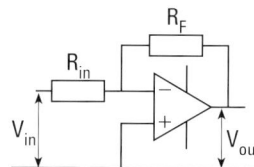

- **Current amplification to drive an output device**
  Use a transistor matched to the power requirements of the output device.

Electronic novelties and toys

A toy or novelty should be fun and amusing. The electronics don't have to be complex. You can use input and output components in unusual ways. Use the special features of electronics – small size, low cost and range of different outputs.

Situations

ELECTRONIC JEWELLERY

Use electronics to create something that's a bit different, incorporating electronics into everyday objects.

Sensing input signals

In an electronic musical instrument the inputs to the system will be used to choose the notes or sounds. Think of ways of 'playing' the instrument that are unusual. For other toys the inputs will depend on the purpose of the device. Think of ways of surprising or intriguing young children with inputs. With novelty devices the inputs can be hidden to make the device operate unexpectedly.

Producing output signals

As with other features of a novelty device, look for ways to use outputs in unusual or surprising ways.

Electronic processing

A special feature of many novelty devices is the need to keep the electronics very compact. One way to do this is to use specialist components that contain most of the circuit you need on an IC. For example:

- **Melody, sound and noise generators**

  These have one or more tunes (or other sounds) pre-programmed into them. They can often directly drive a piezo transducer or, with a few extra components, a loudspeaker.

- **Voice record and play back ICs**

  These can record/playback a few seconds of audio. Some versions allow for a delay or echo to be added to the playback.

- **Organ IC**

  Will play a small range of notes (typically 15). Some ICs also have built-in tunes and the ability to record short sequences from the keyboard.

- **Function generators**

  Used to create waveforms over a wide range of frequencies. Can be used to generate audio tones.

- **Display driver for bar graph display**

  To drive 10 LEDS as a bar display, use a '3914' IC.

- **Counters**

  Used with a pulse generator a counter will produce a repeating sequence that can be used to drive LEDs.

Security devices

A security device is used to keep something valuable safe. It warns the owner if someone tampers with it. Or it may provide an alarm when it detects a danger – a child who has wandered off or the presence of an intruder. These devices often use proximity sensors.

Situations

Many security products are already on the market so look for gaps in the market and find situations where few, if any products, are available.

Sensing input signals

With a tamper alarm you can keep sensors hidden to stop a thief avoiding them – or make them obvious to put thieves off. If the leads to a sensor are cut, the alarm should be triggered.

You can make your own tamper sensors from a range of materials. Tamper alarms may use a code, input through switches, to arm and disarm them.

A proximity alarm may be triggered when something is either too close or too far away. Infrared or ultrasound signals and sensors may be used.

Producing output signals

The output signal will alert the user to the danger. A tamper alarm may have some of the following additional features:

- an intrusive signal to attract the attention of other people and to deter the thief;
- a delay to allow the user to deactivate the alarm or to provide time to catch the thief.

Remember that there are rules about the duration and volume of noisy alarms.

Electronic processing

Your alarm will need some of the following features:

- **A latch to keep the alarm on once triggered**
  A thyristor will provide simple latching on an analogue signal and also act as a driver for the output device. For more complex digital systems use a digital latch. Don't forget to include a reset.

- **A delay after triggering**
  Use either an RC network or a digital delay.

- **Coding and decoding of arm and disarm**
  Input from a keypad can be coded using digital logic. You could arrange for the alarm to be triggered if the wrong code is entered.

- **High frequency pulse generator**
  For use with ultrasound transmitters. The frequency should be around 40 kHz.
  Use matched receivers and transmitters for ultrasonic or infrared proximity sensors.

- **Programmable ICs**
  For a complex digital circuit, program the alarm control into a single IC.

Control systems

To control something effectively, you need to do more than simply switch outputs on and off; you need to know the effect of this switching. The results of the output need to be fed back into the control system.

Situations

Control systems are important in many manufacturing situations which you can investigate by producing a small-scale version of the factory with the same control features. This is often the way such control systems are designed. Many warehouses use robot fork lift trucks to access stock. You can investigate the control systems required by using small scale models and simulation. Museums are using animated figures to bring their exhibits to life. They all use mechanical and electronic control.

You need to think about what you want to control and what the control has to achieve.

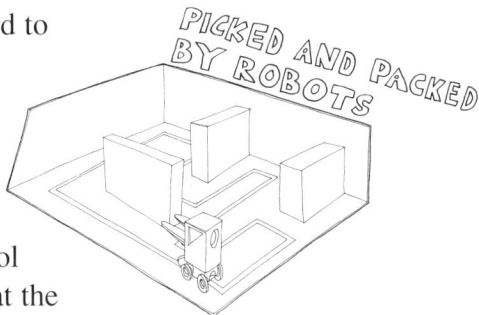

PICKED AND PACKED BY ROBOTS

Sensing input signals

Significant inputs for your control system will be feedback signals, giving information about how effective the control is. Without feedback, control is inaccurate so the inputs will depend on what you are controlling, as shown below.

- In temperature control temperature will be an input.
- If the system is controlling movement, the amount of movement will be an input.

Digital sensors can be used where the output of the control system has to be kept within limits. For more accurate control use analogue sensors.

Producing output signals

The output of a control system will be matched to what you are controlling, for example, a heater for controlling temperature or a motor for movement.

Electronic processing

Your control system will need some of the following features:

- **Comparison of reference and feedback signals**
  For analogue control use an op-amp configured as either a summer or difference amplifier. For digital control with an analogue input use a comparator. To combine digital signals use logic gates.

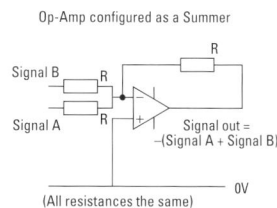

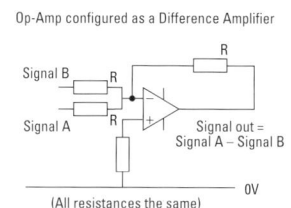

Op-Amp configured as a Summer

Signal B
Signal A
R
R
R
Signal out = −(Signal A + Signal B)
0V
(All resistances the same)

Op-Amp configured as a Difference Amplifier

Signal B
Signal A
R
R
R
Signal out = Signal A − Signal B
0V
(All resistances the same)

- **Analogue control of an output**
  A power amplifier will provide analogue control for a lamp or heater. For motors which run poorly at low voltages either use pulse width modulation (this involves pulsing the output on and off – the more time the signal is off the slower the motor will go) or a stepper or servo motor.

- **Programmable ICs**
  For a complex digital circuit, program the control system into a single IC.

Communicating

A communication system is used to transmit information from one place to another. Receivers are used to 'collect' information that is being transmitted by others. You need to design both the transmitter and receiver.

Situations

In each situation you need to decide what information needs to be transmitted and received, and how this information will be carried – radio waves, light waves, infrared, ultrasound along a wire, etc.

GIRLS WIN RADIO CONTROL CAR RALLY

Sensing input signals

There are two places where you might need sensors:

- as information enters the communication system;
- at the receiving end of the system.

The first of these depends on the kind of information you want to transmit. To transmit sound via radio waves you need a microphone to sense the sound and convert it to electrical signals. For infrared or ultrasound signals you simply need a switch to turn on the transmitter.

The sensor for receiving the communicated information depends on how it is being transmitted. A radio signal is detected using an aerial. For infrared and ultrasound are detected by sensors that are matched to the transmitter.

Producing output signals

There are also two places where you need to produce signals:

- to transmit the information;
- to communicate the information.

The first of these depends on the transmission medium you are using and the second on the kind of information you want to communicate.

Electronic processing

Your communication system will need some of the following features:

- **A radio receiver**
  Both AM and FM radios can be bought on a single IC that needs just a few extra components.

- **Remote encoders and decoders**
  Matched ICs can be used for generating and decoding information for remote transmission. These can be used with both ultrasound and infrared transmitters.

- **Audio amplifier**
  Used for amplifying and audio signal before transmitting it.

- **Power amplifier**
  To amplify an audio signal and drive a speaker.

- **Counter to count events communicated over a distance**
  A wide range of counter ICs is available, for example the '4029' is an IC that counts in tens.

- **Display driver for 7-segment or bar graph display**
  To drive 10 LEDS as a bar display, use a '3914' ic. Each 7-segment display needs a driver to convert a set of four digital signals into signals for the displayed number. There are also ICs that combine counting and driving.

Designing to improve quality

It is unlikely that your electronic product will be so good that it cannot be improved. Here are five areas that you should consider:

- manufacturing in quantity;
- durability;
- maintenance and repair;
- disposal;
- sustainability.

Designing for manufacture

Answering these questions will help you to refine your product so that it is easier to manufacture.

- **Can the number of parts be reduced?**
  Sometimes a group of simple components can be replaced by a single component – often by using an IC. Using fewer parts will save on manufacturing time.

- **Are all the parts the simplest possible shape?**
  This relates particularly to the enclosure; simple shapes are easier and quicker to produce than complex shapes.

- **Can some parts be bought ready made?**
  This saves on manufacturing time and equipment.

- **Can identical parts be produced more efficiently?**
  Always consider using CAD/CAM. If this is inappropriate, develop ways of making several parts simultaneously.

- **Is assembly rapid and foolproof?**
  The fewer the parts and the fixings, the more rapid the assembly. Redesigning parts so that they can only fit together in one way decreases assembly time and prevents mistakes.

- **Can any processes be eliminated or reduced in time?**
  Some parts of the enclosure and PCB may need to be finished to fine tolerances; for other parts this will not matter. Make sure that you are always working to an appropriate degree of accuracy. Remember, the greater the accuracy the longer the time taken.

Designing for durability

What parts are likely to wear out, break or become damaged during typical use? How can the design of these parts be changed to make them last longer?

Here are some possibilities.

- **Change the shape of the part**
  Radius corners and edges are less likely to crack or snag.

- **Change the thickness of the part**
  Thicker parts are stronger.

- **Change the material the part is made from**
  Some materials are stronger or less brittle and will break less easily. Some materials are more resistant to corrosion or rotting.

- **Change the finishes used**
  Give each part a protective finish suitable for the working conditions. Pay particular attention to protecting electrical parts from moisture.

- **Reduce friction between moving parts**
  Ensure that moving parts are well finished and that lubrication is provided where necessary. Include bearings that will reduce wear. Choose materials that run smoothly together.

- **Increase the specification of components**
  Components that are used close to their current or voltage limits will have a shorter life. Components that are getting hot will last longer with a heat sink.

Designing for maintenance and repair

Some parts are likely to wear out, fail, break or become damaged during typical use.

The design of a product can be changed in the following ways.

- **Improve the ease of access**
  Access panels are one way of doing this. They need to be the right size, in the correct position and easy to remove and replace. This is particularly important for batteries and fuses.

- **Improve the ease of removal and replacement**
  The way that parts are held in place is important here. Parts force-fitted together are unhelpful because they are difficult to prise apart. Keyways, grub screws and spring clips are more useful.
  Components that are more likely to fail should be mounted in sockets so that de-soldering is unnecessary.

Designing for disposal

At the end of its useful life a product will usually be thrown away. It will become increasingly important for the design of products to achieve the following.

- **Ease of dismantling**
  This allows useful parts to be reclaimed and re-used. It also allows different types of material to be separated for recycling.

- **Ease of material identification**
  This allows materials to be recycled.

- **Ease of recycling**
  As well as the above, materials should be chosen that can be recycled easily.

Designing for sustainability

Many designers are now beginning to take a much broader view of the impact of their work on the world and its resources. They are looking at their designs with a view to minimising impact on the environment.

This has some interesting consequences. For example, many modem manufacturers are designing modems that can be upgraded as new features are developed – and as new technologies allow data to be transmitted at higher speeds. This means that customers will not need to buy a new modem when they become dissatisfied with the performance of their current model, so the bulk of materials used in the body and PCB will have a much longer life. This, in turn, means that less plastic (from oil) is used and PCB manufacture, with its large amount of waste chemicals, is reduced.

This approach will be particularly applicable to a wide range of other products that use information technology. The idea of upgrading is already familiar in computer software. It is likely to be applied to many other everyday products, such as cars, domestic heating systems, washing machines, cookers, computer systems, music centres, phones and faxes.

For many designers this will mean rethinking their approach to design and adopting a modular approach. For you, starting out as a designer, the opportunity is there for you to begin thinking in this way from the first. Read the IPAS Case Study (page 62) to find out about product life cycle analysis.

A simple buggy

The picture shows an exploded view of a toy buggy made to look like a mouse. It is controlled remotely. The controller is connected to the buggy by ribbon cable. At the bottom of the page are pictures showing the circuit diagram for the toy and how the circuit can be modelled with boards.

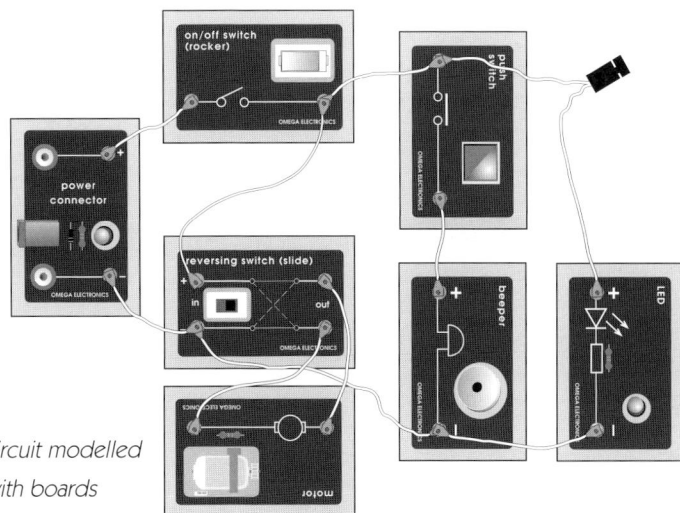

This chapter looks at the things you might need to think about when designing the electrical circuit for such a toy. These are some key points to note.

- The LED eye circuit, a buzzer circuit and a motor circuit are in parallel to one another.

- The 'eyes' come on when the toy is switched on; they act as 'power on' indicators.

- The LEDs have a protective resistor.

- The on switch is a single pole/ single throw toggle switch.

- The eyes can be made to 'blink' with a push-to-break switch.

- The mouse 'squeak' is controlled by a push-to-make switch in parallel with the buzzer.

- The mouse can be made to stop and go forwards or backwards with a double pole/triple throw slide switch.

- The buggy is powered by a battery. This is in the control unit to keep the toy light and fast moving. A child would have to run to keep up with it.

- The circuit diagram shows how the components are connected together; not how they are laid out in the toy and the controller.

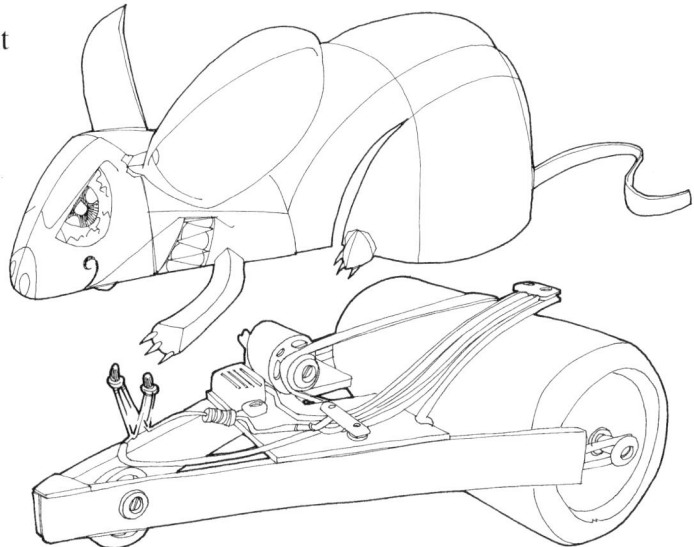

The circuit diagram

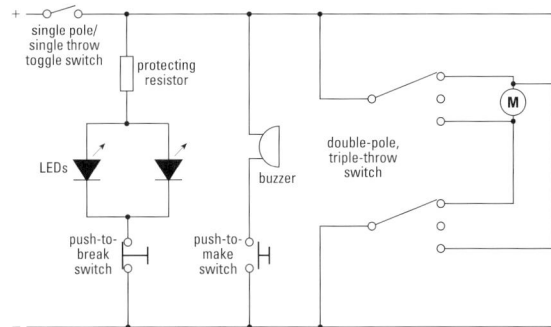

Circuit modelled with boards

Using light sources

There are two reasons for including light sources in a design: first, to provide illumination and, second, as an indicator, perhaps to show that something is switched on. You can use bulbs for illumination but, as they usually get hot, you need to design in ways for the heat to escape. You can wire bulbs into a circuit either way round.

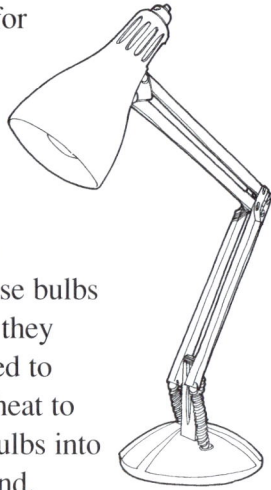

The holes on the shade allow the hot air to escape

Use LEDs (light-emitting diodes) for indication. They don't need much current and stay cool, but give much less light than a bulb. An LED only conducts electricity in one direction, so it has to be placed the correct way round in the circuit. Usually a resistor is put in series with the LED to limit the current flow through it.

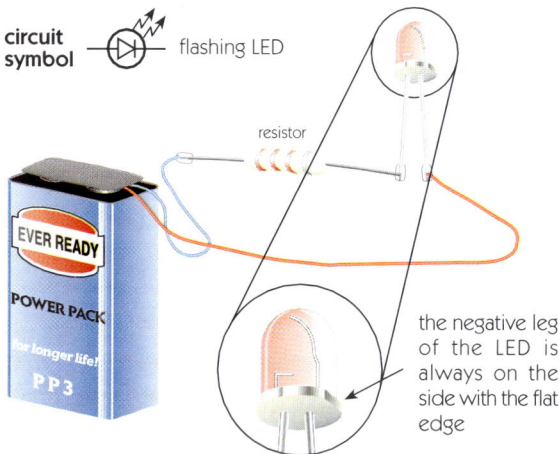

circuit symbol — ordinary LED

circuit symbol — flashing LED

resistor

the negative leg of the LED is always on the side with the flat edge

Wiring a light emitting diode

If a design has more than one light source, these will usually be connected in parallel. Each source will be at full brightness and can be switched independently. Connecting lights in series reduces the current through them and they are dimmed. This is not often useful. A single current-limiting resistor can be used with multiple LEDs if they are switched together. In this way a saving on components can be made, as shown in the circuit for the mouse buggy.

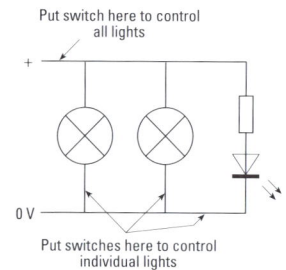

Put switch here to control all lights

Put switches here to control individual lights

Circuit diagram

Components wired in parallel

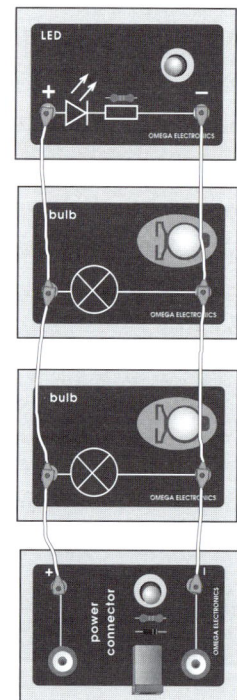

Modelled circuit

Resistors

Resistors limit the flow of current in a circuit. They are also used in pairs, called a potential divider, to control the potential difference (voltage) in a circuit. This is described on page 142. There is more information about different kinds of resistor on page 156, and about calculating with resistance on page 163.

Reading the resistor colour code

Four coloured bands round a resistor show its resistance in ohms. The first two bands give the value, the third is a multiplier, the last, slightly separated from the others, gives the tolerance – or accuracy – of the value. The key for the colour coding is shown below.

On the value bands the colour values are:

Black	0	Green	5
Brown	1	Blue	6
Red	2	Violet	7
Orange	3	Grey	8
Yellow	4	White	9

On the multiplier band the colour code is:

Silver	x 0.01	Brown	x 10	Yellow	x 10 000
Gold	x 0.1	Red	x 100	Green	x 100 000
Black	x 1	Orange	x 1000	Blue	x 1 000 000

On the tolerance band the colours have these values:

Silver	±10%	Red	±2%
Gold	±5%	Brown	±1%

Resistors come in fixed and variable forms

The value of this resistor is 22 x 100 = 2,200Ω or 2.2KΩ accurate to ±5%

Use the information to work out the value of these resistors:

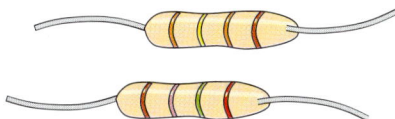

Using switches

Switches are used to turn circuits, or parts of circuits, on or off and to swap between different circuits. There is a variety of ways that switches can be operated and packaged.

Switches come in many shapes and sizes

The electrical operation of a switch is described by the number of poles and throws that it has and whether it latches (stays in the switched position by itself) or not.

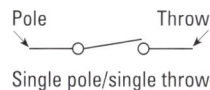

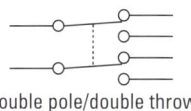

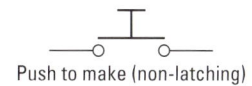

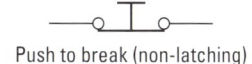

Symbols for five different sorts of switch operation

Combining switches

Connecting switches in series means that they all have to be closed for an electrical connection to be made. If switches are in parallel then closing any of them will produce an electrical connection.

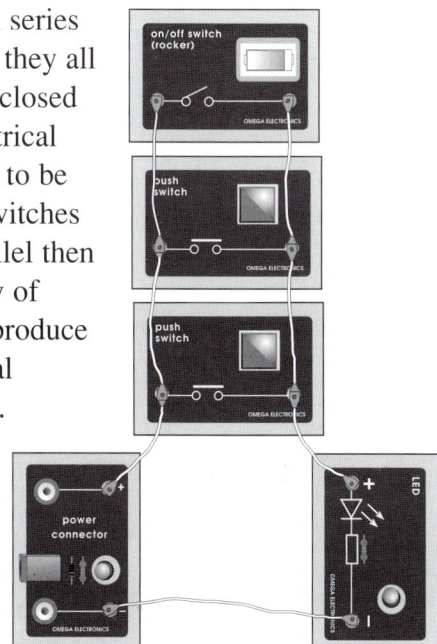

Controlling a motor

Changing round the power connections to a d.c. motor will make it rotate the opposite way. Instead of swapping round the wires to reverse the motor, a reversing circuit is used to swap the power connections. See page 130 for more information on the different types of motor available. Motor speed control is described on page 148.

A double pole/triple throw switch
(so that there is a 'motor off' position)

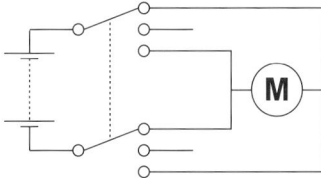

▶ *Can you see how this switch reverses the direction of the current through the motor?*

Providing power

In an electrical circuit there are components driven by electrical energy. This energy can be provided by a battery. A battery is a store of electrical energy. Larger batteries store more energy. Higher voltage batteries deliver the energy more quickly. Sometimes a low voltage supply from the mains can be used.

Different components need energy to be supplied at different rates. For example, a battery powering an LED will last longer than the same sort powering a bulb. Many components work between fixed voltages.

Sam used this information to work out the battery she needed for her bike alarm as shown below.

It's got to use a battery – not mains!

The alarm is tamper proof – so it's a bit of a pain to change the battery

Size is more important than weight – the alarm is compact and any battery that fits will be light enough

The siren will run on any supply between 6V and 12V

When the siren sounds it uses a lot of current – but the rest of the time the battery is only powering a single LED

I'd prefer to use a rechargeable to cut down on waste – it would also be cheaper to run

Rechargeables 'die' very suddenly; perhaps I should include a test button to check whether the battery needs charging

"The pp3 is right for size and voltage. Now I've got to choose between rechargeable and alkaline"

See page 155 for more details on batteries.

Choosing mechanisms

Some electronic products contain moving parts and for this you will need to use mechanisms to carry out the movements. If you design and make a model control system to simulate the operation of an industrial plant or a moving exhibit for a museum, you will also need to use mechanisms. You can use the chart below to choose a mechanism to give the required movement from a rotating input.

For this mechanical function		You can use
	from rotating to linear	wheel and axle, rack and pinion, screw thread, rope and pullet, chain and sprocket
	from rotating to reciprocal	crank, link and slider (4 bar linkage), cam and slide follower
	from rotating to oscillating	crank, link and slider (4 bar linkage), cam and lever follower, peg and slot
	from rotating to intermittent rotating	Geneva wheels (a cam plus a peg and slot)
	increased rotational speed	gear train
	decreased rotational speed	gear train
	reverse direction of rotation	gear train
	change axis of rotation	bevel gear, worm and wheel

You can use a battery plus an electric motor or a wind-up clockwork motor for the rotating input. These means of input are compared in the table below.

Input	Turning force	Turning speed	Power source	Cost
clockwork motor	low/medium	low	human muscle work stored in spring	medium
electric motor	low	high	battery	low

Choosing electric motors

You will probably provide the rotational input to any moving parts by means of an electric motor. You can use the information in the table to choose an electric motor suitable for your design.

	Very light duty no gears	Light duty with built-in nylon gears	Medium duty with built-in steel gears
Size (mm)	20 × 20 × 40	40 × 40 × 80	40 × 40 × 100
Cost	very low	medium	high
Source	Maplins	Radio Spares	Radio Spares
Operating voltage	6-12V	12V	12V
No load speed	8700rpm	70 rpm	130 rpm
Turning power	very low	medium	high

A working example

The simple model shown here is controlled by an electronic system. It is part of an exhibition to show the history of cargo handling. The electronics control the motors in the crane so that it rotates from the ship to the shore and raises and lowers the jib and hook. You can see that gearing mechanisms are used to reduce the rotational speed of the electric motors.

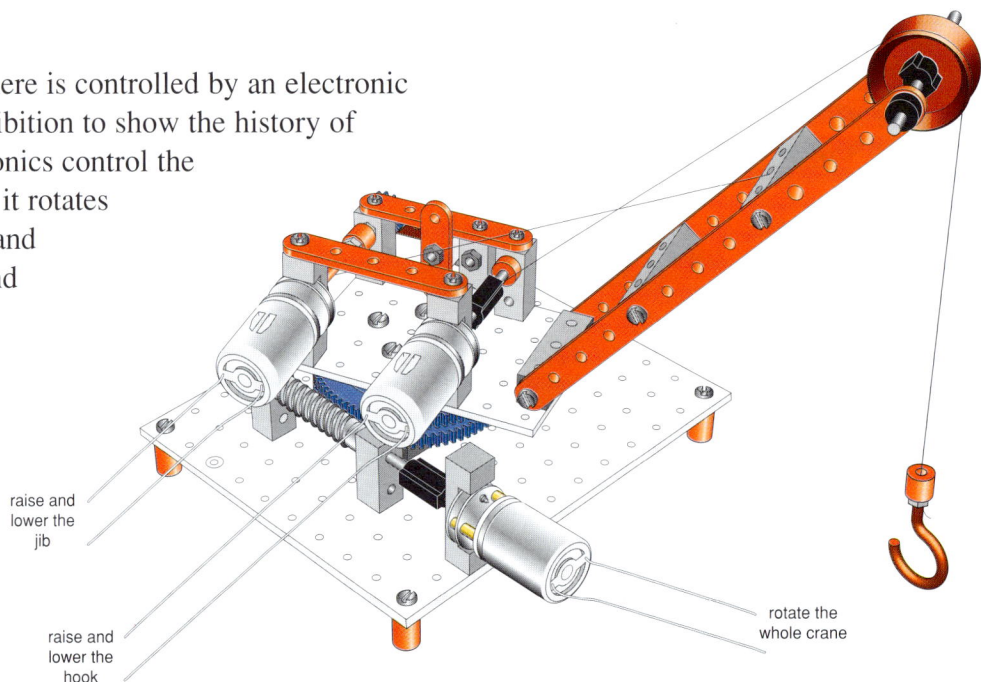

raise and lower the jib

raise and lower the hook

rotate the whole crane

The picture shows a baby incubator being used in a hospital. It warns if the baby's temperature gets too high or too low. These monitors are very sophisticated but at their heart is a straightforward system. The way this system works can be described with a system diagram.

Electronic systems are drawn using a system diagram that has three kinds of subsystem:

- **input subsystems** that use a sensor to change a physical signal into an electronic signal;
- **output subsystems** that use an actuator to change an electronic signal into a physical signal;
- **process subsystems** that change or combine electronic signals.

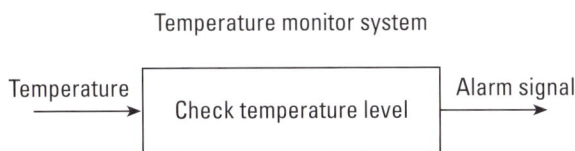

Temperature monitor system

◗ The system diagram describes in a visual way what the monitor does

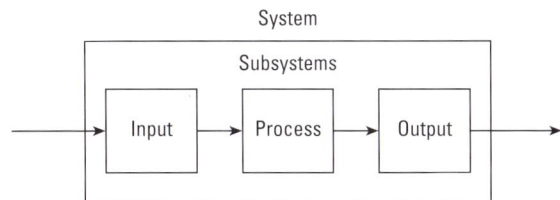

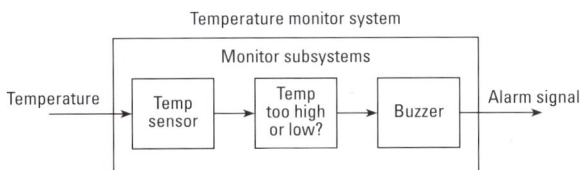

◗ Looking at the subsystems helps to explain how the monitor works

All the signals within an electronic system are electronic signals. The input and output signals are usually other physical quantities.

Understanding system diagrams

System diagrams are drawn using blocks and arrows. Arrows represent a signal moving through the system. Each signal carries information about a physical quantity. Blocks represent parts of the system (subsystems) that change signals. The function of a block is always well defined.

Subsystems can:

- convert a signal from one type to another;
- change the size or value of a signal;
- combine signals.

Some Physical Quantities

Quantity	Measured in
Time	second (s)
Distance	metres (m)
Speed	metres per second (m/s)
Acceleration	metres per second squared (m/s^2)
Force	newtons (N)
Pressure	pascals (Pa)
Light level	lux (lx)
Temperature	degrees Celsius (°C)
Sound level	decibel (dB)
Angle	degrees (°)
Voltage	volts (V)
Current	amps (A)
Energy	joules (J)
Power	watts (W)
Frequency	hertz (Hz)

Using system boards

System boards can be used to design and model electronic circuits.

Each board performs one electronic function and can be represented by one block in a system diagram.

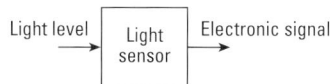

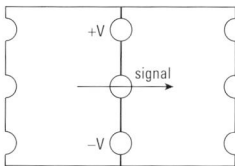

The boards are joined with a link that holds them together, connects the power supply and carries the signal between boards.

Each circuit also needs a power supply. Output boards usually need a driver to boost the signal power as most process boards can't provide much power. These two boards aren't shown in system diagrams.

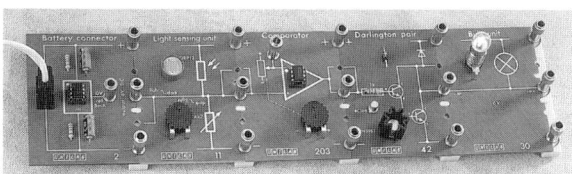

Electronic signals

Electronic signals are voltages. The signal level can vary between a high limit and a low limit. An analogue signal can have any voltage level between high and low. Digital signals can only be at fixed voltage levels; in the system boards digital signals are always either high or low.

Indra caused an analogue change by covering a light sensor in her circuit. Before she covered it the light level and electronic signal were high. As she covered it the light level and signal level dropped. When she uncovered the sensor both the light level and electronic signal rose.

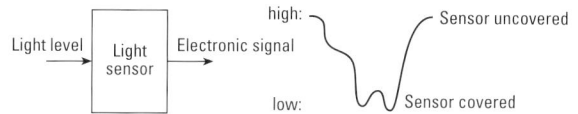

Lucas caused a digital change by pressing a switch in his circuit. Before he pressed the switch the electronic signal was low, when he pressed it the signal went high, when he released it the signal went back to low.

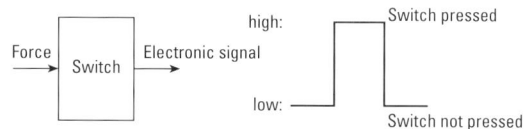

Designing electronic systems

Try asking yourself these questions about the signals in the system.

- What are the input signals?
- What are the output signals?
- What has to happen to the signals between the input and the output of the system?
- Are the signals digital or analogue?

> Well, the input signal has to be a light level. When it gets dark I want the lamp to come on – so the output signal is also a light level.
>
> The process subsystem needs to provide a high signal when it is dark.'

Next choose subsystems that provide the signal changes that you need.

Inputs

You need to choose an input board that can change the input into an electronic signal. So, if the input is light, you will need a light sensor input board.

Some input boards can be used upside down, for example, using a light sensor upside down turns it into a dark sensor.

A light sensor and a dark sensor

Outputs

The range of actuators is not very large so choosing an output board often needs a bit of imagination to see how the available boards can be used to provide the required output signal.

Process

Process subsystems are the heart of an electronic system. The next sections of this chapter describe some of the most common subsystems.

Using transistors

A transistor subsystem is important. You can use it as an electronic switch and as a driver.

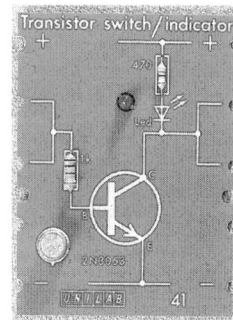

Unless the input signal is 0.6V or above, the transistor stays switched off and the output signal is low

If the input signal is 0.6V or above, the transistor switches on and the output signal is high.

The LED on the board shows the state of the output signal – on for high, off for low.

Usually the input signal is only a small current but the output signal is a much larger current so the transistor board can be used as a driver. It can switch output boards that need a big current even though the signal into the transistor is a small current.

The comparator

A very small change in an analogue signal coming into this process unit gives a large change (between high and low) on the output. This subsystem is used for the following:

- converting an analogue signal into a digital signal (digital process boards only work reliably if their input signal is digital);
- providing a large change in signal level when the input signal only changes slightly (sensor boards such as moisture and temperature sensor boards give small output signals).

◗ *These boards require digital input*

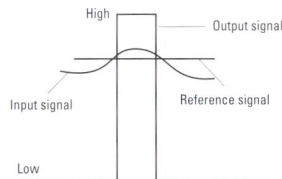

◗ *The comparator board. When the input signal is higher than the reference signal the output signal is high. The output signal is low the rest of the time. The subsystem has a thumb wheel on it. This is used to adjust the level of the reference signal*

Electronic timing

A time delay in an electronic circuit is often useful. You can create a delay with a delay unit or a 555 monostable board.

◗ *The delay unit. This board is most useful when something needs to be turned on or off **after** a period of time. The time delay can be varied between 3 and 10 seconds with the thumb wheel.*

◗ *The monostable board. If you need a wider range of time delays, use a 555 monostable. This allows you to choose a resistor/capacitor pair to give the time delay desired. See page 147 for help on working out time delays. These boards are most useful when something needs to be turned on or off for a short period of time.*

Electronic counting

Electronic systems can be used for counting. Counting systems are always digital and they count digital pulses.

These pulses can come from:

- a sensor (this needs to be either a digital sensor or an analogue sensor used with a comparator to give a digital signal);
- a pulse generator or astable.

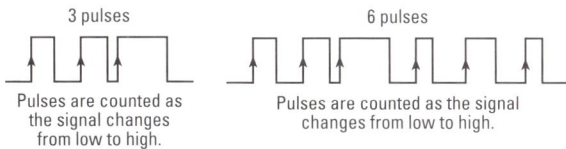

3 pulses

Pulses are counted as the signal changes from low to high.

6 pulses

Pulses are counted as the signal changes from low to high.

▶ *If these pulses were counted, the count would be 3*

▶ *If these pulses were counted, the count would be 6*

Pulse generator board

This board produces regular pulses that are on and off for the same amount of time. If you use a 555 astable board the mark (when the signal is high) and space (when it is low) can be different lengths of time. The proportion of time that the signal is high is called the 'mark-to-space ratio'. Varying the mark-to-space ratio is the best way to control a motor's speed. The lower the ratio (the more time that the signal is low), the slower the motor. The alternative method of reducing the size of the signal to the motor is much less effective.

▶ *System boards for counting have an input signal that is a series of digital pulses. Inputs to reset a display to zero and to choose between counting up and counting down are usually available.*

Binary, decimal and hexadecimal

People usually count in decimal. This is base 10; there are 10 different number symbols (0-9). Numbers larger than 9 are written by adding extra columns (10s, 100s 1000s, etc). Computer systems usually count in binary or base 2 (with just two number symbols: 0 and 1). A digital electronic signal represents a single binary digit (a 'bit') with 'low' being '0' and 'high' being '1'. For numbers higher than 1 additional signals (or 'columns') are used. The extra columns are 2s, 4s, 8s, 16s, 32s, etc. Sometimes four binary signals are grouped together and used to represent a hexadecimal (base 16) number. Hexadecimal numbers larger than 9 are written using the letters A-F. This is summarised in the table below.

Decimal	Binary	Hexadecimal	Decimal	Binary	Hexadecimal
0	0	0	9	1001	9
1	1	1	10	1010	A
2	10	2	11	1011	B
3	11	3	12	1100	C
4	100	4	13	1101	D
5	101	5	14	1110	E
6	110	6	15	1111	F
7	111	7	16	10000	10
8	1000	8	17	10001	11

Digital logic

Digital electronic signals can be processed and combined using logic subsystems. **Inverters** 'turn the signal over'; from high to low or low to high. This is also called a 'NOT' function. **Gates** combine signals according to logical rules. The behaviour of a logic subsystem is described by its truth table. In truth tables '1' represents a high signal and '0' a low signal. Here are some examples.

Input	Output
0	1
1	0

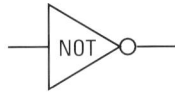

Symbols and truth tables for 2-input
AND, OR, NAND, NOR, XOR

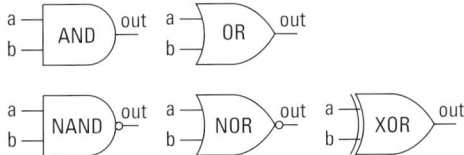

Inputs		AND	NAND	OR	NOR	XOR
a	b					
0	0	0	1	0	1	0
0	1	0	1	1	0	1
1	0	0	1	1	0	1
1	1	1	0	1	0	0

Bistables have an output that can be set to either high or low – they are a simple form of memory. The various types of bistable respond to input signals in different ways.

- A latch will provide a high output once it has been triggered. This will stay high whatever happens to the input – until it is reset.

- A flip-flop copies the signal on its input over to the output only when its clock input goes high.

- A plain bistable changes the state of its output every time its clock input goes high.

These boards often have 'set' and 'clear' inputs which force the output to high or low.

Analogue processing

Operational amplifiers ('op-amps') can combine and change the size of analogue signals. These subsystem boards must be linked to 0V so that their signals vary between −2.5V and +2.5V. An amplifying subsystem increases the size of the input signal. The amount of increase, or 'gain', can be controlled with a thumb wheel.

A non–inverting amplifier board with block diagram

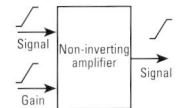

An inverting amplifier increases the signal size in the same way but also inverts the signal. A summing amplifier adds the two signals on its inputs.
A difference amplifier subtracts one of its input signals from the other.

SBRT4, SBRT5

Subsystem Chooser Charts

Analogue signal   Digital signal

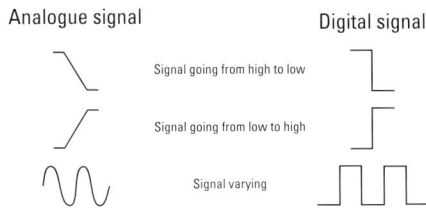

Signal going from high to low

Signal going from low to high

Signal varying

Inputs: for changing a physical signal into an electronic signal

Physical signal   *Subsystem*

Magnetism

System function: closes a reed switch in a magnetic field. Invert to give high when there is no magnetism.

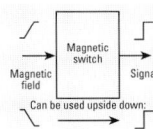

Proximity

System function: closes a reed switch when a magnet is close. Invert for high when magnet is far away.

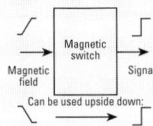

System function: gives a high signal when IR light is reflected back to the switch. Use with remote input board.

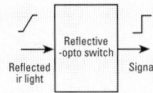

Movement

System function: mercury ball opens/closes switch when it is tilted. Use with remote input board.

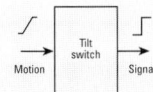

Rotary motion

System function: turning of potentiometer varies electronic signal.

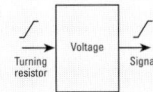

System function: gives a high signal when IR light is transmitted across slot. A disc with alternate opaque and transparent sections will provide a changing signal as it rotates through the slot. Use with remote input board.

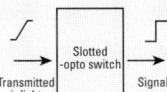

Force

System function: when switch is pressed output signal goes high. Invert to give low when pressed.

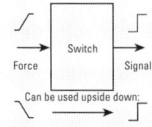

System function: as above but operated by smaller force. Use with remote input board. Invert to give low when pressed.

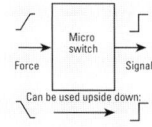

System function: as above but gives 'clean' input for counting. Provides two signals, one the inverse of the other.

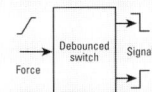

Time

System function: produces a pulse train between about 0.5 to 500 Hz. Note that there is no input signal apart from time. Use 555 astable to control mark:space ratio.

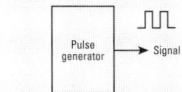

Light or dark

System function: converts light level to electronic signal. Invert for dark sensing.

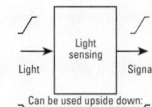

Moisture, liquid level

System function: converts moisture level to electronic signal. Use comparator to control range of operation.

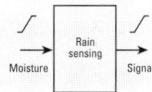

Sound

System function: converts sound level to electronic signal. Follow by sound level adaptor to give analogue signal related to input amplitude.

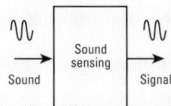

Temperature

System function: converts temperature to electronic signal. Use with comparator to adjust sensitivity.

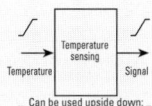

Radio signal

System function: converts radio signal to electronic signal. Radio receiver demodulates the signal.

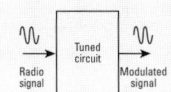

Electronic devices as systems

9

Outputs: for changing an electronic signal into a physical signal

Physical signal   *Subsystem*

Light

System function: converts electronic signal to light signal, requires transistor driver. Use for illumination.

System function: converts electronic signal to digital light signal, LED is on transistor driver. Use for indication.

System function: converts digital signals from counter or analogue-to-digital converter to digital display of number, requires no driver.

Sound

System function: converts electronic signal to on/off (digital) sound signal, requires transistor driver.

System function: converts electronic signal to analogue audio signal, requires power amplifier.

Rotary motion

System function: converts electronic signal to motion, requires Darlington or bi-directional driver. Can be reversed, use pulses to control speed.

Precision rotary motion

System function: converts electronic signal to motion, requires servo driver.

System function: converts electronic signal to motion, requires stepper driver. Motor turns in fixed steps.

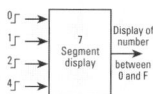

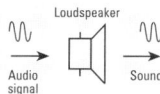

Linear motion

System function: converts electronic signal to motion, output is digital and requires Darlington driver.

Pneumatic control

System function: converts electronic signal to motion, output is digital control of a pneumatic valve. Requires Darlington driver.

Magnetism

System function: converts electronic signal to magnetic field. Output is analogue and requires Darlington driver.

Electrical switch

System function: converts electronic signal to movement of switch, requires transistor driver.

Liquid flow

System function: converts electronic signal to pumping of liquid from one place to another. Can be switched by relay for digital control or high power driver for pulsed analogue control.

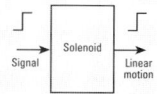

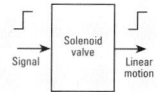

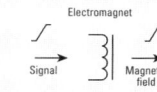

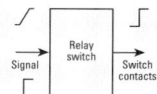

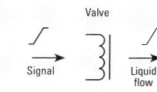

System function: converts electronic signal to control of liquid flow. Can be switched by relay for digital control or high power driver for pulsed analogue control.

138 SBRT1, SBRT2

Drivers: providing power for an output

Features	*Driver*

Low power – up to 0.25A, for analogue or digital signals. Switches on when signal in is higher than 0.7V. Includes LED.

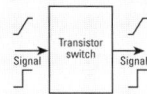

Medium power – up to 0.5A, for analogue or digital signals. Switches on when signal in is higher than about 1V.

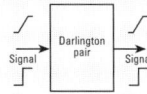

High power – up to 3A for analogue or digital signals.

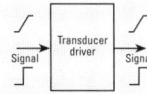

For full analogue control of motor speed and direction – up to 0.75A, ±2.5V max. Requires separate 6V supply.

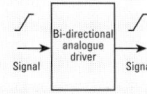

High power full analogue or high speed digital switching. Uses a solid state driver which switches 6A at rates up to 10 kHz. Requires separate 12V supply. For pulsed motor speed control.

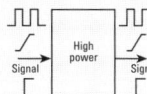

For precise position control of a motor within 180°. Input is analogue signal ±2.5V. Uses matched servo motor.

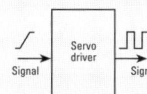

For audio amplification to drive a loudspeaker, ±2.5V max.

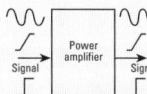

For continuous stepped position control of a motor. Input is digital pulses. Uses matched stepper motor.

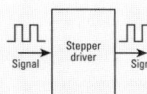

For electrical switching of secondary circuits. switches up to 24V at 1A.

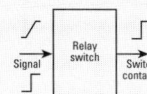

Hybrid processes: with mixed analogue and digital inputs and outputs

Function	*Process*

Convert analogue signal to digital. System function: the output is high if the input signal is higher than the threshold signal. The threshold level can be set.

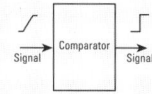

System function: Inverts input An input above 3V gives a low output, otherwise the output is high.

Truth table

IN	OUT
Over 3V	0
Under 2.5V	1

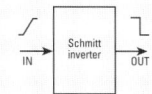

System function: similar to above above but two analogue inputs are combined following the NAND rule.

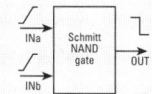

System function: produces a 4 bit digital signal, representing the size of the input, between 0-15 in binary form. Can be linked to 7-segment display to show hexadecimal value of input.

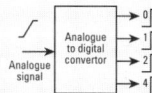

Create analogue delay from digital signal

System function: creates falling or rising analogue signal from digital trigger.

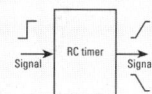

Digital processes: with digital inputs and outputs

Function   *Process*

Combine signals

System function: the combination rules are described by each gate's truth table.

Truth table

INa	INb	OUT
0	0	0
0	1	0
1	0	0
1	1	1

AND gate

Truth table

INa	INb	OUT
0	0	0
0	1	1
0	0	1
1	1	1

OR gate

Truth table

INa	INb	OUT
0	0	1
0	1	1
1	0	1
1	1	0

NAND gate

Truth table

INa	INb	OUT
0	0	1
0	1	0
1	0	0
1	1	0

NOR gate

Truth table

INa	INb	OUT
0	0	0
0	1	1
1	0	1
1	1	0

Exclusive OR gate

Invert signal

System function: signal on output is opposite of input signal. High <-> low.

Truth table

IN	OUT
1	0
0	1

Inverter

Remember a signal

System function: latch output stays high once triggered until it is reset. Triggered by input signal going high.

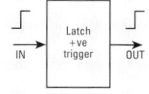

Latch +ve trigger

As above but triggered by input signal going low.

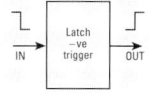

Latch –ve trigger

System function: bistable output inverts (high <-> low) when clock input goes high. Set and reset inputs can force the output to high or low.

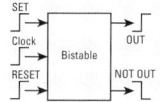

Bistable

System function: as above but flip-flop output set to state of input on clock pulse.

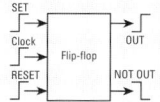

Flip-flop

System function: delay output goes high for short period when input goes high. 555 monostable allows longer delays.

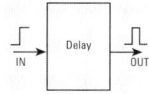

Delay

Count pulses

System function: counts and displays input pulses. Count (0-9) is shown on 7-segment display and available as four signals along with carry out signal. Other inputs allow count up or down and reset.

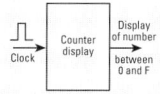

Counter display

System function: as above without display. Displays count on 4 LEDs. Can count in bases 10 and 16. Socket for 7-segment display.

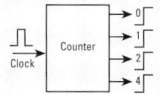

Counter

Control pulses

A gate can be used to stop or allow pulses to pass.

System function: an AND gate will pass pulses at input a if input b is high. Otherwise the output will be low.

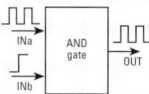

AND gate

System function: an OR gate will pass pulses at input a if input b is low. Otherwise the output will be high.

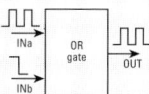

OR gate

SBRT1, SBRT2

Electronic devices as systems

Analogue processes: with analogue inputs and outputs

Function   *Process*

Combine signals

System function: the output is the sum of the signals on its two inputs. Output ranges between ±2.5V.

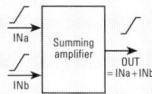

INa
Summing amplifier
INb
OUT = INa + INb

System function: as above but the output is the difference between the signals on its two inputs.

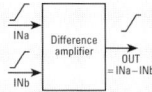

INa
Difference amplifier
INb
OUT = INa − INb

Amplify a signal

System function: the output is the size of the input multiplied by a gain which can be set to between about 1 and 10. Output ranges between ±2.5V.

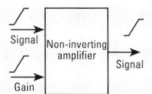

Signal
Non-inverting amplifier
Gain
Signal

As above but it also inverts the signal.

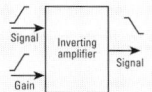

Signal
Inverting amplifier
Gain
Signal

Transmit a light signal

System function: produces an analogue light signal that is a copy of the input signal, for transmission along optic fibre.

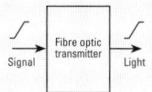

Signal
Fibre optic transmitter
Light

Receive a light signal

System function: receives an analogue signal from an optical fibre and reproduces it as an electronic signal.

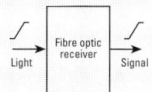

Light
Fibre optic receiver
Signal

Receive a radio signal

System function: demodulates the signal from the tuned circuit to produce an audio signal.

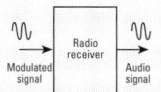

Modulated signal
Radio receiver
Audio signal

Receive an audio signal

System function: converts the audio signal from the sound sensor into analogue signal that is proportional to the average level of the audio signal.

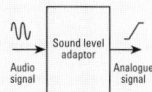

Audio signal
Sound level adaptor
Analogue signal

Create a linear signal

System function: a positive input creates a steadily falling output from 0V. A; negative input creates a steadily rising output from 0V. Both the input and the output range between ±2.5V.

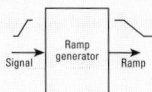

Signal
Ramp generator
Ramp

Investigating transistors

There are many different types of transistor, but you only need to know about two or three for most purposes. If you need something special you can choose it from a catalogue.

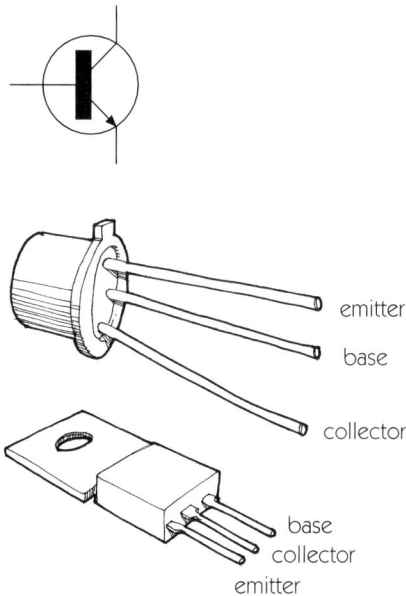

emitter
base
collector

base
collector
emitter

Transistor as a switch

The commonest use for a transistor is to switch an output device on or off depending on the state of an input signal.

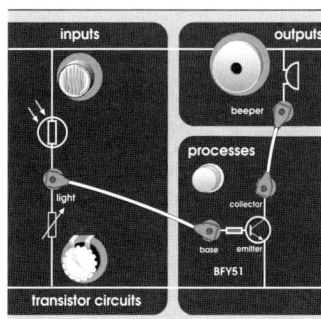

The LDR and variable resistor are in a potential divider. The light level controls the resistance of the LDR. As this changes the voltage at the input to the transistor changes and this switches the transistor; the transistor switches on when the base voltage is above 0.7V.

This kind of circuit will work with many different sensors in the place of the LDR to switch a range of output devices.

There are two important points to note about the transistor in this circuit.

● It has a resistor in series with the base to limit the current.

   A typical resistor value is 10 kΩ. Use Ohm's law to find the right resistor for a particular base current and supply voltage (see page 163).

● It has a maximum current that it can carry – this must be enough to drive the output device on.

This circuit does have some limitations.

● The transistor switches on gradually between about 0.6 and 0.8V. A sensor that only provides a small change in signal, for example a thermistor, will not switch on the output cleanly.

● The transistor may not supply sufficient current to drive the output device. The current flowing into the base of the transistor is amplified at the output. If the potential divider passes only a very small current to the base of the transistor, the resultant current at the output may be too small to drive the output.

Swapping over the sensor and resistor in the potential divider reverses its action – in this case changing the circuit from one which switches on in the light to one which switches on in the dark.

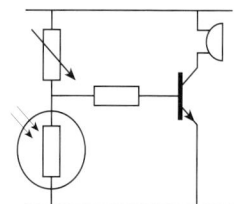

IBRT1, CCRT3

Transistor as a voltage amplifier and inverter

The transistor is a voltage-controlled switch and it acts as a voltage amplifier.

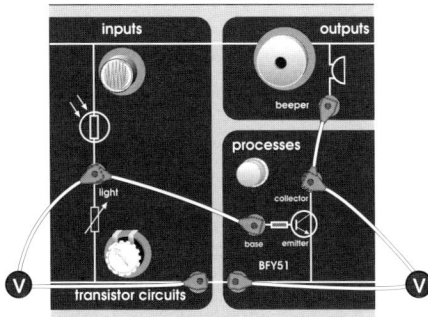

Measuring the base and collector voltages gives results like this.

Base voltage	Collector voltage
0.6V	5V
0.8V	0.1V

So a small change of 0.2V at the base produces a larger change of about 5V at the collector. Note, too, that as the base voltage gets larger, the collector voltage gets smaller. The transistor has inverted the voltage. This can be used to improve the switching from a thermistor.

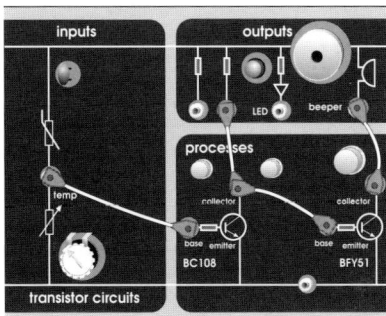

The small voltage change produced by the thermistor is amplified to give clean, and inverted, switching of the buzzer.

Transistor as a current amplifier

A transistor amplifies its base current. This amplification is called its gain.

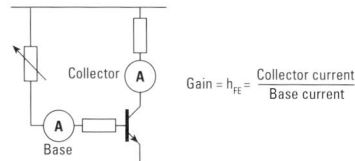

$$\text{Gain} = h_{FE} = \frac{\text{Collector current}}{\text{Base current}}$$

This amplification can be used to improve the switching from a low current sensor such as an LDR.

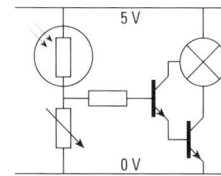

Both transistors amplify the current from the LDR; the total amplification is the gain of the two transistors multiplied. Two transistors used like this are called a Darlington pair and can be bought as a single, three-legged, component.

Field effect transistors (FET)

FETs look the same as normal (bipolar) transistors and are used as voltage amplifiers. The voltage on the gate controls the current between the source and drain and very little current passes through the gate.

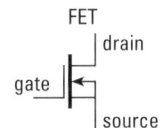

Thyristors

These can be used as a latching transistor. When the signal on the gate rises above 2V the thyristor switches on and stays switched on until the current passing through it is switched off.

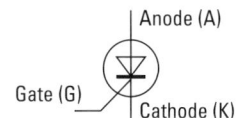

Investigating comparators

A comparator is an op-amp optimised to give clean and rapid switching. Single comparators are 8-pin ICs. ICs with two or four comparators are also available.

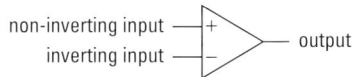

The inputs to the comparator can be either analogue or digital. The output is always digital.

The state of the output is decided by comparing the level of the two input signals. It is:

high when the signal on the non-inverting input is the largest;

low when the signal on the non-inverting input is the smallest.

Almost no current passes into the comparator from the inputs.

Voltage amplification

With a comparator a very small change in input signal level can switch the output between high and low.

This makes it useful for amplifying the signal from components that produce quite small changes in signal level.

Here the comparator is an alternative to using a transistor as a voltage amplifier.

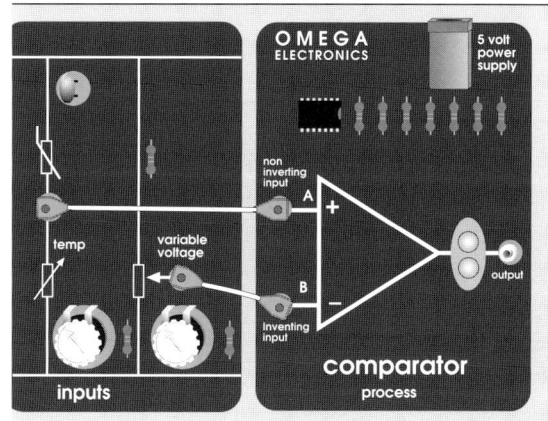

This circuit has two variable resistors. One, in series with the thermistor as a potential divider, adjusts the signal level from the sensor for a particular physical signal. The second, on the inverting input, controls how high the sensor signal has to be to switch on the output; it is a reference signal.

In most situations just one of these variable resistors gives sufficient control of the circuit.

IBRT2

Investigating components

Analogue to digital signal conversion

The voltage amplification circuit can also be used to convert an analogue signal to a digital signal.

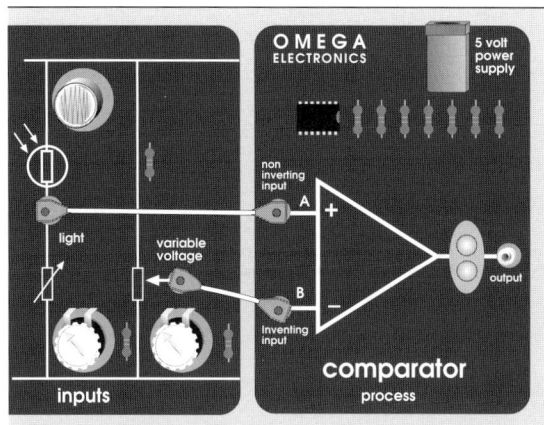

This is necessary when feeding signals into a digital component.

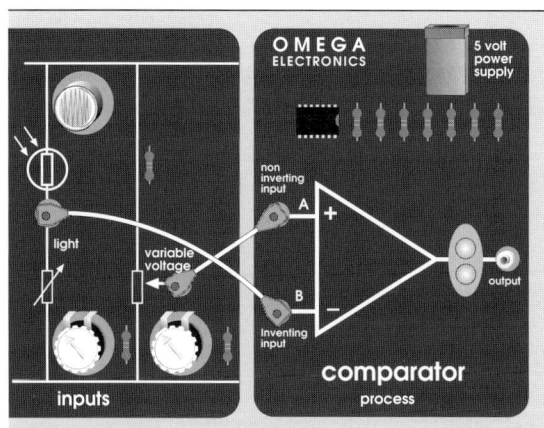

Swapping over the inputs to the comparator, as shown above, converts the circuit from a light to a dark sensor. Both circuits switch over at the same light level.

Comparing signals from two sensors

The circuit shown compares the signals from two temperature sensors. If the left-hand sensor is warmer, the comparator output is high.

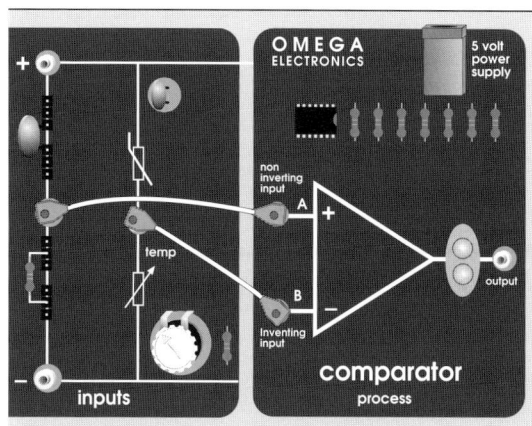

Investigating timing circuits

Resistor capacitor networks

A simple timing circuit can be created by arranging for a capacitor to charge up, or discharge, through a resistor.

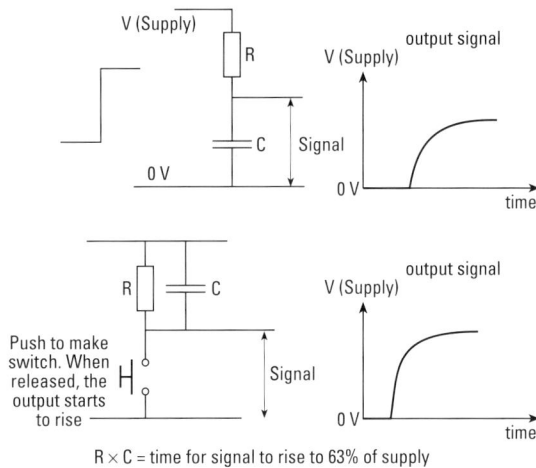

V (Supply)
R
C
Signal
0 V

V (Supply)
output signal
0 V
time

R
C
Push to make switch. When released, the output starts to rise
Signal

V (Supply)
output signal
0 V
time

R × C = time for signal to rise to 63% of supply

To stay off for the delay time

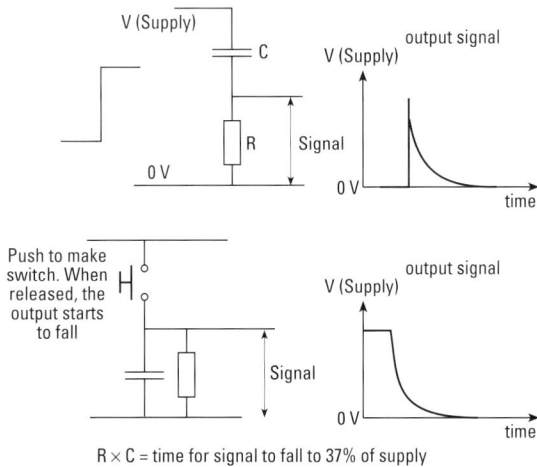

V (Supply)
C
R
Signal
0 V

V (Supply)
output signal
0 V
time

Push to make switch. When released, the output starts to fall
Signal

V (Supply)
output signal
0 V
time

R × C = time for signal to fall to 37% of supply

To stay on for the delay time

For these timing equations to work, R must be in ohms and C in farads, see page 164.

Timer ICs

A number of ICs are available for producing accurate timing circuits. These provide digital outputs, unlike an RC network where the output is analogue.

A common timer is the 555 IC.

This can be made to create a wide range of different outputs by using it with a few extra components.

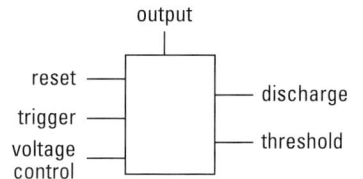

output
reset
trigger
voltage control
discharge
threshold

555 monostable

A monostable circuit gives a high signal for a period of time but always returns the output to low eventually.

When the trigger switch is pressed the output goes high for a short period. Any signal that goes below 1.7V will trigger the pulse. This output can drive low-current devices such as an LED or buzzer. Other devices will need a driver.

The time that the output is high depends on the values of R and C:

$$\text{Time} = 1.1 \times R \times C$$

If R is a variable resistor, this time can be adjusted.

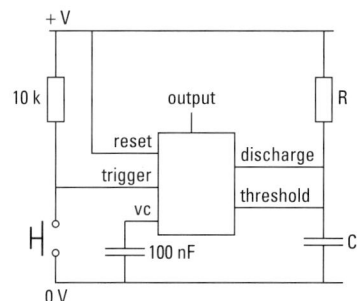

+V
10 k
output
R
reset
trigger
vc
discharge
threshold
100 nF
C
0 V

555 bistable

A bistable circuit can be switched between high or low.

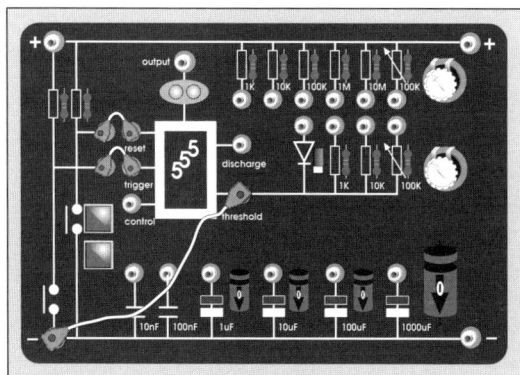

A high trigger signal (from Sw1) sets the output high; a high reset signal (Sw2) makes the output low.

Examples of use include digital latching and debouncing a switch.

555 astable

An astable circuit (or oscillator) constantly switches between high and low states.

Note that the circuit has no input; the output oscillates between high and low by itself.

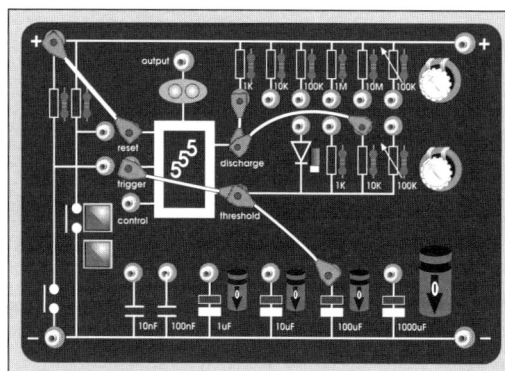

The time that the output is high depends on R1, R2 and C:

$$\text{Time high} = 0.693 \times (R1 + R2) \times C$$

This is called the 'mark' of the pulse.

The time that the output is low depends only on R2 and C:

$$\text{Time low} = 0.693 \times R2 \times C$$

This is the 'space' of the pulse.

As long as the value of R1 is less than a tenth of R2 the mark and the space will be roughly equal; the ratio of mark to space will be 1.

Making R2 variable allows the frequency of the pulse to be varied.

If the frequency is between about 20 Hz and 20 000 Hz, it will be an audio signal. This can be used to drive a piezo transducer to produce a tone.

Controlling the mark:space ratio

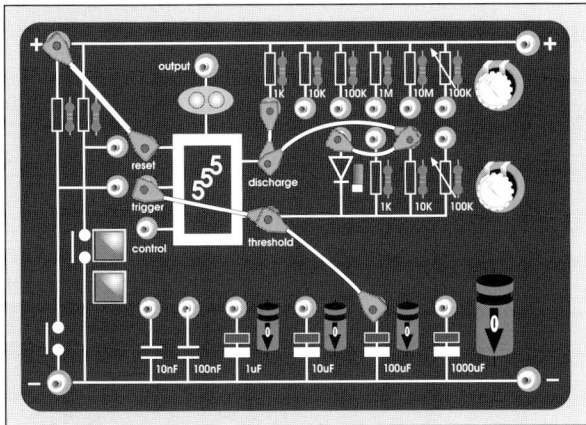

The diode added to this circuit changes the equation for the time high so that R2 no longer affects it:

$$\text{Time high} = 0.693 \times R1 \times C$$

The equation for the time low is not changed.

If R2 is variable, the time low, and thus the mark:space ratio, can be varied. Making R1 variable would allow the time high to be varied.

A circuit like this, operating at a frequency of at least 100 Hz, can be used for adjusting the speed of a motor or the brightness of a lamp. Because it can switch high currents rapidly, a field effect transistor is a good output driver for this circuit.

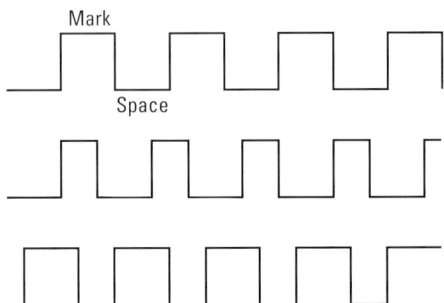

Mark

Space

Mark:space ratio $= 1 : 1 = 1$. Motor at medium speed

Mark:space ratio $= 1 : 2 = \frac{1}{2}$. Motor at low speed

Mark:space ratio $= 2 : 1 = 2$. Motor at high (but not full) speed

Investigating logic circuits

Remember that the signals in logic circuits are always digital.

Combinational logic

Logic gates (page 136) can be combined to make circuits whose output depends on the input signals.

Truth table are used to describe these logic circuits. They can also be used to help with the designing of logic circuits.

NAND logic

Circuits that use lots of different gates can be inefficient to make for two reasons.

Integrated circuits contain multiples of the same gate. Where few of these gates are used a circuit has lots of half-used chips in it.

Buying one kind of IC in bulk is cheaper than buying small amounts of IC's.

Often NAND gates are used in combination to create all the other logic functions.

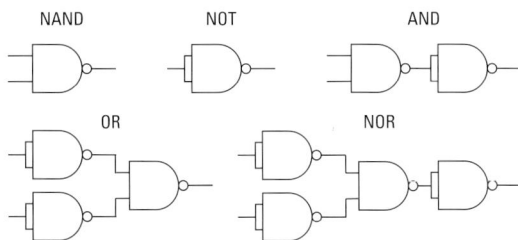

Sequential logic

In sequential logic circuits a change in the output signal is caused by a change in an input signal. The final output depends not only on the input signals but on the previous state of the output signal itself.

A simple sequential circuit is a bistable made from two gates:

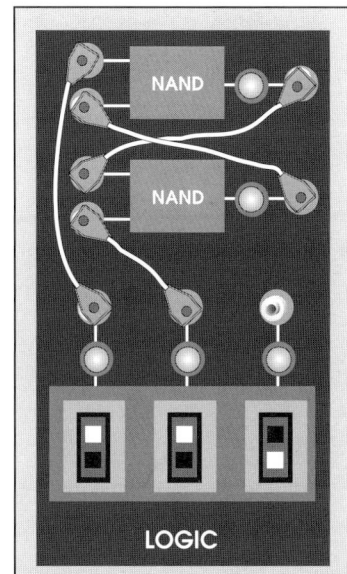

When the 'set' (or S) input goes high the output (Q) goes high. When the 'reset' (R) input goes high the output goes low. Nothing changes when either input goes low again. This simple SR flip-flop acts a memory or latch.

To use a flip-flop in a circuit it is better to use one on an IC rather than build it from chips. For example the D-type flip-flop stores the signal on its data (D) input when the clock (Ck) goes high.

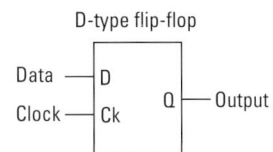

D-type flip-flop

Investigating counting circuits

The signals in counting circuits are digital pulses, see page 147. A series of D-type flip-flops can be used to count pulses.

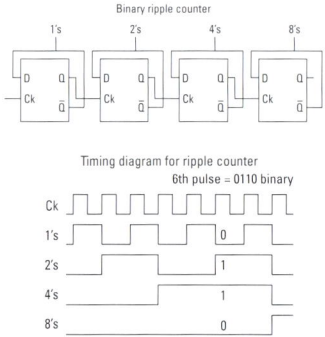

Binary ripple counter

Timing diagram for ripple counter
6th pulse = 0110 binary

Here are some points to note about this circuit.

- The 'Q̄' output is the NOT of the 'Q' output.

- Every time the clock signal goes high the 1's signal changes. Although a regular pulse chain is shown, any rising signal at any time will cause counting.

- The 2's signal changes each time the 1's signal goes low. the 4's signal changes when the 2's signal goes low and the 8's signal changes when the 4's signal goes low.

- The timing diagram shows how the count of the pulses is shown in binary (see page 000).

This counter will count from 0 to 15 (F in hexadecimal) and then restart at 0.

This number can be displayed on a 7-segment display – this uses a decoder IC to turn the binary number into signals to switch the LEDs in the display.

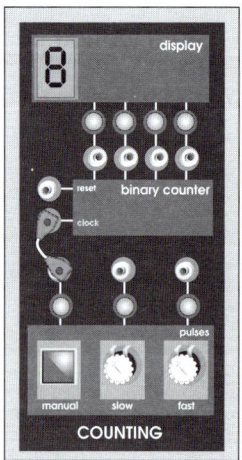

As is often the case in digital electronics, complicated circuits like counters can be bought on a single IC, as can a circuit that both counts and drives a 7-segment display.

These ICs usually have inputs that allow control of various features, including:

- whether the count goes up or down when a clock pulse is detected;

- a 'carry' output to drive a second counter;

- a reset that forces the count to zero.

Resetting a counter

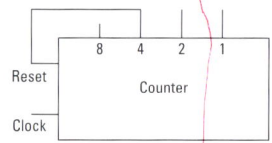

The reset can be used to force the counter automatically to restart counting at zero at some other number than 15. For example, to reset at 4, link the 4's output to the reset.

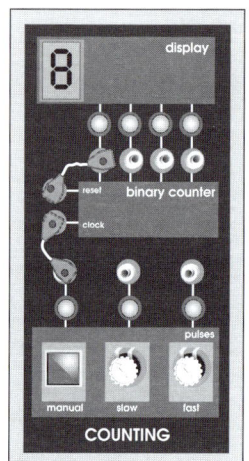

Often resetting at 10 is wanted. This needs a few extra components because the counter doesn't have a 10's output.

Ten is '1010' in binary so the reset needs to happen when the 8's signal is high and the 2's signal is high.

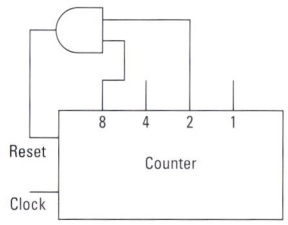

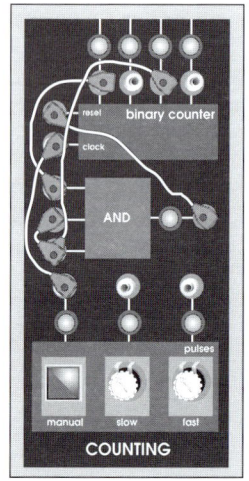

Measuring a voltage

A voltmeter is used to measure the difference in voltage between two places in a circuit. The proper term for a voltage is potential difference. The measurement is in volts (V).

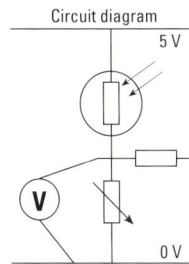

Circuit diagram
5 V
V
0 V

▸ *To measure the voltage between two points in a circuit, hold a voltmeter lead firmly on each of those points.*

Voltage measurement checklist

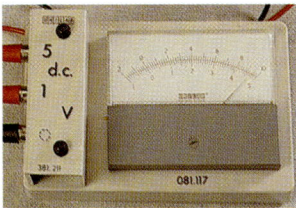

- Use a meter with the correct range. The range is the highest voltage that the meter can read. It must be higher (but not more than about twice as high) than the circuit's power supply voltage.

- Connect the meter across the part of the circuit where the voltage is being measured. Don't change the circuit connections at all.

- Connect the meter the correct way round. The meter will have two sockets and one will be labelled '+' (and often also coloured red). This positive side of the meter always connects to the positive side of the voltage being read.

Measuring current

An ammeter is used to measure the flow of current at a point in a circuit. The measurement is in amps (A).

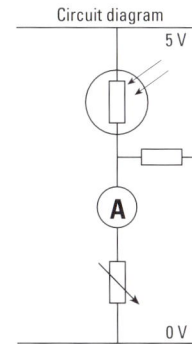

Circuit diagram
5 V
A
0 V

▸ *To measure the current in a circuit, make a break in the circuit and connect the ammeter in series with components that the current is flowing through*

Current measurement checklist

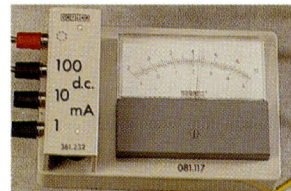

- Use a meter with the correct range. The range is the highest current that the meter can read. If the right range is not known, start with a high range meter. Use the reading on this meter to show what lower range can be used safely.

- Connect the meter into the circuit where the current is being measured.

- Connect the meter the correct way round. (See Voltage measurement checklist.)

Reading analogue scales

Use these hints to help you.

Make sure you know the value of one division on the scale. Some scales have this marked.

Read to the nearest $1/2$ division.

Assume the accuracy of a reading is ±1 unit (unless the meter has its accuracy marked).

If the needle moves to the left, then the positive and negative leads are the wrong way round.

Monitoring signals

Using a multimeter

A multimeter can measure voltage, current and resistance. For each type of measurement there is a choice of ranges. The positive lead uses specific sockets for different measurements.

Multimeter checklist

- Decide on the type of measurement (voltage, resistance etc.). Check whether it is alternating or direct current (ac or dc).
- Place the positive (red) lead in the correct socket for the measurement.
- Choose the highest range available for the measurement. Choose ac or dc if necessary.
- Connect the multimeter into the circuit correctly for the type of measurement – in exactly the same way as a standard meter.

If the reading is at the low end of the scale, adjust the range setting to get a more accurate reading. Use the lowest range that the value being measured will fit on.

Reading digital scales

Use these hints to help you.

- Check what units the scale is showing. This is marked on the meter or range selector.
- A '–' shows that the positive and negative leads are the wrong way round.
- A '1' on the left of the display indicates that the measurement value is too high to display.
- Accuracy may be less than the number of decimal places shown. Check the user notes.

Measuring resistance

An ohmmeter is often an option on a multimeter and is used to measure the resistance of components or other parts of a circuit. The measurement is in ohms (Ω). You can use this option for continuity testing. Continuity testing is checking that there is a continuous current path between two points, so you can test the tracks of a PCB to ensure that there are no breaks (open circuits) along them. If there is continuity i.e. no breaks, the reading is zero ohms. You can also check for short circuits between the tracks. Continuity testing is useful for testing fuses and checking for breaks in wiring.

Component testing

Measuring the internal resistance of a component can be useful. For example:

- checking that a diode has low resistance in one direction only confirms that it works properly;
- for measuring the changing resistance of a sensor in circuit design.

Using an ohmmeter

Use these hints to help you.

- Adjust the needle to 0Ω if necessary.
- Test items must be disconnected from a power supply and other components (the ohmmeter has its own supply).
- An analogue scale is very non-linear – the most accurate readings are for low resistances.

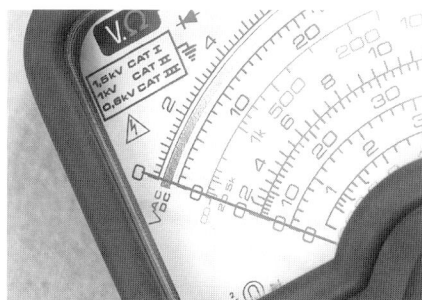

Measuring signals in systems

Electronic signals are voltages. So the signal level between subsystems can be measured as a voltage. One way to do this is to use a signal level display board. This plugs into the connector and displays the signal level on an LED display.

▶ *LEDs indicate whether the signal level is high or low. Some probes show when a signal is pulsing*

Digital signals

The measurement of digital signals only needs to distinguish between high and low. A logic probe is a cheap instrument that does this.

▶ *The state of digital signals between subsystems are shown by a probe that fits the connector*

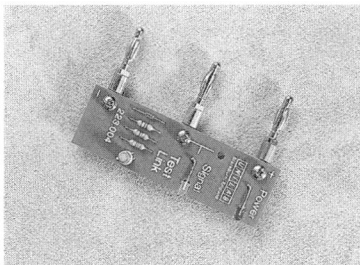

Using an oscilloscope

Signals that are changing rapidly (more than about once per second) cannot be read accurately with a meter or LED display. An oscilloscope is an instrument which can show such rapid changes in voltage. A bright dot moves across the oscilloscope screen at a fixed rate (controlled by the 'timebase'). At the same time the dot is moved up and down the screen by the changing voltage. The result is a 'graph' of the changing voltage drawn on the screen.

Both time and voltage measurements are read by using the divisions marked on the screen. The timebase and range settings show, respectively, how many seconds and how many volts each division is worth.

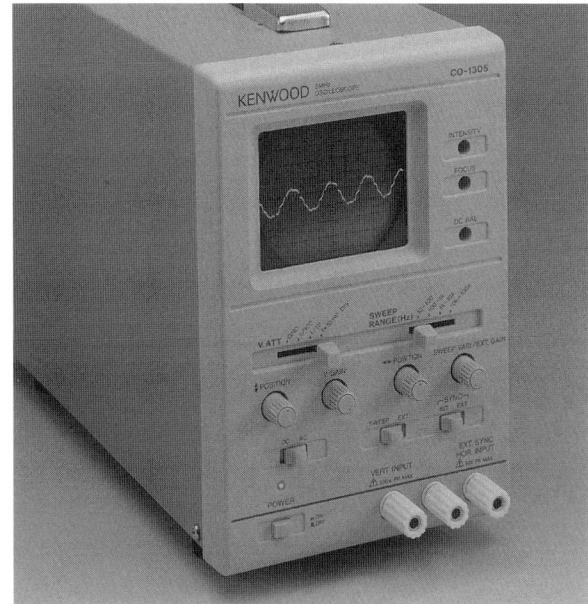

Oscilloscope checklist

Use these hints to help you.

- After switching on wait a few seconds until the dot appears.
- Adjust the dot so that it is in the middle of the screen, focused and just bright enough to be seen.
- Set the range to about 2V/cm; this ensures that any signal being measured is visible.
- Connect the probes to the circuit; the display will simply be inverted if these connections are the wrong way round.
- Adjust the time base so that between two and five cycles of the signal are displayed.
- Adjust the range to the lowest that fits the signal in the display. Using too low a range crops the signal display but causes no damage.

Signal generators

A signal generator produces a regularly varying signal. This can be used to produce a controlled input to a circuit that is being tested.

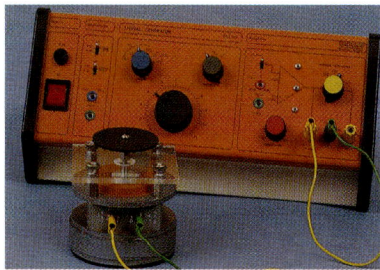

Computer datalogging

A datalogger can store signal readings from a sensor over a period of time. These readings can be displayed and analysed using a computer.

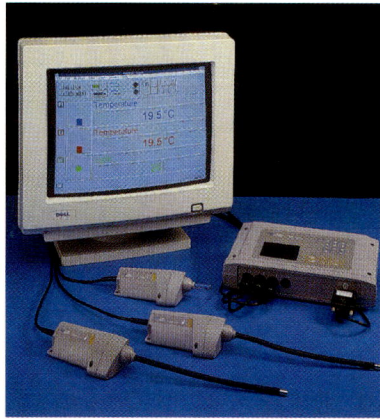

Measurement chooser chart

The two main reasons for needing to make measurements are:

- evaluation – checking that a circuit works properly and to specification;
- fault-finding – to discover why a circuit is not working.

You can use this chooser chart to decide on appropriate methods.

Evaluating a prototype

Size of signal	Test unit, logic probe (for digital signals),voltmeter
Value of signal or other voltage	Voltmeter
Shape of changing signal	Oscilloscope
Current at a point in a circuit	Ammeter – need to insert meter into circuit
Current between system boards	Ammeter – need to insert meter between boards

Evaluating a finished circuit

Size of signal	Logic probe (for digital signals), voltmeter
Value of signal or other voltage	Voltmeter
Shape of changing signal	Oscilloscope
Current at a point in a circuit	Can't be measured directly. Measure voltage and resistance between two points. Use Ohm's law (see page 163).

Fault-finding in a prototype

Size of signal	Test unit, logic probe (for digital signals), voltmeter
Value of signal or other voltage	Voltmeter
Shape of changing signal	Oscilloscope
Current at a point in a circuit	Ammeter – need to insert meter into circuit
Current between system boards	Ammeter – need to insert meter between boards
Continuity	Ohmmeter, continuity tester

Fault-finding in a finished circuit

Size of signal	Logic probe (for digital signals), voltmeter
Value of signal or other voltage	Voltmeter
Shape of changing signal	Oscilloscope
Current at a point in a circuit	Can't be measured directly. Measure voltage and resistance between two points. Use Ohm's law (see page 163).
Continuity	Ohmmeter, continuity tester
Resistance of components	Ohmmeter. Components will need de-soldering

You can use the information in these Chooser Charts to choose the components you need.

Power supplies Chooser Chart

Batteries and cells

Zinc carbon	Low current infrequent use	Low cost
Zinc chloride	Medium current regular use	Medium cost
Alkaline	High current regular use	High cost
Nickel cadmium	Medium and high (not low) current	High outlay, low lifetime cost Rechargeable

Note that where batteries have the same voltage, larger batteries will last longer

Symbols   battery   cell (1.5 V)

The standard sizes of batteries are:

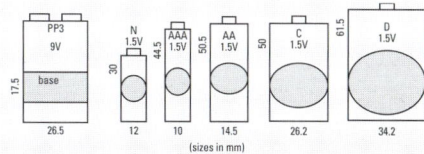

PP3 9V / N 1.5V / AAA 1.5V / AA 1.5V / C 1.5V / D 1.5V

(sizes in mm)

Battery holders

Holders and clips are available for standard size batteries. These enable connection of a battery to a circuit.

Clips and holders make connection simple

Solar cells

Powered by light energy – most effective in sunlight	For low current, low voltage applications	High outlay, zero running cost

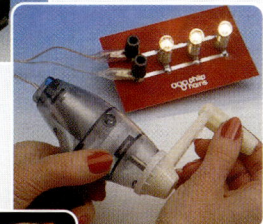

Typical output, for single cell in sunlight; 100mA at 0.45V

Lead acid battery

Rechargeable while in use Typical 5 year life	For high current, constant use 6V, 12V voltage	High outlay, low running cost

Generator

Powered by rotation	For low current, low voltage applications	High outlay, zero running cost

Low voltage supply

Mains powered so not portable	For high current, constant use flexible voltage	High outlay, low running cost

Calculating with power supplies

When power supplies are connected in series the voltage increases and the current is not affected.

When power supplies are connected in parallel the available current increases and the voltage remains the same.

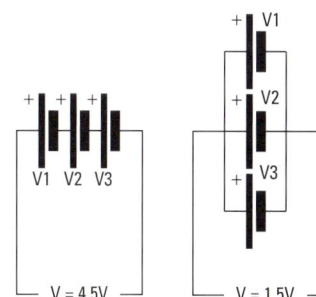

V1 V2 V3   V = 4.5V

V1 V2 V3   V = 1.5V

Resistors Chooser Chart

Fixed resistors

Values from 1W
to 10MΩ
(10 million Ω)

Only fixed values are available. e.g. E12 series has 12 values:
1, 1.2, 1.5, 1.8, 2.2, 2.7, 3.3, 3.9, 4.7,5.6, 6.8, 8.2 with multiples of 10 to
1 MW.

The tolerances on fixed values usually cover the values in between.
If exact values are required, resistors can be combined, see page 163.
If the tolerance on a 10Ω resistor is 10%, then its value could be in the
range 9–11W. The range for an 8.2Ω resistor would be 7.38–9.02Ω and
for a 12Ω resistor 10.8-13.2Ω

See page 127 for resistor colour code

Resistors with a large power rating are physically larger so that they can better absorb the heat generated

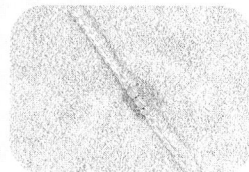

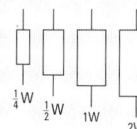

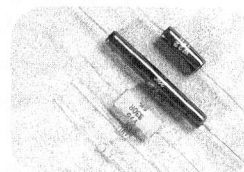

Various types
available

Choice based on balancing the accuracy and power rating required
against the cost. Power ratings range from 0.125W to 25W. If a resistor
generates more power than it is rated at, it will overheat and be
damaged.

$\frac{1}{4}$W $\frac{1}{2}$W 1W 2W

To limit current

Use the Resistor Equation to calculate current through a resistor,
see page 163.

To control voltage

Potential (or voltage) divider. Use two resistors in series to divide a
voltage into two parts, see page 163.

10 V
R1   V1
R1   V2
0 V

Variable resistors

Max values from 100Ω to 2MΩ

Each type typically has 9–12 values covering the range.

potentiometer   preset

Initial circuit adjustment

Presets.
Miniature variables for situations where adjustment will be infrequent

Regular control
of voltage or current

Potentiometers
Options include: maximum power rating, accuracy, inclusion of switch,
rotary or slide control, linear (resistance change constant along range)
or logarithmic (greater sensitivity at low resistance)

Knobs

Potentiometers are supplied with a standard spindle but no knob.
A wide range of different styles is available.

Capacitors Chooser Chart

For: storing charge, smoothing a dc supply, timing (with a resistor), suppressing interference, passing ac and blocking dc, filtering particular frequencies.

Low capacitance (up to 10µF)	Non-electrolytic
	More accurate, higher resistance and larger than electrolytic equivalents
	Connected either way round in circuit
	Higher capacitances are more expensive than electrolytic equivalents
High capacitance (1µF to 0.1F)	Electrolytic
	Must be connected with '+' connection
	always positive (can't be used with ac)
	More compact than equivalent
	non-electrolytic
For tuning. (up to 150 pF)	Variable non-electrolytic
	(Variable electrolytics not available)

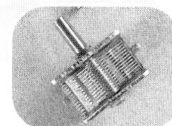

Diodes Chooser Chart

Diodes conduct in only one direction – the 'forward' direction. When a diode is conducting there is a voltage drop of about 0.7V across it.

For: steering signals, rectifying ac, protecting other components.	A diode is specified by its maximum forward current and maximum reverse voltage. Higher ratings are more expensive, but if in doubt use a higher rating.

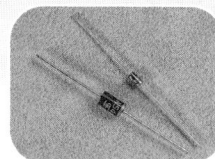

anode → cathode

Connectors Chooser Chart

Temporary e.g. external sensor or output	Jack pug/socket Available sizes; 2.5, 3.5 and 6.35mm 2 (mono) or 3 (stereo) wire PCB mounting sockets available
DC power 12V max	Power plug/socket including internal switch to disconnect a battery when plug is inserted Available sizes; 1.3, 2.1, 2.5, and 3.1mm PCB mounting sockets available
Semi-permanent Multiple line	Screw terminal blocks D series sockets and plugs Shape ensures connection is correct way round. Available are; 9, 15, 19, 23, 25, 37 and 50 way versions.

For connecting to batteries see Battery Chooser Chart (page 155).

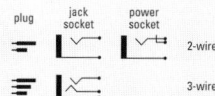

Component information

Switches Chooser Chart

Electrical characteristics

Only switches while operated	Non-latching Push-to-make, push to break	e.g. to hold an alarm off or on a keypad	a push-to-make switch
To switch between on and off	Single pole single throw	e.g. an on/ off switch	a push-to-break switch
To switch between two circuits	Single pole double throw	e.g. stair lighting circuits	a single-pole, single-throw switch
To switch between multiple circuits	Single pole multiple throw	e.g. selecting mode of operation	a single-pole, double-throw change-over switch
To switch two signals	Double pole double throw totally isolating	e.g. reversing a motor or a power supply	a double-pole, double-throw change-over switch
To switch multiple signals between multiple circuits	e.g. Triple pole double throw to reverse and switch off a motor		a double-pole, triple-throw switch

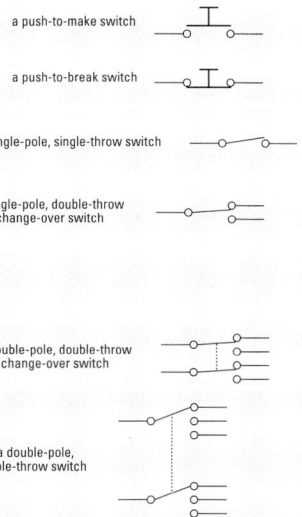

Physical characteristics

Switches are packaged in a wide variety of ways.

This chart describes the most common but omits colour options and some rarer switch types.

Push	Usual form for non-latching. Also as foot switches
Membrane	Simple non-latching switch, often used for switch arrays
Toggle	Wide range of switch types
Slide	Wide range of switch types
Rocker	DPDT is usually most complex type
Rotary	Often single pole multiple throw. May be lockable (with key)
Dip	Array of miniature switches for infrequent use
Micro	For automatic systems – only a small force causes switching. Available as a plain push switch and with a lever or roller.
Sensors	Switches that are operated by environmental changes include reed, vibration and tilt. See page 159 for more information
Illuminated	Incorporating a light source to indicate the switch position
Knobs	Some switches are supplied with a standard spindle that a range of knobs will fit. See page 156 for knobs.

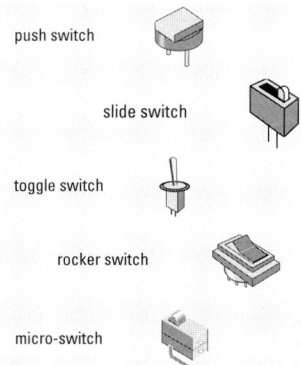

push switch

slide switch

toggle switch

rocker switch

micro-switch

Sensors Chooser Chart

Detecting (sensors may be digital or analogue and need not be linear)

Magnetism	Reed switch	
	Closed when close to a magnet.	
Proximity	Reed switch (see above)	
(without touching)	Reflective opto switch.	reflective opto switch
	Infrared light reflected into sensor indicates object is close	
	LDR; light level drops when shaded	
Visible	Light dependant resistor (LDR)	photo transistor light-dependent resistor
Light	Resistance drops as light level rises	
	For fast response use a photo transistor which also provides a higher current and requires fewer components	
Infrared	IR detector. A photo transistor, usually matched to an IR emitter	
Heat	Thermistor, resistance drops as temperature increases	thermistor bimetallic strip
	Bimetallic strip, bends as temperature rises, used as a switch	
Moisture or	Moisture sensor; on when wet	float pivot
liquid level	Float operates microswitch at a set level	liquid micro switch
		moisture sensor
Turning	Tilt switch	
	Cam hitting microswitch	
	Slotted opto switch, use a rotating disc with	
	alternating clear and opaque sections in the slot	
Linear motion	Slotted opto switch, use a strip with holes or notches in the slot	
Force	Microswitch (see page 158)	
	Membrane switch (see page 158)	
Time	Count pulses from an astable (page 147)	
	Use turning motion of clock mechanism	
Sound	Microphone	

Measuring (requires analogue sensors, preferably with linear outputs)

Visible Light, Infrared	Photodiode with op-amp (see also page 162)	
Temperature	LM35, a temperature sensor IC that gives output of 10 mV per °C	5 V
	Either 0-100°C or –40-110°C	LM35 Signal
		0 V
Humidity	Humidity sensor (non-linear)	potentiometer
Liquid level	Float operating potentiometer	
Motion, rotary	Potentiometer (see page 156) Slotted opto switch, (see above)	float
Motion, linear	Slide potentiometer (see page 156)	liquid pivot
Sound	Microphone, needs circuit to convert audio signal to analogue signal proportional to amplitude	
Force	Strain gauge, resistance changes as it is stretched	

Component information

Output transducers Chooser Chart

To produce:

Illumination — Bulb. Usually requires correct holder (which makes bulb changing easier). Brighter bulbs require higher current

Indication — Light emitting diode (LED). Available as red, yellow or green in a range of brightnesses

Flashing LEDs include protective resistor (also available for steady LED)

LED arrays typically contain 10 LEDs

Distance signalling — IR LED. Usually matched to an IR detector

Rotary motion — Dc motor. Usually need to drive load through gear train to reduce speed and increase torque.

Stepper motor. Turns in precise steps (7.5°) controlled by digital signals.

Servo motor. Allows precise positional control over about 180° using an analogue signal. Low speed, high torque.

Linear motion — Motor via appropriate mechanisms

Solenoid. Produces large force over small distance, rapidly, in one direction. Available as pull or push

Sound — Buzzer. Fixed amplitude and frequency

Piezo sounder. Requires 500 Hz signal. Amplitude can be controlled

Loudspeaker: requires audio signal, full control of amplitude and frequency

Bell. Loud, fixed frequency and amplitude

piezo sounder   buzzer

loudspeaker   bell

Electrical switching — Relay. Wide range available, must be matched to current and voltage being switched. See page 158 for electrical characteristics of switches.

SPDT

Fluid control — Pump. Moves liquid or gas from one place to another. Control speed in same way as dc motor

Solenoid. Armature pressing on flexible tubing can restrict flow through the tube.

Pneumatic solenoid valve allows electrical control of a pneumatic circuit

Magnetism — Electromagnet. Produces a magnetic holding force while current is applied

Display of numbers or letters — Moving coil meter. Shows strength of signal by movement of needle.

LED display. Available as 7-segment or dot matrix. Range of sizes.

Liquid crystal display (LCD). Uses less power than LEDs but not visible in dark

CCRT1

Processes Chooser Chart

Transistors

For driving an output, or for amplifying a signal. There are a very large number of different types of transistor. Things to think about when choosing a transistor:

Type	Bipolar (npn) or Field Effect (FET)
npn	amplifies current,
FET	amplifies voltage.

These are interchangeable in most circuits. But the FET passes a very low input current and this makes it useful when an input signal cannot provide a high current, for example a touch switch.

What gain (for npn)?	How much the current is amplified
	collector current = base current x Gain

The collector current drives the output device. Make sure that the base current will be amplified enough to give the current the output device needs.

Maximum current	How much current can pass through the collector.

Make sure that this maximum current is more than the current needed by the device being driven.

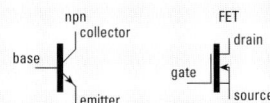

All transistors have three legs. Use a data sheet or catalogue to help you identify which leg is which

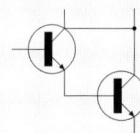

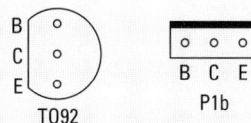

Darlington pair

A matched pair of transistors

npn transistors usually have either a high gain with a low maximum current or a high current with a low gain. A Darlington pair combines a high gain transistor with a high current transistor. This gives both high gain and high current. Note that Darlington pairs are packaged with three legs, like a single transistor.

Useful information about transistors and Darlington pairs

Type	Identifying code	BC168	ZTX450	TIP122
Casing	What shape is it	T092	T092	P1b
Material	What it's made from	npn silicon	npn silicon	npn silicon
Max voltage	Maximum circuit voltage	30V	60V	100V
Max base current	Current flowing into base	0.2mA	4m A	1mA
Max collector	Current flowing into collector	100mA	1A	5A
Max power	Maximum power it can dissipate	300mW	1W	65W
Gain typical	At a particular collector current	650@2mA	300@150	5000@2A
Application	What the transistor is for	General purpose	Fast power switching	Darlington pair

Thyristors

Use for simple latching

Maximum current	How much current can pass from the anode to the cathode

Make sure that this maximum current is more than the current needed by the device being driven.

Thyristors have three legs so they look similar to transistors. They are also called 'silicon controlled rectifiers' (SCRs)

Processes Chooser Chart

For processing analogue signals

Operational amplifiers (op-amps)

Supply range	The voltage range required
	The maximum of this range must be higher than the supply used in the circuit
	Many op-amps need a dual rail supply (for example two 9V batteries in series)
	Using one requiring a single rail supply may lead to a simpler circuit
Output voltage	The signal level at the co-amp output
	This about 80 per cent of the input voltage
Output current	The current that the output can supply
	This needs to be high enough to drive the next stage of the circuit

If you are using more than one op-amp in a circuit, use a dual or quad package to minimise the number of components and ensure good matching

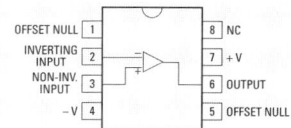

Analogue to digital conversion

For turing an analogue signal into one or more digital signals

Comparator	For a one bit digital signal
	Comparators are an op-amp. Use a dedicated component as this provides fast and accurate switching from high to low on a single rail supply.
Multi bit	To gave a binary value for the analogue signal A to D converters with 6 to 16 digital outputs are available in both TTL and CMOS versions (see below).

If you are using more than one comparator in a circuit, use a dual or quad package to minimise the number of components and ensure good matching

Digital to analogue conversion

Multi bit	To give an analogue signal from a binary value D to A converters with between 6 and 16 digital inputs are available in both TTL and CMOS versions (see below).

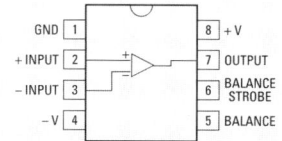

Because of the large number of digital lines used when converting between analogue and digital, the integrated circuits used have a lot of legs!

For processing digital signals

Digital integrated circuits

TypeTTL or CMOS
    TTL (ICs prefixed by '74')
    CMOS (ICs prefixed by '40')

Each has a similar range of functions available. The main advantage of CMOs is that the ICs do not need a stabilised power supply so they can be run straight from a battery.

Comparing TTL and CMOS		
	TTL	CMOS
Supply	5±0.25V	3–15V
High	2.4–5V	70–100% of supply
Low	0–0.7V	0–30% of supply
o/p current		
– source	1.6mA	4mA (at 5V)
– sink	16mA	4mA (at 5V)

CCRT1, CCRT3

Equations Chooser Chart

Ohm's law

$$V = I \times R \quad I = \frac{V}{R} \quad R = \frac{V}{I}$$

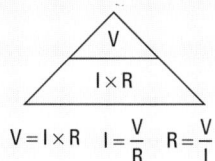

Ohm's law links a component's resistance to the current through it and the voltage across it. If two are known, the third can be worked out.

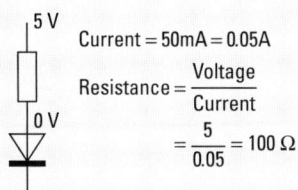

5 V

0 V

$$\text{Current} = 50\text{mA} = 0.05\text{A}$$

$$\text{Resistance} = \frac{\text{Voltage}}{\text{Current}}$$

$$= \frac{5}{0.05} = 100 \ \Omega$$

Combining resistors

If the resistors are in series, simply add the resistances together. If they are in parallel then the inverses have to be added – and don't forget to invert the final answer!

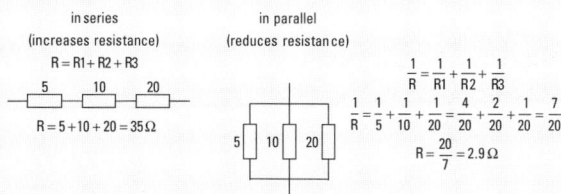

in series
(increases resistance)

$$R = R1 + R2 + R3$$

5   10   20

$$R = 5 + 10 + 20 = 35\Omega$$

in parallel
(reduces resistance)

$$\frac{1}{R} = \frac{1}{R1} + \frac{1}{R2} + \frac{1}{R3}$$

5   10   20

$$\frac{1}{R} = \frac{1}{5} + \frac{1}{10} + \frac{1}{20} = \frac{4}{20} + \frac{2}{20} + \frac{1}{20} = \frac{7}{20}$$

$$R = \frac{20}{7} = 2.9\Omega$$

Potential divider

Two resistors in series divide a voltage into two parts. As the resistance of R1 increases, the voltage across it gets bigger. If one of these resistors is a sensor, the sensor can control the signal.

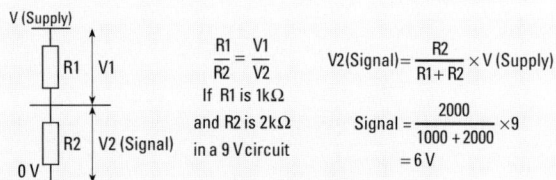

V (Supply)

R1   V1

R2   V2 (Signal)

0 V

$$\frac{R1}{R2} = \frac{V1}{V2}$$

If R1 is 1kΩ
and R2 is 2kΩ
in a 9 V circuit

$$V2(\text{Signal}) = \frac{R2}{R1 + R2} \times V(\text{Supply})$$

$$\text{Signal} = \frac{2000}{1000 + 2000} \times 9$$

$$= 6 \text{ V}$$

Power equation

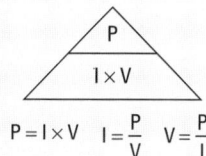

$$P = I \times V \quad I = \frac{P}{V} \quad V = \frac{P}{I}$$

This links the power generated by a component to the voltage across it and the current through it. If either two are known, the third can be worked out

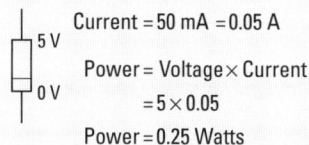

5 V

0 V

$$\text{Current} = 50 \text{ mA} = 0.05 \text{ A}$$

$$\text{Power} = \text{Voltage} \times \text{Current}$$

$$= 5 \times 0.05$$

$$\text{Power} = 0.25 \text{ Watts}$$

I need to know the power produced in this diode so I can pick the right type

I need at least a 0.25W diode

I need to limit the current through this LED circuit to 50mA

The circuit voltage is 5V

I will use ohms law

Right, I need a 100W resistor

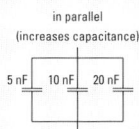

Component information

Combining capacitors

If the capacitors are in parallel, simply add the capacitances together. If they are in series then the inverses have to be added – and don't forget to invert the final answer!

in parallel
(increases capacitance)

5 nF | 10 nF | 20 nF

$C = C1 + C2 + C3$
$C = 5 + 10 + 20 = 35nF$

in series
(reduces capacitance)

5 nF | 10 nF | 20 nF

$\dfrac{1}{C} = \dfrac{1}{C1} + \dfrac{1}{C2} + \dfrac{1}{C3}$
$= \dfrac{1}{5} + \dfrac{1}{10} + \dfrac{1}{20}$
$= \dfrac{4}{20} + \dfrac{2}{20} + \dfrac{1}{20} = \dfrac{7}{20}$
$C = \dfrac{20}{7} = 2.9nF$

Time delays with resistors and capacitors

$Time = C \times R \text{ (seconds)}$

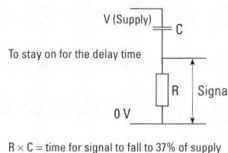

To stay on for the delay time

$R \times C$ = time for signal to fall to 37% of supply

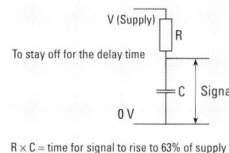

To stay off for the delay time

$R \times C$ = time for signal to rise to 63% of supply

$Time = R \times C$
$So\ C = \dfrac{Time}{R}$
$= \dfrac{5}{15000}$
$= 0.0005\ F$
$= 500\ \mu F$

Transistor gain

$$h_{FE} = Gain = \frac{\text{Collector current}}{\text{Base current}}$$
$$\text{Collector current} = Gain \times Base\ current$$

This is how much current amplification the transistor provides. The symbol for Gain is h_{FE}.

Base current I_b
= 5 mA = 0.005

Transistor gain = 150
I_C = Gain × Base current
= 150 × 0.005
= 0.75 Amps

Emitter current = I_e = Collector current + Base current
= $I_c + I_b$
= 0.75 + 0.005
= 0.755 Amps

Op amp gain

$$Gain = \frac{\text{Voltage out}}{\text{Voltage in}}$$
$$\text{Voltage out} = Gain \times Voltage\ in$$

This is how much signal amplification the op-amp provides. This depends on the op-amp configuration. The configuration shown is an inverting amplifier. Note the minus sign which shows that the signal is inverted. The gain can be increased by making RF larger.

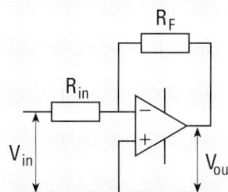

$$Gain = \frac{V_{out}}{V_{in}} = \frac{-R_F}{R_{in}}$$

Radio information

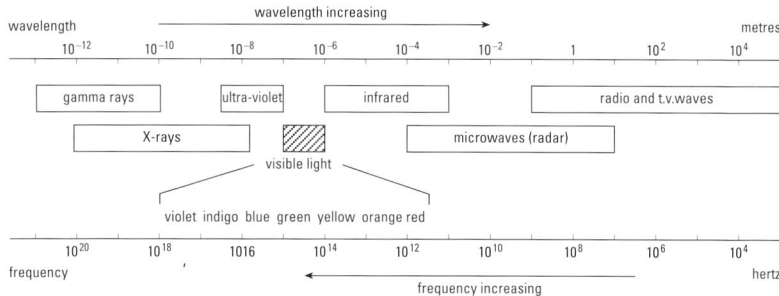

The electromagnetic spectrum

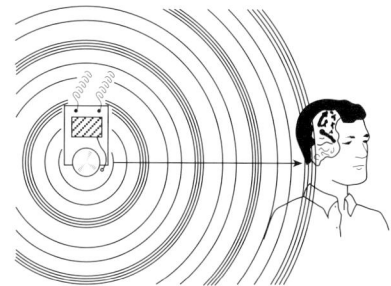

Hearing sounds

Radio waves

All forms of radiation can be described in terms of their wavelength. The different forms of radiation make up the electromagnetic spectrum. This is shown in the panel above. Radio waves are part of the electromagnetic spectrum. You can see that they have long wavelengths. At the opposite end of the spectrum is radiation with very short wavelengths – gamma rays. Visible light – electromagnetic radiation that we can see – occupies only a very narrow band of the electromagnetic spectrum. Electromagnetic radiation can travel through empty space.

Sound waves

Sound waves are not electromagnetic radiation. They cannot travel through empty space. They need a physical medium – solid, liquid or gas. Sound waves are produced by vibrations which cause the medium through which they travel to vibrate. When we hear sounds it is because these vibrations are causing the ear drum in our ears to vibrate. These vibrations are interpreted by the brain as sounds.

Transmission and reception

Radio waves can be used to transmit sound signals across wide distances. First the sound wave has to be converted to an electrical audio signal by a microphone. Then this signal has to be put onto a radio signal which can carry the sound across space. This is called modulation. This radio audio signal is then amplified and sent out across space although we cannot hear the sound. This process is called transmission. In order to hear the sound the modulated radio wave has to be received, amplified and the electrical signal converted back into audio. This is called demodulation. The audio signal is then amplified and converted to the sound that we hear by means of a loud speaker. This process is called reception. The transmission and reception processes are summarised in the block diagram below.

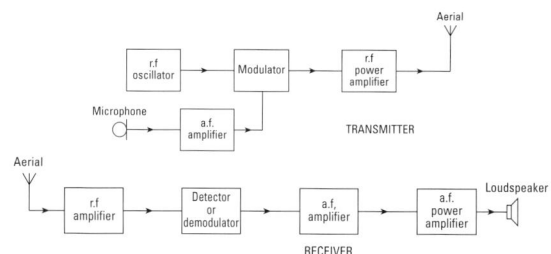

Transmission and reception

(a.f = audio frequency, r.f = radio frequency

Modulation

There are two ways to modulate radio waves – amplitude modulation (AM) and frequency modulation (FM). In amplitude modulation the audio signal is combined with the radio signal so that the amplitude of the radio wave changes with the frequency of audio signal from the microphone. In frequency modulation the audio signal is combined with the radio signal so that the frequency of the radio wave changes with the frequency of audio signal from the microphone. These processes are summarise in the diagram below.

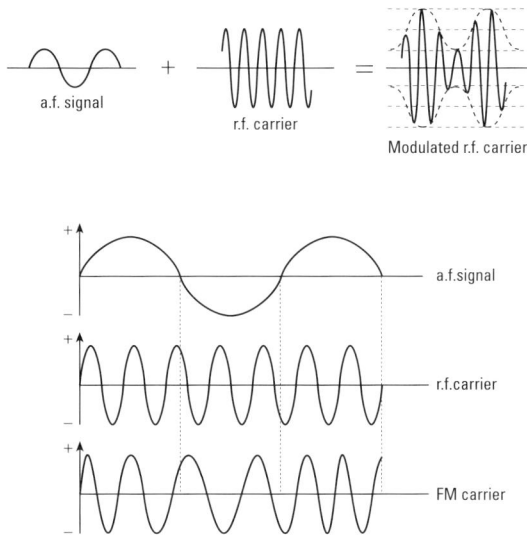

The TEP radio – a simple FM radio receiver circuit

a.f. signal + r.f. carrier = Modulated r.f. carrier

a.f.signal

r.f.carrier

FM carrier

Two ways to modulate radio waves

FM radio circuit

The circuit diagram for a simple FM radio receiver is shown below. It uses a single integrated circuit with a minimum of external components to receive and demodulate the radio signal and a general purpose audio amplifier integrated circuit to drive the loudspeaker.

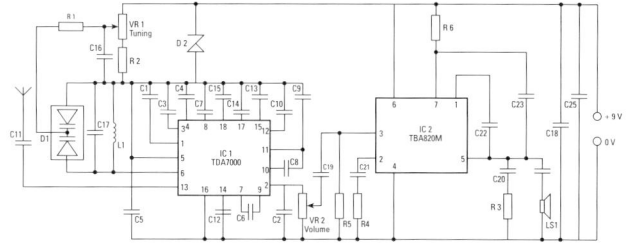

Radio control

An interesting application of radio technology is the use of simple transmitters and receivers to control models – planes, boats and cars. Such models are interesting examples of multiple technologies in action. Consider the radio-controlled car shown on the right. The hand-held transmitter unit sends signals which control the following functions:

- speed of travel;
- forward and reverse;
- left and right steering.

The transmitter uses a crystal oscillator to provide the radio control signal. This operates on the 27 MHz band. Other crystals for radio control operate at 418 MHz. The transmitter controls the speed of travel by altering the mark:space ratio of the signal transmitted. If there is a high mark:space ratio, the signal is on far more than it is off and the motor rotates rapidly. If there is a low mark:space ratio, the signal is off more than it is on and the motor rotates slowly. Inverting the signal reverses the direction of rotation of the motor. The receiver unit can read the mark:space ratio and so control the speed of the motor. The receiver unit can also receive signals which operate the servo motor that controls the steering.

Ready to go

The body shell is just for show

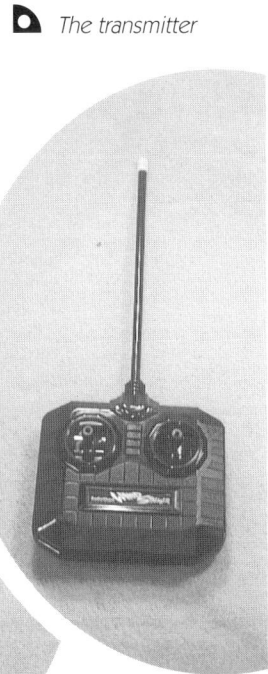

The transmitter

The receiver circuit is more complicated than the transmitter

Inside the transmitter

The drive system is completely detachable

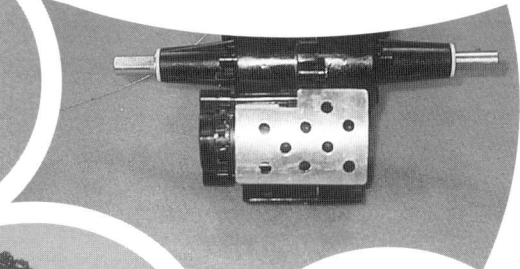

This large heat sink is used to cool the motor

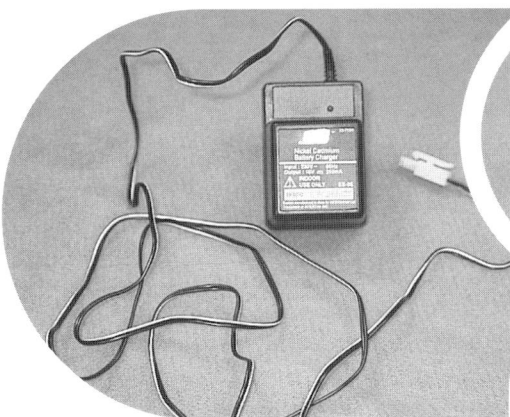

The wheels fit together, trapping the tyre in position

Battery charger

Compression springs are used for the suspension

14 Programmable ICs

Microprocessors

Integrated circuits (ICs) that can be programmed have been available for many years now. The microprocessor at the heart of a personal computer is a programmable IC. When a control program is written using control software, it is this microprocessor that runs the program. Microprocessors are quite expensive and need a lot of other ICs alongside them before they can be used, but fast modern computers rely on them.

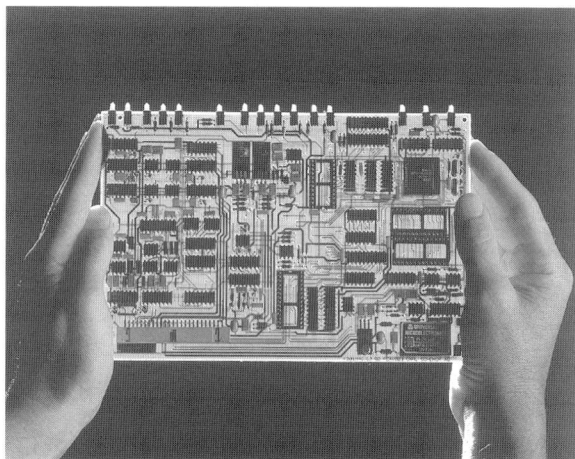

The heart of a computer is the microprocessor

Microcontrollers

A microcontroller is an IC that includes a microprocessor plus memory that can hold and run a program, timers, counters, inputs and outputs. You can think of it as a computer on a chip. The memory on these ICs can be either 'EPROM' (erasable programmable read only memory) that can be used many times or 'OTP' (one time programmable) that can only be programmed once. EPROMs are used while programs are being developed. OTPs, being cheaper, are used in final products.

Often these microcontrollers are called PIC chips after one of the most common families of microcontroller. ICs like this are less powerful than microprocessors, but they are small, and cheap, enough to be included in all kinds of products. The cheapest OTP microcontrollers cost less than a pound and even more powerful versions only cost a few pounds.

An EPROM chip. Note the window in the chip that enables the program to be erased with UV light

Both these modern domestic products incorporate a microcontroller

PICRT1, PICRT2

Microcontrollers in industry

Microcontrollers are used to control production lines and processing plants in all kinds of industries.

The controllers used in industry are called programmable logic controllers (PLCs).

In different industries the same controller might get very hot or cold or be in a very humid or dusty place. So PLCs are designed to be very robust to withstand this range of environments.

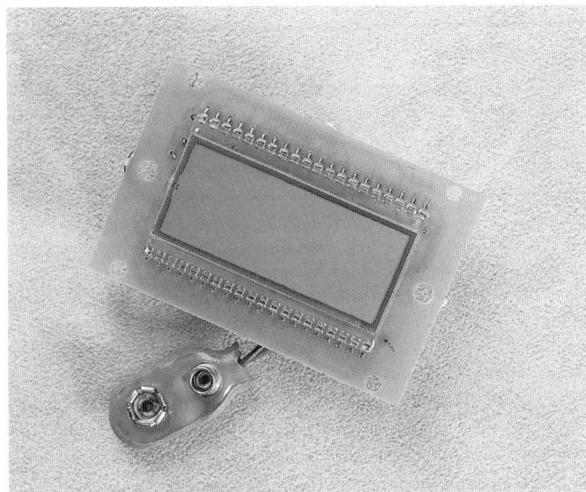

A programmable logic controller (PLC)

PLCs are modular. A basic PLC will have a fixed number of inputs and outputs under its control. Extra features, such as additional inputs and outputs, digital to analogue converters, analogue to digital converters, links to computers or other PLCs, modems or extra memory, can all be added by plugging the appropriate module into the PLC's communication 'bus'.

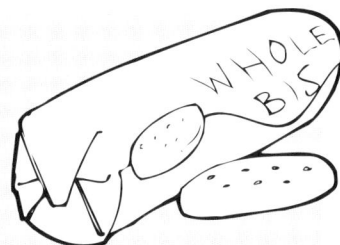

All these products are manufactured on production lines using microcontrollers

Creating a program

The program for a microcontroller is written on a desktop computer.

There are different types of computer control program available. The most common are as follows.

1 Written commands

A series of written instructions are obeyed one after the other in a fixed order. Groups of instructions can be named as procedures.

2 A flowsheet

Similar to the written commands but with the instructions enclosed in boxes. Different boxes represent different kinds of instruction and the flow from box to box is shown by arrowed lines.

3 Systems diagrams

Programs are written by joining together function blocks with signal lines. This is very like designing an electronic circuit using system boards. The emphasis is on what signals are going into and coming out of the system and what blocks are needed to change the signals.

4 Ladder logic

This is the method used to program PLCs in industry. The diagrams look very different to system diagrams, but the idea is very similar. Input signals are on the left of a diagram and outputs are on the right. In between these are functions that combine and change signals. The links from the inputs to the outputs look like the 'rungs' of a ladder.

```
TO ALARM
IF  INPUT A < 100
    THEN  BURGLAR
ELSE ALARM
END

TO BURGLAR
SWITCHON 3  ;(Plays growling sound)
WAIT 10
SWITCHOFF 3
ALARM
END
```

Written command programming

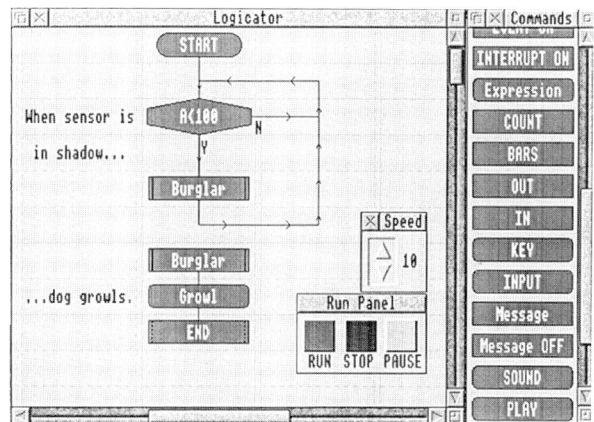

Flow chart programming

Ladder logic programming

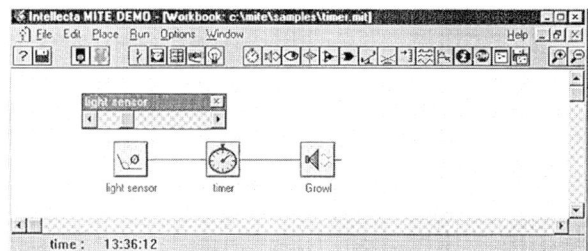

Systems diagram programming

Testing a program

Programming an OTP chip is irreversible – if the program is wrong, the chip has to be thrown away. So testing is very important. There can be up to three stages of testing.

Simulation

The program is tested within the computer – using the mouse or keyboard to provide inputs and showing the state of outputs on the screen.

Computer control

The program is tested by running it on the computer using real input and output devices. These are connected through an interface box. External control components, such as mechanisms or pneumatic systems, also need to be tested at this stage.

EPROM

The final stage of testing is to put the program into an EPROM version of the chip. The chip is then placed into a prototype of the actual product. In this way the working of the entire device can be tested and evaluated. Even if one of the other stages of testing is missed out, the EPROM testing must happen. Only when this testing is finished is the program put into the final, OTP, IC.

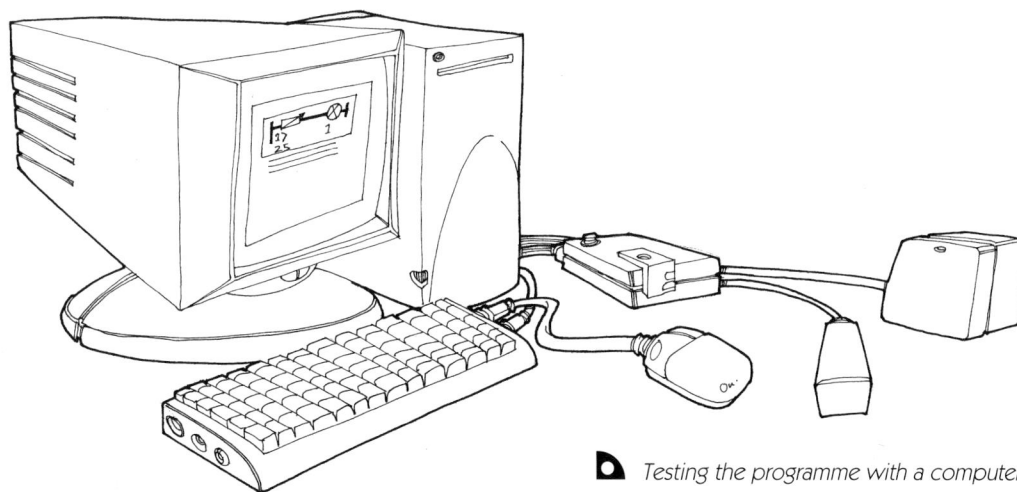

Testing the programme with a computer

Writing a program for a microcontroller is just the first step. The program then has to be transferred into the EPROM or OTP memory on the IC.

An IC is programmed using a programmer board. This connects the computer where the program has been written to the chip and provides the correct signals for it.

EPROM memory can be erased by exposing the IC to UV light. An EEPROM (electrically erasable PROM) can have its memory erased electrically by the same programmer board.

Once the program is on the IC it will stay there, even if no power is provided, until it is erased.

Product opportunities

Traditionally, a complex electronic circuit has been both large and expensive. When electronic circuits get too complex, engineers start to use computers which, though expensive, are very flexible. The exciting thing about programmable ICs is that they are both cheap and small but also very flexible. This means that they can be designed into everyday products. This opens up new opportunities for design.

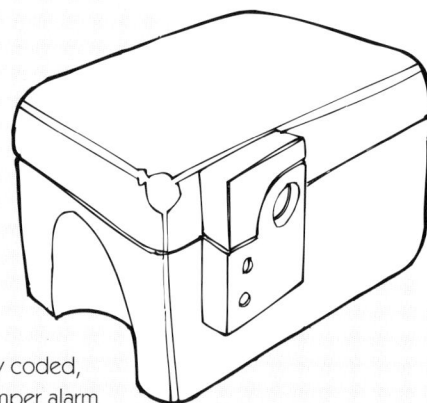

A security device—a key coded, lockable box with a tamper alarm

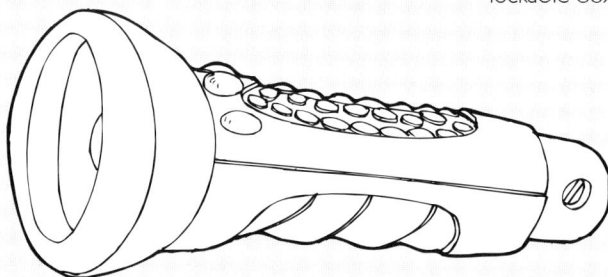

A communicating device—a morse torch, a button for every letter

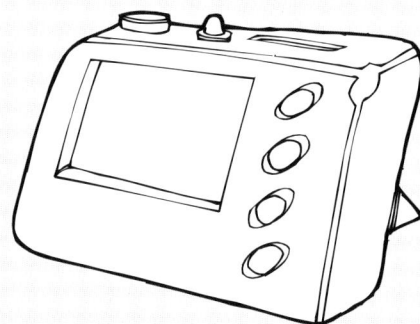

A measuring device— a digital chess clock

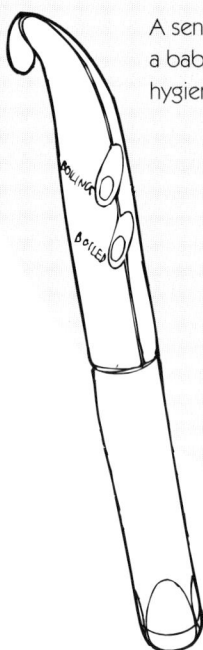

A sensing device— a baby bottle hygiene monitor

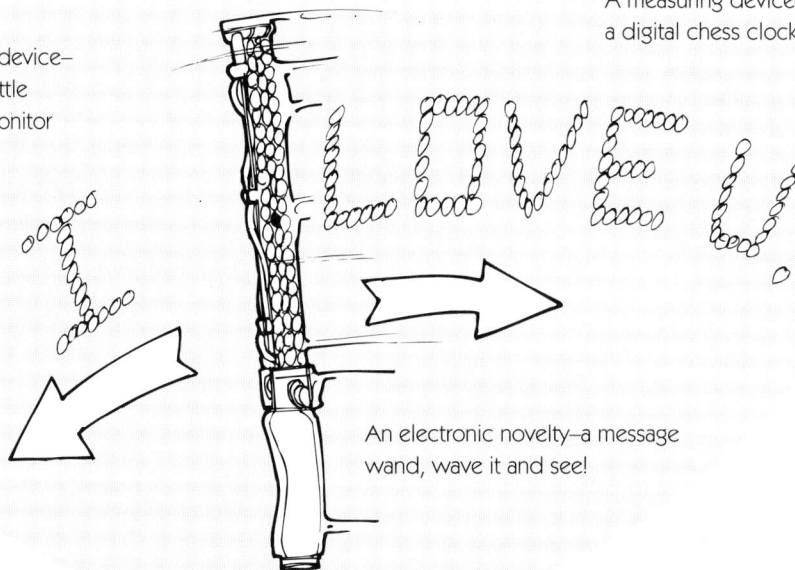

An electronic novelty—a message wand, wave it and see!

Electronic assembly

Components are connected to one another by joining their legs together. This can be done directly or through a wire. To make a good electrical connection the metal of the legs or wires must be held firmly together.

Temporary connections

You can use physical force to hold the legs or wires together with:

- crocodile clips;
- terminal blocks;
- plugs and sockets (for example, a jack).

(See page 157 for more information on temporary connections.)

Permanent connections

You can solder the legs or wires together as shown in the panel. After soldering, check each joint by looking closely to see if there are any 'dry' joints. A magnifying glass will be useful. In a dry joint the solder has not 'wet' the connecting pieces and there is only a poor electrical contact and a weak physical contact. You can also use a continuity meter to test that the electrical connection is good – see page 152.

Poor ('dry') joint   Good joint
PCB
Wire

Make sure your joints aren't dry!

1 Remember to strip the plastic insulation from the end of a wire. Twist the ends of stranded wire together.

2 Make sure the joint is clean. Use wire wool to clean off dirt or grease.

3 Be safe! Wear goggles. Keep the soldering iron away from all mains cables.

4 Many components are damaged by heat. Crocodile clips used like this act as a heat sink – they absorb the heat. A small pair of pliers can be used instead.

5 The crocodile clip also holds components steady while they are soldered.

6 To solder: first hold the iron against the electrical joint to heat it up. Then apply the solder so that a small amount melts and flows around the joint. Then remove the solder. Finally, remove the iron. Let the solder harden before the components are moved.

7 Remove any spare wire or leg with a side-cutter.

Making the product

Printed circuit boards

Almost all products that use electronics have printed circuit boards (PCBs) in them. A PCB is used both to support components and to make connections between them. The electrical connections on a PCB are made with copper 'tracks' (between components) and copper pads (where components are soldered).

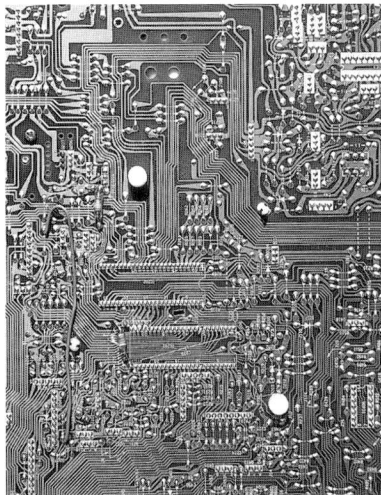

◖ PCB for a CD player

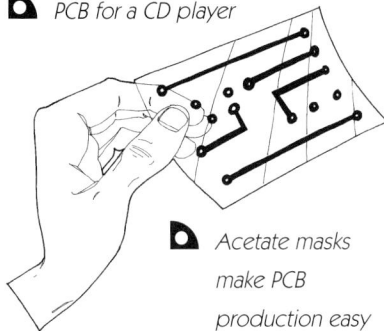

◖ Acetate masks make PCB production easy

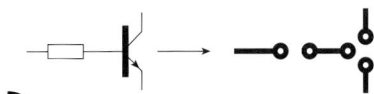

◖ Can you see how the circuit diagram becomes the PCB layout?

Designing a PCB

The shape of a PCB will be influenced by the shape of the enclosure it needs to fit into – in return, the enclosure shape may be influenced by the size of the PCB, see page 113.

Often input and output components need to be on the outside of the enclosure. Where possible, a PCB and its enclosure are designed so that these components are on the PCB and fit through holes in the enclosure.

The circuit on a PCB is printed using a 'mask'. The mask can be drawn directly onto copper-covered board with a special pen.

Alternatively, the mask can be printed onto clear acetate. In this case a photo-sensitive, copper-covered board will be used for the PCB.

The design of a mask comes either from a circuit diagram or a system diagram.

PCB design software – a drawing program with special tools for tracks and pads – is the easiest way to draw out a high quality mask. Computer aided design (CAD) software like this allows mistakes to be changed and produces a high quality and accurate drawing. Many PCB design programs have libraries of masks for system functions. Most PCB design software also has tools for drawing out circuit diagrams. It also allows you to put writing on the mask – for example, a name to identify the designer or company.

◖ Using CADCAM for PCB design

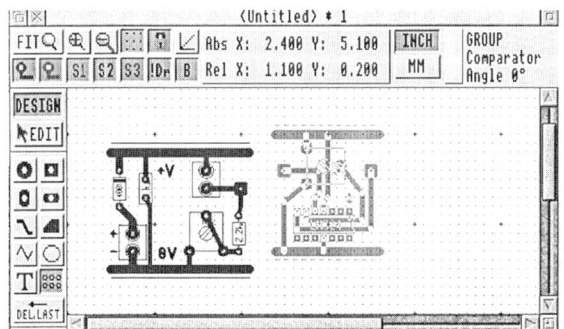

MfRT1, MfRT2,

Making a PCB

A PCB is made from a sheet of glass-reinforced plastic (GRP) covered with a thin copper layer. The circuit is formed by using a mask. This protects the copper where the tracks and pads are to be, while the rest of the copper is etched away. Photo-resist board has a light-sensitive layer on top of the copper, which is protected by a black plastic film.

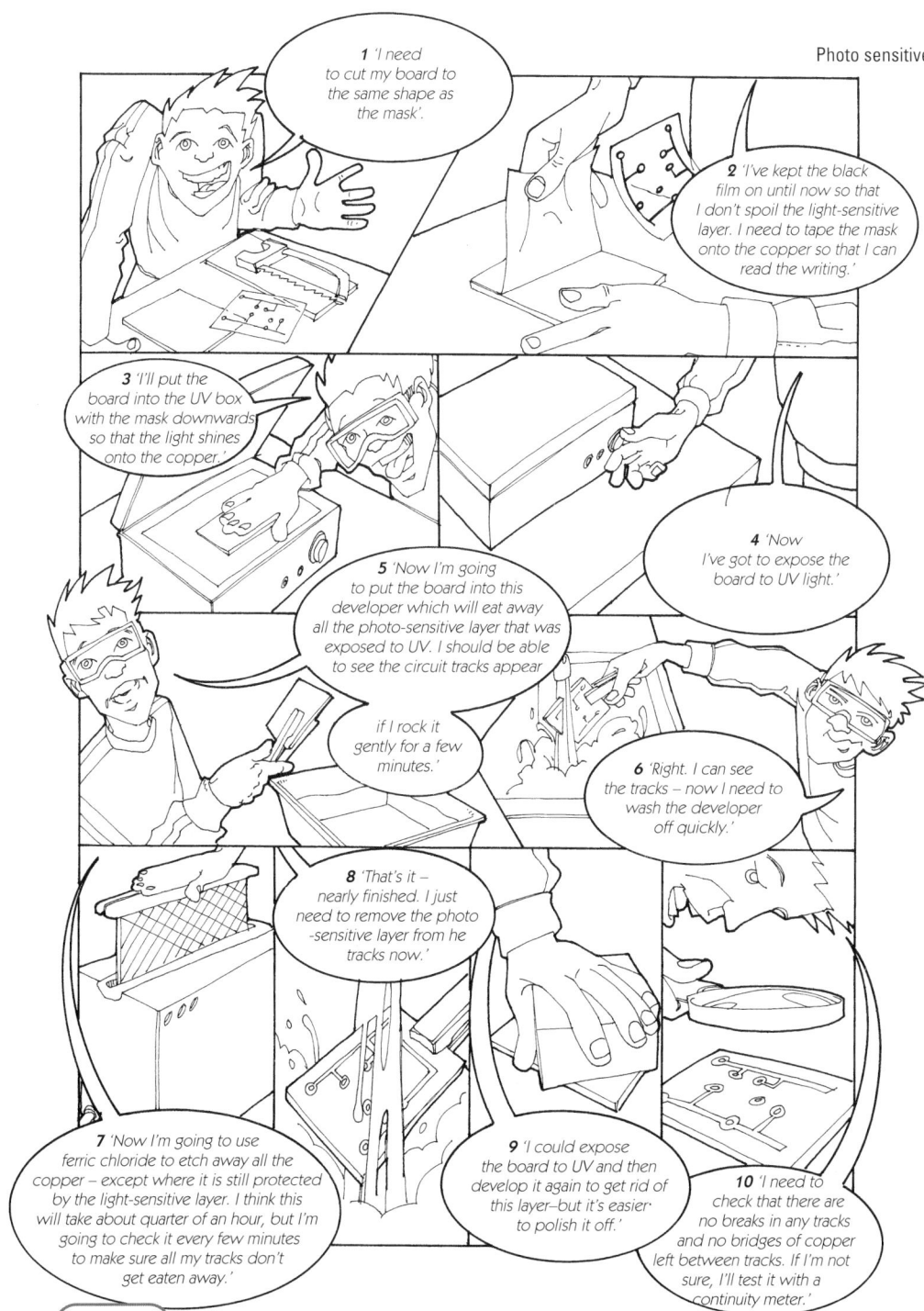

Putting components in place

Holes are drilled in the PCB, through the centre of each pad, so that components can be mounted onto the board. Component legs go through these holes so that the component is on the opposite side to the copper.

▶ Drill so that the components will fit through as shown.

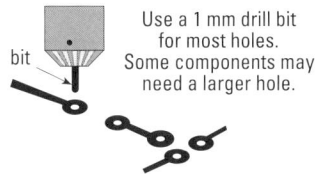

bit

Use a 1 mm drill bit for most holes. Some components may need a larger hole.

Any unwanted bridges between tracks can be carefully scraped away with a sharp knife. A gap in a track can be repaired by soldering a short length of wire across it. Before soldering (see page 173) a component into place, check that it is:

- the correct component;
- the right value;
- the right way round;
- a component that can be soldered directly onto the board.

Some components may be damaged by heat. In particular, integrated circuits ('chips') and transistors usually have a holder soldered to the board. The component is inserted into the holder afterwards.

▶ Chip holders make life easy

After each component has been soldered, the joint should be tested (page 173).

Being systematic

Solder in a few components at a time and then test that part of the circuit. If there are faults, they will be found more quickly this way. There will also be fewer parts of the circuit to examine when searching for the cause of the fault.

If the circuit has been designed using system functions then follow these steps.

1. Solder in the components for one subsystem at a time. Start with the power connection and then work from input to output.
2. After a subsystem has been built, test that it works properly before soldering in the components for the next one.
3. Connect power through the power connector. Use a voltmeter to check that the supply voltage is reaching the subsystem.
4. Next test the signal out of the subsystem. The system design for the circuit will have details about the signals for each subsystem.
5. If you discover a problem or fault, put it right before you build the next subsystem.

Finding faults

If you are trying to find a fault try these ideas.

- Disconnect the power supply first.
- Check each new soldered joint with a continuity meter.
- Check that each new component is correct. De-solder and replace any mistakes.
- Check that components are the right way round. De-solder mistakes. If it is a transistor or 'chip', then it will probably no longer work, so replace it. Other components can be reused.

If you can't trace a fault, ask for expert help; don't just carry on adding further components.

Surface mounting components

Modern electronic production uses 'surface mounting' to put components on a PCB. Here the components are placed straight onto the copper tracks and pads.

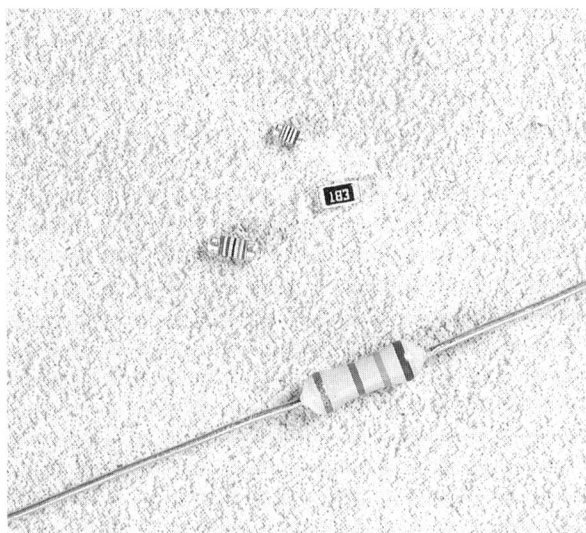

Surface mounted components (above) are much smaller

The advantages to industry are that:

● holes don't have to be drilled;

● components can be put in place by robots;

● PCBs can be smaller because the components are smaller.

Using real surface mounting technology uses expensive equipment. However, it is possible to surface mount components designed for through-hole PCBs. One way to do this is simply to solder components onto the copper side of the PCB. Note that it is more difficult to get a good electrical connection this way unless the PCB is designed with more room for the components than usual. Also, the physical connection is not so strong.

A second way to surface mount components is to use adhesive copper track. This sticks down along the lines of a circuit diagram and the components are soldered straight onto the track.

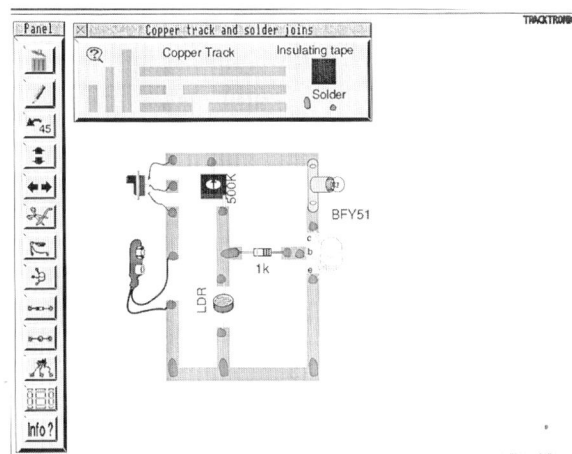

You can draw and print circuits using a computer

The resulting circuits are quite large compared to PCBs but can be made without the photo-etching process. The physical strength of a circuit depends on the material that the track is stuck onto. This copper track can also be used to make membrane switches.

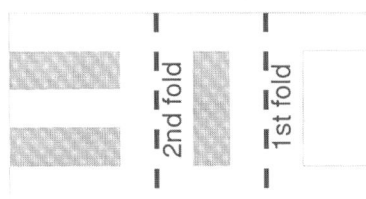

Making the container

Choosing materials

Electronic systems are usually housed in enclosures made from plastic or metal. It is unusual to find electronic products in wooden containers. This is partly due to the traditional appearance of wooden containers, as opposed to the more modern appearance of metal and plastic, but also to the ease of mass manufacturing in metal and plastic. Natural timber and manufactured board are both very useful for making moulds and formers for use with plastics.

You can use this Materials Chooser Chart to select materials for your electronic product.

Material	Description	Thermal conductivity	Electrical conductivity	Cost
Jelutong	fine grained, cream coloured, solid wood	very poor conductor	will not conduct electricity	medium
Pine	stronger grained, cream coloured, solid wood	very poor conductor	will not conduct electricity	low
Medium Density Fibre Board	manufactured from wood pulp mixed with adhesive	very poor conductor	will not conduct electricity	low/ medium
Plywood	manufactured from veneers glued together with grain at 90° to each other	very poor conductor	will not conduct electricity	medium/ high
Aluminium sheet/ tubing	dull silver lightweight metal, resists corrosion from moist air	good thermal conductor	excellent conduction	low/ medium
Steel sheet	strong metal with a silver colour which will corrode if left unprotected in moist air	good thermal conductor	good conduction	low
High impact polystyrene sheet	wide range of colours and thicknesses	poor conductor softens on heating and may deform	will not conduct electricity	medium
Acrylic sheet	wide range of colours and thicknesses	poor conductor softens on heating and may deform	will not conduct electricity	medium/ high
Butyrate tubing	wide range of colours and sizes	poor conductor softens on heating and may deform	will not conduct electricity	medium
PVC tubing	black, white or grey round or square drainpipe	poor conductor softens on heating and may deform	will not conduct electricity	low/ medium

Environmental audit	Availability	Applications
renewable resource; should be from sustainable source; can be found in a form suitable for re-use in school	purchased from a specialist supplier	excellent for moulds as it is very easy to cut, shape and finish
renewable resource; should be from sustainable source; can be found in a form suitable for re-use in school	readily available from most timber merchant	simple frameworks and block models as it is very easy to cut, shape and finish
renewable resource; makes very effective use of all timber taken from sustainable source; can be found in a form suitable for re-use in school	readily available from most timber merchant	block models, vacuum forming molds, small bases as it is hard, and keeps edges well
renewable resource; makes very effective use of all timber taken from sustainable source; can be found in a form suitable for re-use in school	high quality birch (finish) plywood is more difficult to source	medium to large enclosures, flat cut out figures, back boards as it is strong and stable
finite resource can be recycled; new stock may contain recycled material; can be found in a form suitable for re-use in school	quite easy to source from metal stockholders	medium to large enclosures as it is easy to cut and bend. and can be fixed with blind (pop) rivet or epoxy resin, but cannot be soldered easily
finite resource can be recycled; new stock may contain recycled material; can be found in a form suitable for re-use in school	quite easy to source from metal stockholders	medium to large enclosures as it can be brazed and welded but hard to bend, and cut
finite resource from petrochemical processing may contain recycled material; can be recycled; may be found in a form suitable for re-use in school	available from specialist plastics suppliers	small enclosures as it is suitable for vacuum forming and joining with solvent adhesive
finite resource from petrochemical processing; may contain recycled material; can be recycled; may be found in a form suitable for re-use in school	available from specialist plastics suppliers	mainly useful for an assembly of flat pieces though it can be line bent or drape formed
finite resource from petrochemical processing; may contain recycled material; can be recycled; may be found in a form suitable for re-use in school	available from specialist plastics suppliers	small enclosures as it is easy to cut and trim; join with solvent adhesive
from petrochemical processing; may contain recycled material; can be recycled; may be found in a form suitable for re-use in school	available from builders merchants	small enclosures as it is easy to cut, join with solvent adhesive

Making the product

Making your own enclosure

This section describes the techniques you may need to use to make an enclosure for your electronic system. You can use the information in this section to choose the techniques that you require to make your design. You will need to get detailed advice and guidance from your teacher on the safest ways to carry out these techniques.

Assembling from tubing and end caps

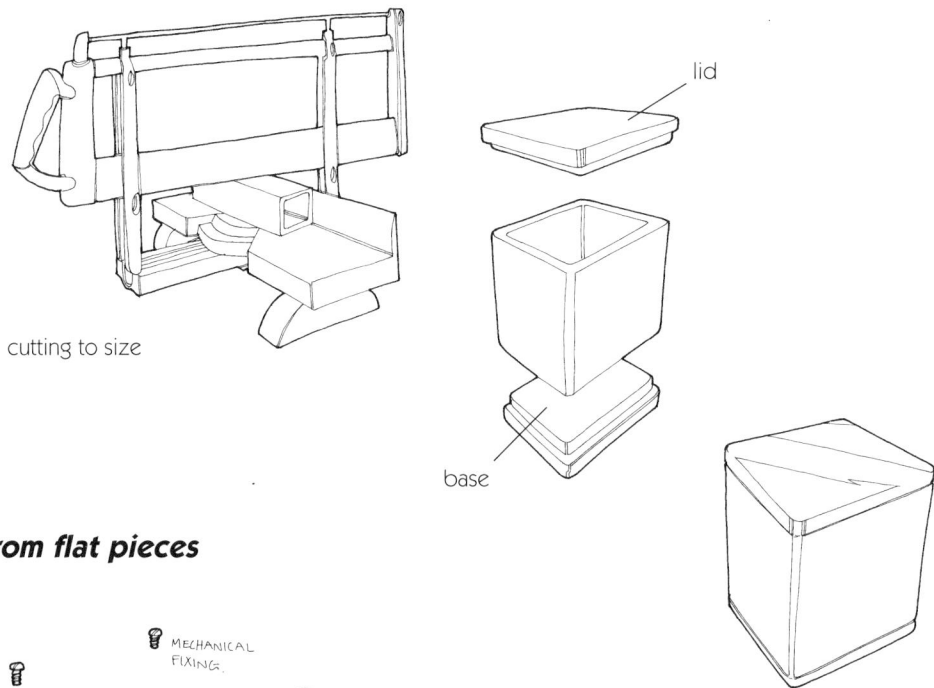

cutting to size

lid

base

Assembling from flat pieces

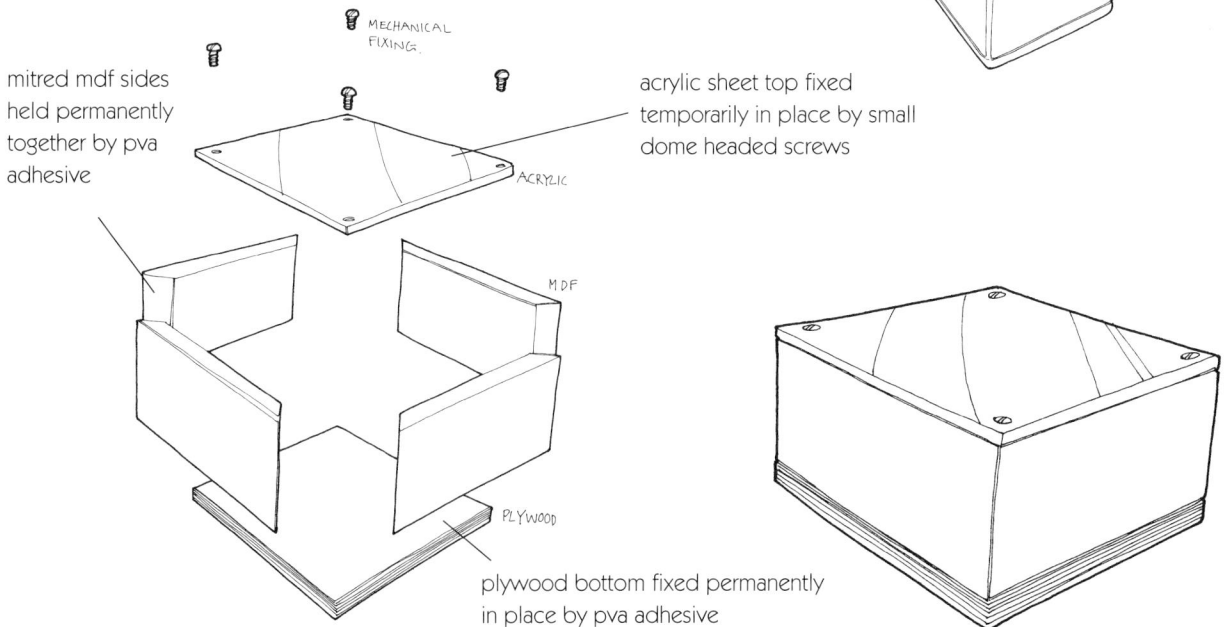

MECHANICAL FIXING.

mitred mdf sides held permanently together by pva adhesive

acrylic sheet top fixed temporarily in place by small dome headed screws

ACRYLIC

MDF

PLYWOOD

plywood bottom fixed permanently in place by pva adhesive

Drape forming acrylic sheet

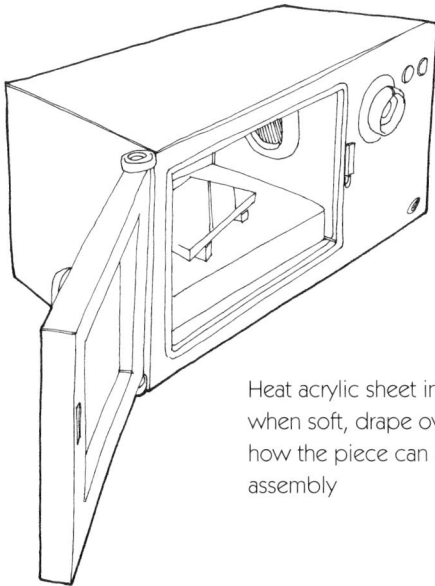

Heat acrylic sheet in an oven and, when soft, drape over former. See how the piece can be used in an assembly

Line bending acrylic sheet

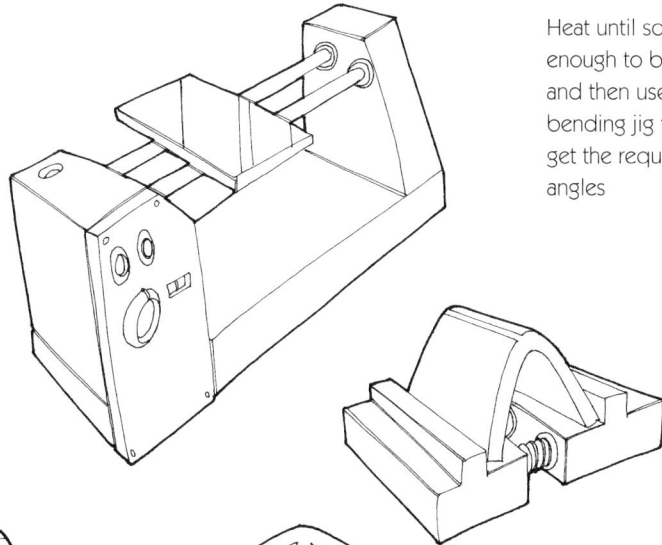

Heat until soft enough to bend and then use a bending jig to get the required angles

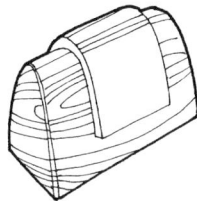

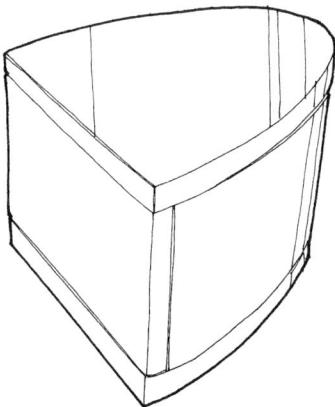

Assembling from shaped pieces of different materials

sheet metal top bent over folding bars held in place by small self-tapping screws base and sides formed by line bending acrylic sheet

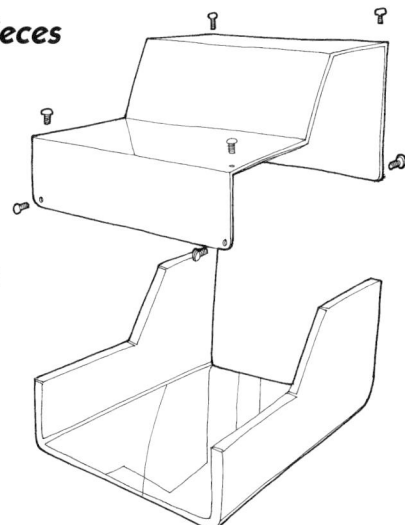

Making the product

Forming from a single sheet of metal

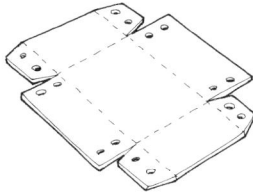

cutout, finish and
drill the sheet

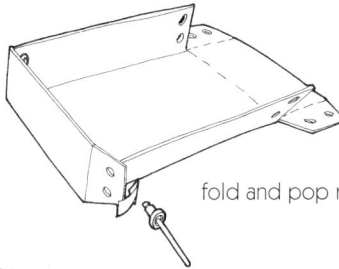

fold and pop rivet

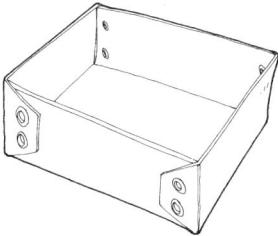

Forming more complex shapes

You can make the mould for more complex
shapes by using Plasticine or clay as
shown here.

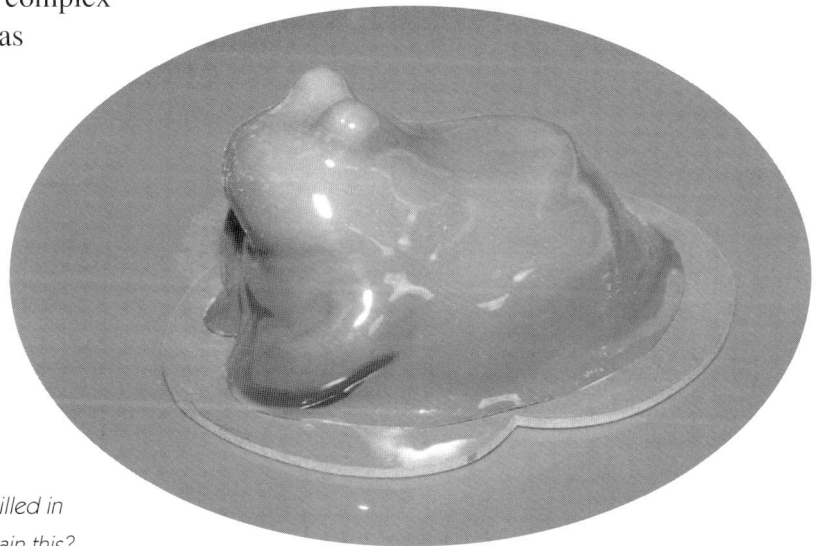

Forming from a sheet of thermoplastic material

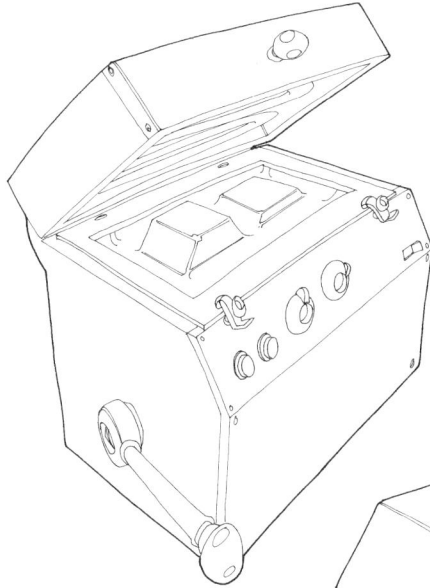

Vacuum
forming the
base to fit the
enclosure

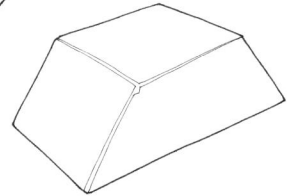

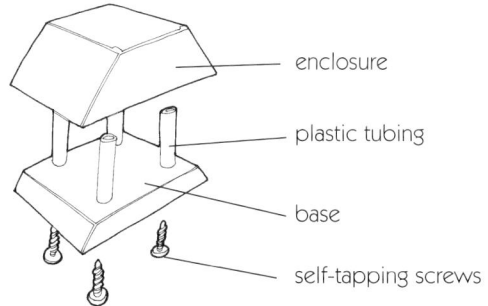

enclosure

plastic tubing

base

self-tapping screws

The Plasticine mould for this frog was chilled in
the refrigerator before use. Can you explain this?

Fitting to a surface

Components which need to be fitted to a surface may have different individual requirements. Some will need a hole made, many will click or snap into place and others will need a mechanical fixing such as a machine screw and nut.

If components are housed on a panel or movable part of an enclosure, you will need to consider the connections between them and other working parts. It may be possible to make a neat connection with a ribbon cable.

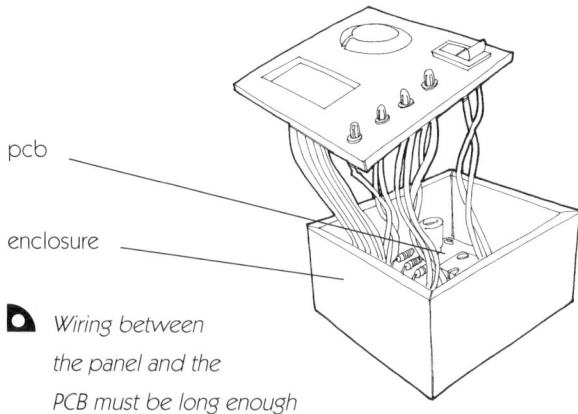

pcb

enclosure

◨ *Wiring between the panel and the PCB must be long enough*

Many components, such as this variable resistor, need a hole to be drilled. The component fits on the inside of the surface and the nut and lock washer are fitted from the outside to hold the component in place.

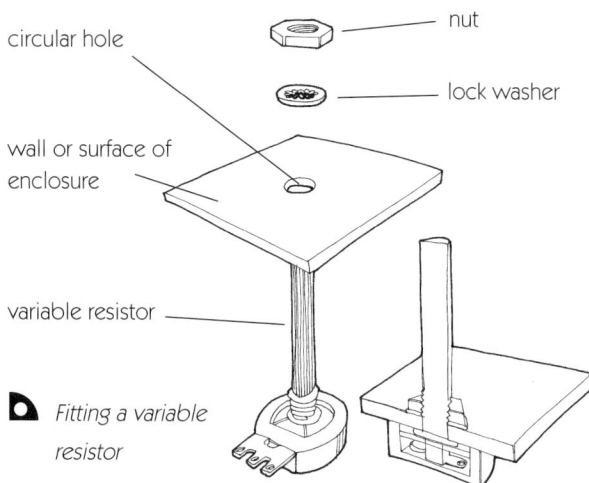

circular hole

nut

lock washer

wall or surface of enclosure

variable resistor

◨ *Fitting a variable resistor*

This rocker switch needs a rectangular hole, It has spring clips moulded into its body. These open out on the inside of the hole after the switch has been snapped into place.

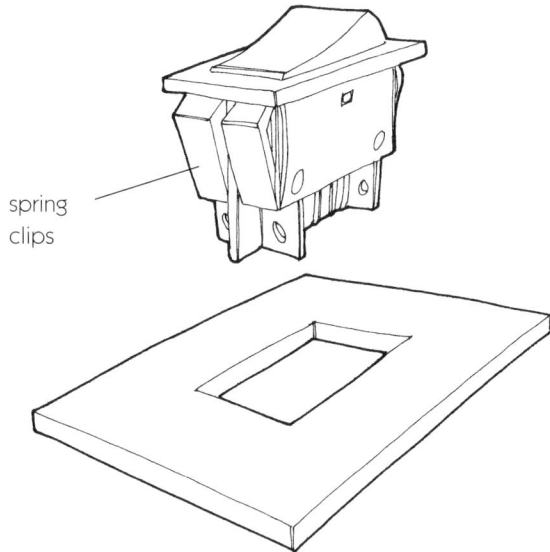

spring clips

◨ Fitting a rocker switch

Making the product

Any wires which need to pass through a surface made out of plastic or metal must be protected from abrasion against the edge. A rubber grommet will locate on the edges of a hole.

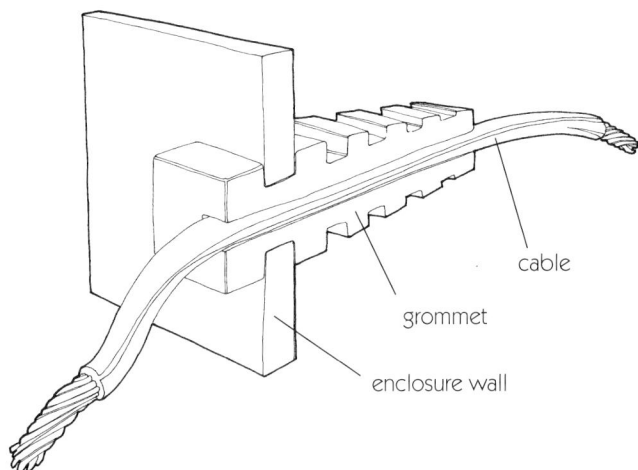

cable

grommet

enclosure wall

▶ *Using a grommet prevents wear*

LEDs can be mounted to a surface with a clip or a cover. The clip or cover fits inside a hole which is drilled. The LED is snapped into place from the inside to lock the clip or cover in place.

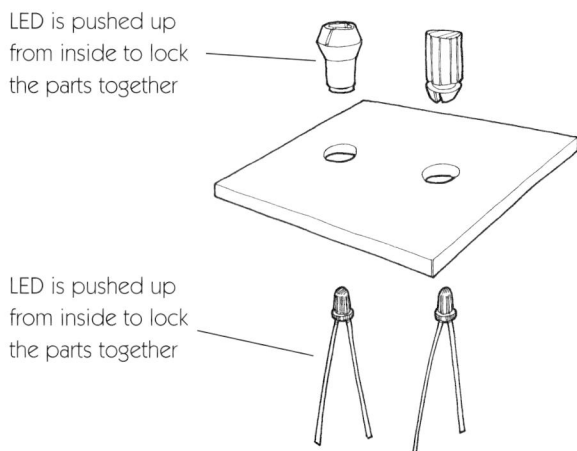

LED is pushed up from inside to lock the parts together

LED is pushed up from inside to lock the parts together

▶ *Fitting LEDs*

A loudspeaker is fitted from the rear of a panel and a grill cloth or moulded grill is fitted to the front. A less expensive option is to fit the loudspeaker behind a matrix of drilled holes or slots in the panel.

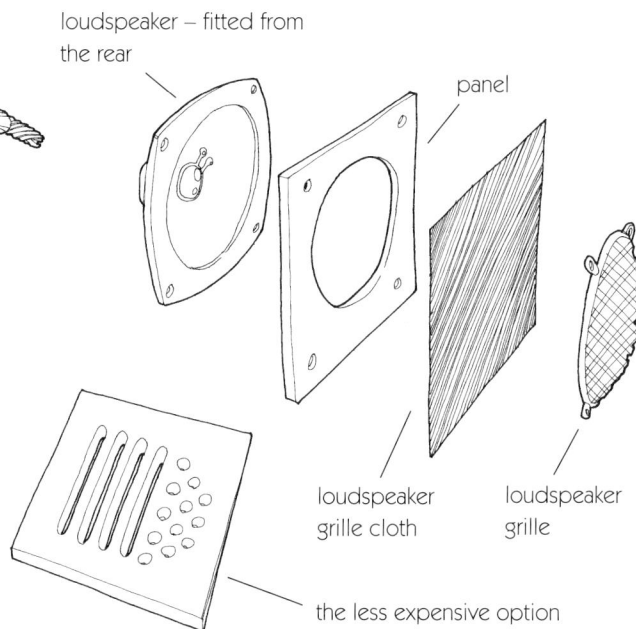

loudspeaker – fitted from the rear

panel

loudspeaker grille cloth

loudspeaker grille

the less expensive option

Display modules come with their own PCB. The module fits through a rectangular slot from the inside. Four screw holes are used to fasten the PCB to the surface. A bezel can be fitted from the outside to improve the appearance.

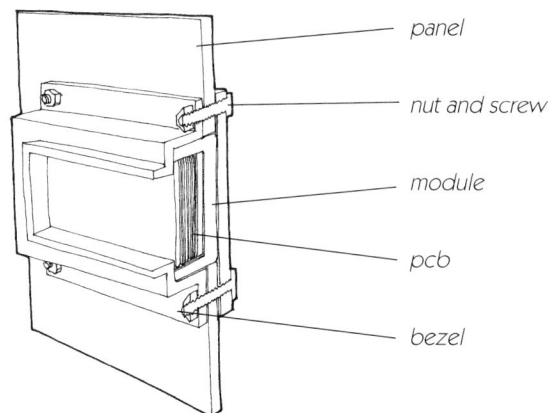

panel

nut and screw

module

pcb

bezel

Fitting things inside

You will need to consider the way in which the parts of your system are contained inside the enclosure. The examples in the panel show a number of possibilities.

Internal fitting

1 Things can be held in place with mechanical fixings.

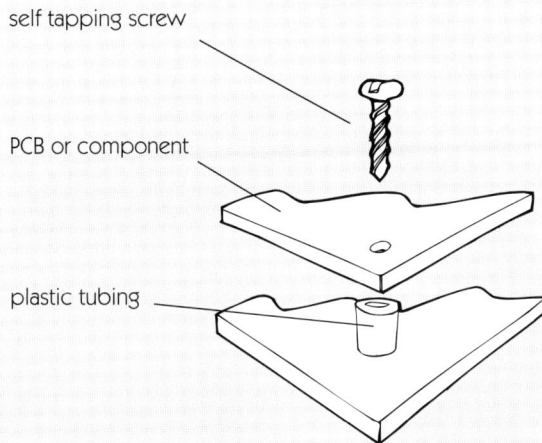

self tapping screw

PCB or component

plastic tubing

2 Guides can be glued to the inside of an enclosure. A PCB or component can then slot into place.

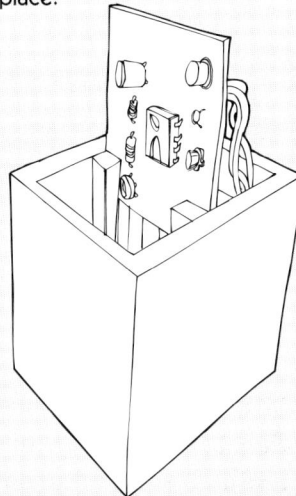

3 Individual compartments can be made on the inside of an enclosure.

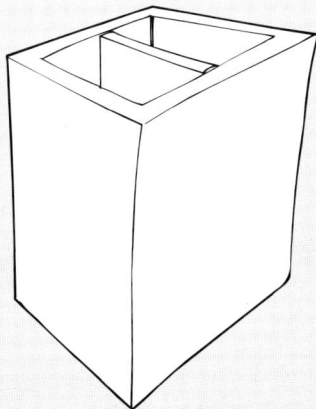

4 It is possible to fasten all of your electronics to a base and then to fit an enclosure over the top.

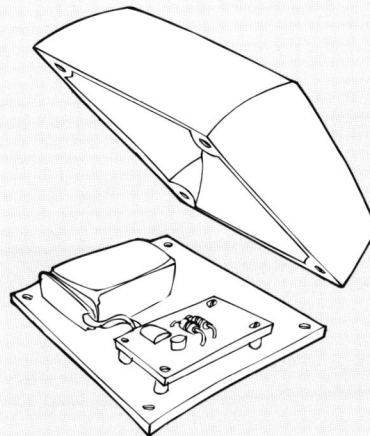

Buying in

You may be able to buy in all your requirements for an enclosure. A wide range of boxes is available from suppliers, as shown in the panel, and many come with slots to hold PCBs and dividers to make separate sections.

It is quite possible to start with a fairly conventional box and finish with an innovative design. This process is called customising and you can use any of the following techniques:

- changing the shape by removing material;
- changing the shape by adding material;
- changing the texture by abrading the surface;
- changing the texture by adding new material;
- changing the colour by spraying;
- adding interest with stick-on decorations.

The pictures show just what can be achieved.

You will also be able to find a range of accessories which can be attached to an enclosure you have bought or made. These hinges, catches and handles give a professional appearance to a case-like enclosure which needs to be portable. Small rubber feet will stop an enclosure from slipping on a surface and scratching it.

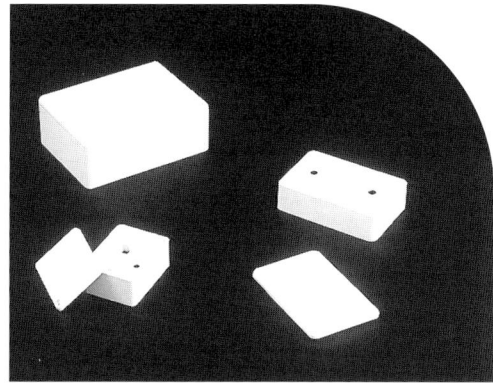

▶ *Enclosures*
before and after customising

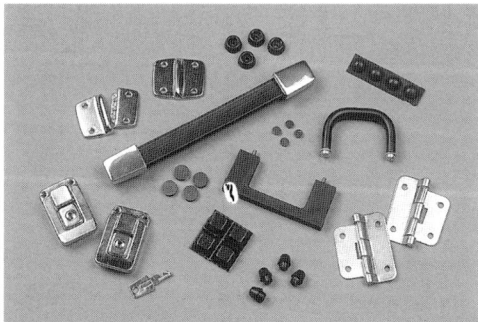

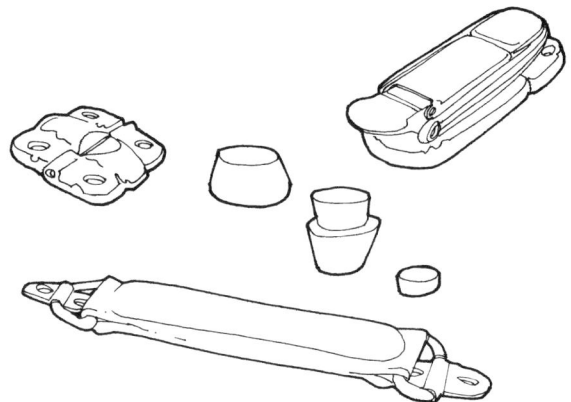

Important ideas

To avoid accidents and harm, you need to think about:

- hazards;
- risks;
- risk assessment;
- risk control.

A **hazard** is anything which might cause harm or damage. The chance of a hazard causing harm or damage is called the **risk**. You can work out how big the risk is by thinking about whether the harm or damage is likely to happen. This is called **risk assessment**. **Risk control** is the action taken to ensure that the harm or damage is less likely to happen.

Safety in the workplace

No workplace is risk free and the Health and Safety at Work Act ensures that employers identify the risks, assess them and then actively seek ways of controlling those risks. This will involve identifying safe practice and providing both training and supervision to ensure it is carried out. The workers do, of course, have to follow the procedures laid down.

A useful way of looking at this problem is shown in the diagram.

The diagram shows these elements:

- the workplace environment;
- light and ventilation (the window in the diagram);
- the means of access (getting in);
- the means of egress (getting out);
- the machinery (plant);
- the handling, storage and transportation of articles and substances;
- the people working in the workplace.

The diagram shows that risk assessment has to take into account the interactions of all the elements.

It is often the **interactions** that get forgotten. People and things move around. It is these interactions that affect health and safety. For example, a small pile of bricks stays still. Someone might trip over it, so it represents a hazard. Once the bricks start to be moved, however, they can become an even greater hazard – they can cause strain injuries through lifting, head and feet injuries through being dropped, and so on. So, if bricks are around people, and can therefore interact with people, the people must wear hard hats and steel-toe boots.

In electronic product manufacture there are many potential hazards. You will recognise many of these because they apply just as much to working with electronics in school or at home. How would you assess and control the risks? As a worker, what could you do to ensure safe and healthy working?

Index

Addison Wesley Longman Ltd
Edinburgh Gate, Harlow, Essex, CM20 2JE, England and Associated Companies throughout the World

First published 1997
ISBN 0582 31775 4

Set in ITCKabel and Times
Designed and produced by Pentacor plc, High Wycombe, Bucks, HP12 3DJ
Illustrations and other materials by Nathan Barlex, Hugh Neill, OIL, Pentacor plc and Anoop Dinesh Shah
Picture researcher Louise Edgeworth
Editor Lesley Young
Indexer Richard Raper/Indexing Specialists
Printed in Great Britain by Scotprint Limited, Musselburgh, Scotland

The Publisher's policy is to use paper manufactured from sustainable forests

Project Directors
Executive Director Dr David Barlex
Co-directors Prof. Paul Black and Prof. Geoffrey Harrison

Contributors

David Barlex	Debbie Howard	Ann Riggs
Michelle Bell	John Plater	Torben Steeg
Terry Bendall	Judith Powling	Ruth Wright
Brenda Hellier	Stephanie Richards	

We are grateful to the following for permission to reproduce photographs and other copyright material:

BBC Copyright ©, page 29; BayGen Power Europe Ltd, page 53; British Toy & Hobby Association, page 44 below right; Trevor Clifford, pages 7, 108, 168 below right, 174 right; Draper Tools Ltd, pages 37, 38, 39 (photo: Trevor Clifford); Economatics (Education) Ltd, pages 142, 143, 144, 145, 146, 147, 149, 150; Mary Evans Picture Library, pages 24 above, 28, 32; GT Autoalarm, page 49; Intermediate Technology, pages 58 above (Jeremy Hartley), 58 centre & 61 above (Lindel Caine), 58 below, 60, 61 below (Caroline Penn); London Transport Buses, pages 54, 55, 56, 57; London Transport Museum, pages 24 below, 25, 26; PA News/Martin Keene, page 31 above; Popperfoto, page 30; Powergen plc, page 35; Sanyo, page 116; Science Photo Library, pages 92, 131, 168 above left, below left & above right, 174 left; Tony Stone Images/Ian Shaw, pages 8, 9; TECTRIX Bikemax (photo: Sport Inter-Media Ltd), pages 40–41, 42; Telegraph Colour Library/Benelux Press, page 20; Tomy UK Ltd, pages 43, 44 above & below left; TRIP/Helene Rogers, page 48; Unilab, pages 127, 128, 130, 132, 133, 134, 135, 136, 151, 153, 154, 155, 156, 157, 169, 177; Unipath Ltd, page 33; Daniel Weil (photo: Pentagram Design Ltd), page 114.

The Nuffield Design and Technology Project gratefully acknowledges the support of the following commercial concerns in developing the published materials:

Unilab	BayGen	Hytec
Economatics (Education) Ltd	Draper Tools	Tectrix
London Transport Buses	GT Autoalarm	Tomy
Intermediate Technology		